AF513133

Gender Dynamics in Economic Development of India

GENDER DYNAMICS IN ECONOMIC DEVELOPMENT OF INDIA

By

Kumar Das

Professor, Utkal University, Bhubaneswar

Reference Press

4831/24, Ansari Road, Darya Ganj,
New Delhi-110002
Tel. : 23260807, 41563444
Fax : 011-41563334
E-mail: info@essessreference.com
www.essessreference.com

REFERENCE PRESS
4831/24, Ansari Road,
Darya Ganj,
New Delhi-110 002.

Tel.: 23260807, 41563444
Fax: 41563334
E-mail: info@essessreference.com
www.essessreference.com

© Author

Rs.875/-

All Rights reserved. No part of this publication may be reproduced, stored in a retrieval system, transmitted in any form or by any means, mechanical, photocopying recording or otherwise without the prior written permission of the publisher.

First Published - 2009

ISBN: 978-81-8405-046-2

Cover Design by Patch Creative Unit

Published By Reference Press and printed at Salasar Imaging Systems

PRINTED IN INDIA

Dedicated to

My great Source of Inspiration

Professor Amartya K Sen

The Nobel Laureate,1998

Contents

Preface

Gender inequality is endemic but not enigmatic. Women are always made dependent on social relations. The cultural imperatives do not allow her to think for the 'women as a class'. Because she is brought up in the culture of altruism. Even today man continues to exercises his subtler-control on the family production and reproduction system. It is gradually institutionalized at several spheres: work, culture, customs, religion and education. Therefore liberation of women will not be easy or complete without the destruction of neo-patriarchy . Neo patriarchy reinforces the process of neo-housewifization. The social and economic structures that locks production and reproduction together , perpetrate male dominance and female submission. The liberation of women can only be achieved if all structures in which women are integrated are transformed simultaneously. A modification of any one of them can be offset by a reinforcement of another, so that a mere permutation of the form of inequality is ultimately achieved. We should understand the sexual division of labour as the intersection of two sets of social forces: capitalism and patriarchy. The capitalists extract greater benefits from the existence of sexual division of labor due to cheaper labor cost. Wage is always less than women's marginal productivity. The female works more, gets less. The patriarchy makes her an object , a matter to be possessed, worshiped or condemned. Thus a social transformation, which gives us real modernity is warranted. Modernity does not come from technology or economic development or consumerism. Real modernity implies social prosperity which treats both male female as equal and free human beings.

Effective policy design requires an effective understanding of the gender issues within a broad social framework. Ongoing process of economic development through free market policy is not gender-neutral. It is more divisive and discriminatory. It has winners and losers. Market is never pro-people ,rather it discriminates against the women. Women's economic contribution has been invisibilised in the process of economic development. The slogan of women empowerment is becoming increasingly louder with the ongoing process of disempowering people. There is also the growth of dangerous tendency of the elite to dismiss the deep concern towards poverty and economic vulnerability as the obsession toward egalitarian romantics. The main thrust of globalisation measures is greater commodification of all aspects of everyday life and work. The ongoing development process has inherent tendency to manifest the marginalisation process. Job market is becoming increasingly characterised by the process of casualisation and informalisation. As a result the economic insecurity manifests in job insecurity, food insecurity, nutritional insecurity and educational insecurity etc . It is not very difficult to observe anti-woman bias in the ongoing economic reform process. Therefore poverty can not serve as the proxy for subordination of women. The anti poverty policies can not be expected to necessarily improve the position of women. Money is neither necessary nor sufficient for transforming existing asymmetric gender relations. Thus Gender issue should never be approached with poverty reduction policies. Because this approach believes that women are victims of misdevelopment.

In the contemporary context the globalisation has created an atmosphere of excitement of instant economic growth. It is based on the principle of 'invisible hand'

There is sharper obsession for economic development to be achieved by laissez faire policy .All sectors of the economy are vibrating with economic buoyancy. Whole world is moving ahead with the pragmatism of high tech and excitement of achieving higher economic efficiency. But the society has become too much materialistic and consumption-oriented. These are all direct consequences of the Newtonian paradigm and Darwinian principle of efficiency. The advocates of free marketism focus on "feminization of jobs", globalization of knowledge, and "advancement of technology". But there is inherent gender bias, urban bias and elite-bias in the formulation of macro policies. It is creating a system which is ultimately as centralised and undemocratic as any that can be imposed by the meddlesome bureaucracy.

The debate on state non action on gender issues is ceased. The gender implications are erased from their analysis. With the immense sophistication in methodology that emphasizes exclusively on quantification, uncomfortable issues such as patriarchy has remained as non issue and invisible. Gender concern and discourses survive with in the development bureaucracies which are themselves dominated by men. It is easier for them to ring-fence gender issues as a problem of poverty and to argue against 'feminization of poverty' than to admit the realistic view of gender disadvantage which crosses the boundaries of class and ethnicity. We are myopic to treat gender inequality as a result of poverty and illiteracy. Indian society should not wait till the end of poverty and illiteracy to establish an unisex society. The notion of virtuous woman and domesticity of woman created by the patriarchy has to be demystified. Woman has to be vital but not virtuous. Empowerment of women has to emerge from the society itself through effective health and education. The educational reforms can foster people involvement and participation. It breaks the patronage of patriarchal force and exploitation of the capitalistic power. Participative approach can only break patriarchal approach. Empowerment of women shall automatically ensure entitlement and their capabilities. Gender equality is the sine quo none building a healthy and prosperous society. Unisex society can ensure meaningful inclusive growth and true prosperity.

This book is the product of an organic thinking process. It argues that education and technology should ensure liberation and freedom of thought for all human beings. It should break gradually the shackles of tradition that binds women in the man-made gaol. The gender issue should be delinked both from myopic economics and insensitive politics. There is no substitute for a gender analysis , which transcend class divisions and material definitions of deprivation. Therefore 'adding women' is not necessary, but an insight and rethinking development concepts and practices as a whole through a gender lens is necessary. So mainstreaming gender is imperative and engendering development is warranted.

This book is the outcome of my research of last couple of decades. It also contains revised versions of some of my research papers published in reputed international journals. It also includes my lectures delivered at different professional for a in India and abroad. Later on I observed the convergence of my insightful ideas and common line of my thought in all my seminars presentations. I am thankful to the organizers of those seminars and editors of different journals who have permitted me to published these materials in the form of this book. I express my deep sense of gratitude to my friends and colleagues of Asian University, Bangkok Sanghai University, Hongkong university who have encouraged me to bring out this book. This manuscript could be completed during my sabbatical leave during which I worked as visiting professor of Hongkong university and Sanghai University. Particularly I am thankful to Dr P. Temie, Dr Peter Gruberman, Dr. Suthiporn, Dr. Peter Nijkamp, Dr A. Amin for their useful comments on the earlier draft of the manuscripts. My thanks are also due to my students and research scholars for whom my ideas and lectures have constantly got refined. I am thankful to my better half, my younger brother, Nira, Nirmala, my sons, Leonard, Maynard and Nikhil and for their loving support during the preparation of this manuscript. I thank Mr D.Mahakul for completing the DTP job very neatly and Mr.Sumit Sethi, the publisher for bringing out the book in time.

Kumar Das

1
Introduction

Main stream Economics assume men and women to be abstractly equal, both making rational choice. Gender is not recognised either as an asymmetry or as a system of power relationships. Economics, being the most scientific of all social sciences does not have much to offer either conceptually or methodologically in terms of gender. As economic theory does not systematically analyse the linkage between the mode of production and mode of reproduction, the social reality that it examines, remains clouded by many misconceptions. Economics has rather trivialised the gender issue. Both balance and level of power are ignored. Adam Smith, the father of economics, devoting hardly one page to women in his scholarly tome(1976) rationalised gender roles He argues that material conditions of a family require the care of children by mothers and hence womens' reproductive role was important for a good society. J S Mill [1] advocated egalitarian economic reforms which would promote women's economic autonomy. Women's lower wages he pointed out were unrelated to productivity and were the result of customs and prejudices. He did not perceive the contradictions in capitalism and liberalism which espoused individualism and free entry in the market along with prevalent sexual division of labour.. Webs[2] and other Fabian socialists gave an explanation to lower wage of women, that competition between unmarried and married women, who supplements husband's income pushes down the wages foe all women. Alfred Marshall,[3] propounding the human capital theory says wage depends on labour productivity, which improves with the education is given by the state. At the same time he says mother must be given motherhood skills. Lower wage for women is caused by customs. He did not bother for the inconsistency in his conclusions. A C Pigou[4] too addresses the issue of unequal wages. He ingeniously says women are paid what they deserve. The very segregation of women into women's job makes it difficult to evaluate what is a fair wage. None of these early attempts to grapple with women's economic activity ever find a place in the teaching of history of economic thought.

1.1. ECONOMICS AND WOMEN

Economics as a discipline lacks even a fringe field devoted to the study of women. It is predominantly male dominated. All types of planning and policies are geared to promote economic growth rates . At the most the mainstream economics deals with the problem of female labour .Until women studies gained credibility, until international agencies promoted gender concerns in development aid serious economist avoided gender issues.. This myopia is inherent in any patriarchal organisation and creation of knowledge. Entry of two reputed noble laureates, Amartya Sen [5] and Garry Becker [6] into the field of gender studies enlarged the credibility of feminist economist among the mainstream practitioners.

Dominant paradigm in economic today is the neoclassical one ,which is accepted as mainstream economics. Defining neo classical Economics, as Robbins does as, "the study of the allocation of scarce resources among different and competing ends" is too generalised, since various non neo-classical schools such as the Marxist and Austrian also analyse resource allocation. The ideological and methodological basis of neoclassical economics is impersonal functioning in a free market situation, which automatically brings about an efficient allocation of resources among individuals, who are free and rational, seeking maximisation of profits, as producers and of utility as consumers. With the immense sophistication in methodology that focuses almost exclusively on quantification relevance has been subsumed by method leading to tyranny of methodology that classifies uncomfortable issues such as patriarchy as non issue and thus invisible. Abstractions has reached such levels that reality becomes an exception.

Neo classical economics generally ignores that every economy is characterised by two inter dependent systems- the system of production of material goods and the system of reproduction of the labour force-an patriarchy is fully integrated with production relations and productive forces. Consequently, the central point of economic theory ,is smoothened to such a degree that all class and gender differences are erased from the analysis. Thus economics analysis is gender-neutral. As are technology, market and development- the list is endless. This class neutrality and gender-neutrality postulates a single universal rationality, totally out of keeping with reality. Neo classical economic theory has concentrated more on wage differentials rather than gender segregation, employing mainly models of perfect competition where wages are equal to the values of worker's marginal product. The conclusion of such an analysis is that women's economic situation is a result of tastes and choice of women themselves and of employers etc., acquired through both specialisation of and socialisation by individuals .[7]

The new home Economics developed by Chicago

school [8] extended the theory of comparative advantage to the gender-based division of labour to explain why women specialise in household work. This school argues that the historical division of labour between men and women gives men a natural and inevitable comparative advantage in market activities and women in house work resulting in efficiency gains. Women consciously choose housework due to tougher market conditions. .Further productivity differential is explained by low levels of experience, skills, efficiency and education. Marriage is equated to a two person firm and is defined as a contract in which one partner is the entrepreneur hiring another and reaping residual profits. The two major variations of neoclassical theories based on models of perfect competition that explains wage differentials are overcrowding and human capital. In both a workers wage equals the value of her marginal product. So wage differential exist because of their differing productivities, either due to women's lower level of accumulated human capital or to over crowding with its affiliated implication of a relatively low capital labour ratio. As opposed to the overcrowding approach the human capital approach does not assume that men and women are perfect substitutes. This explains wage and productivity differential through differences in the quality of labour between men and women. Human capital is acquired by workers who invest in themselves through education and training. Cost is compared with returns in terms of wages. This theory thus concludes that as men have invested more in themselves they have more human capital than women and so receives higher wages. This approach ,just like overcrowding approach assumes freedom of choice with out taking into account the restrictions imposed by society on both women's freedom and her choice. Maden's model [9] represent another third approach to gender. It is based upon theory of monopsony.

The monoposonist gives wages lower than the value of the marginal product. The degree of such divergence depends upon the strength of the monopsony elements in labour market. The central component of this model is the relationship between wages and elasticity of labour supply. The less elastic the supply curve of labour the lower will be the wages. Therefore women receive lower wages than men because their supply curve is less wage –elastic. Various econometric studies have been conducted to show the contribution of various factors to the wage gap. But entire neo classical apparatus is not able to explain wage differentials fully even with in the capitalist system.. It fails to explain even the survival issue. The neo classical economic theory states that as wages increases the supply of labour will also increase. This is questionable for women. It is found that women withdraw themselves from the labour market as economic condition improves. It indicates that women work for survival but not out of choice. Studies have identified large number of factors that reduce women's participation in the labour market. These include rise in male earnings, average household size, per capita income, size of landholding, caste, status and agricultural productivity, level of education etc

1.2. GENDER DISCRIMINATION IN INDIA

India is one of the few countries of the world where sex ratio is adverse for females. The sex ratio except few states, has been consistently falling. The child-sex ratio is also declining over the decades. The birth of a girl child has remained the most unwanted and ominous. The female foeticide is still a serious menace in the country. The infant mortality rate is much higher among girls than boys. Son preference continues in both rural and urban area , and among educated and uneducated families. Both father and mother pray God for a male child. Early marriages are rampant in every parts of the country except towns and cities. The female literacy rate in both rural and urban areas has remained lower than the male literacy rate. In the rural areas, the school attendance among girls is very low and school drop out is very high . In the urban areas, on the contrary educated parents consider daughter's education as expenditure while son's education as an investment. The heinous practice of dowry has been increasing ,regardless of the caste and class of the household. The case of bride-burning has been increasing in the society. Mothers are accustomed to all familial tradition and regards their own status as inferior within the family.

The participation of women in the political system of India has remained very low. 'Feminization of job' is a myth. Their economic citizenship has not increased. The dependency ratio in the entire society has remained very high. Therefore percapita income of India has remained low. The productivity of female workers have remained low. The exploitation of casual women workers is very high. The work participation rate among female has remained very low. The wage rate for female workers has remained also very lower. The irony is that all legislations and programmes meant to protect and ensure gender equality have remained only on papers.

Since the beginning of planned development, women have been viewed as a deprived section requiring welfare measures. Indian culture and social ethos have to a large extent been influenced by a patriarchal value system. Given the cultural and social background, whether 73rd amendment off the constitution would be able bring about a significant change in the exiting situation leading to empowerment of women is still an open question. As a result of deeply entrenched social attitudes and practices, women by and large have not been independent decision makers in the country. Their decisions in most cases have been influenced by the wishes and dictates of the male family members. They are always guided by patriarchal social system and therefore are discriminated against in terms of food and health care and education.

There is a shocking aspect of recent census i.e. a sharp decline in the female-male ratio in several states. It is the consequence of female foeticide on a massive scale, if not female infanticide and high female child mortality rates. Bose (2001) observes says, It is unfortunate that even in southern India, except Kerala, the child sex ratio has declined. The 2001 census results fully validates India's population problem in terms of the adverse role of four BIMARU states. The situation has worsened in these backward states. . On the basis of a 50-point decline in the child sex ratio, he classifies Punjab, Haryana, Himanchal Pradesh and Gujarat as DEMARU (Daughter Elimination) States

Gordon Ann et al (2000) look at the characteristics of urban poverty and the effects of the monetized economy on the livelihood of the urban poor of developing countries. Such population often uses natural resources e.g. land, water, agricultural produce and wild resources to support their livelihoods. There are many ways in which livelihoods of the urban poor are bound up with natural resources, even though they are removed from the more obvious rural setting. They analyze such linkages including those provided though employment, consumption, migration the environment and institutions. They take a holistic view and cover both economic and social components affecting livelihoods and associated factors notably with respect to health and education. The final section of the study provides conclusions for policy at the macro level and also with respect to urban infrastructure and planning, governance, employment and safety nets. The development of appropriate policy requires an understanding of the way urban poor people use natural resources, the links they retain with rural areas and how they are affected by agricultural, trade and general macro economic policies.

Despite the shifts to decentralized planning, policy still focuses on treating the symptoms of poverty rather than addressing the underlying causes. They conclude that greater understanding of the underlying causes, addressing livelihood system, inequalities, and environmental degradation and meeting basic needs would seem to be necessary for effective regional development policy. This means empowering local people to manage the resources on which they depend. They identify the opportunities for both external interventions and internal redirections of resources and assessment of the complementarily of contributions and tradeoffs between outcomes (Dalal, 2003). This particular view point calls for an area-based rather than sectoral approach to rural development and supports the devolution of resources and authority to the district level.. Dalal (1995) examining the gender relations in the villages, holds that the caste system and cultural practice of seclusion are important factors shaping the social technology. The separation between paid and unpaid work leads to erroneous perceptions about the economic contributions of male and female within on household promoting the inferior economic and social position of women. Generally upper caste women are more secluded. The unequal status of women extends into labour market where female wage earners trapped in low paying low status jobs. This wage gap result from discrimination, occupational segregation, low educational levels, lack of skills and constrained mobility. Women in rural India endure exploitation from three interlocking systems: gender, caste and class. The poor and low caste women are continuously marginalized in rural areas (Dalal: 41) Being displaced form cottage industries and pushed to the edge of survival have received no benefit from economic reforms. They are crowded in low paying menial and manual jobs of the cities Although women do not improve their economic conditions by migrating to the cities, lack of farm and non farm rural jobs and urban biased export promotion policies intensify rural urban migration. There is no guarantee that adoption of an integrated domestic – market oriented rural economic policy can break the culture of seclusion and the caste barriers that permeate the entire country.

1.3. GENDER EMPOWERMENT

Although gender empowerment has been a buzzword in development circles, the concept has been used in so many different ways by different agents that it remains ambiguous. Conceptualizing power and gender adequately entails understanding its multi dimensional nature, the complex ways in which women experience subordination and the ways in which they negotiate or manage this state of affairs.

The gender gap in indices such as life expectancy, literacy and earning have in fact increased from sixties to eighties in south Asia and Sub Saharan Africa. UNDP developed Gender Development Index(GDI) as a tool to capture gender inequality. It notes the inequalities between men and women on the same variables that make up the Human Development Index related to the over all achievements in that society. It includes three variable: health education and income. It has been criticised on the ground that by considering only three variables, it fails to take into account important dimensions such as the quality of community life access to basic amenities and human rights. Important dimensions relevant for women such as safety and security , household allocation of resources, unpaid labour, mobility constraints and on sexual and reproductive freedom by patriarchal ideology do not find any place. It is argued that rising incomes may not indicate improved status for women. Education and income may be high, there may still be greater degree of violence against women. In a society there may not be overt gender disparities in provisioning for basic needs, but dowry demand may be showing escalation. Recognising the centrality of gender based power imbalances the UNDP has clearly identified the movement towards gender equality as a political process. UNDP's Gender Empowerment Measure (GEM) attempt to reflect women's political participation, their access to professional positions and their earning power. A comparison of GDI and GEM yields interesting results .For example countries like France and Japan are high in GDI but lag far behind on the GEM. Some developing countries like China ,Cuba and Barbados have high GEM ranking than developed countries like Japan, France and Spain. The GEM is also criticised on the ground that it is again based on three variables. It is built on a very narrow conception of empowerment. It does not include legal and human rights nor does it reflect the ways in which cultural constructions of gender identity. Thus it is clear from the above discussion that if one attempts to assess the impact of structural reforms differential on men and women, the conventional parameters used to measure gender disparity is not enough. It is therefore necessary to consider research methodologies that go beyond the quantitative in order to do justice to the complexity of these phenomena.

Dreze and Chen (1995) in their paper contend that the concern for widows cannot be dissociated from those of women in general. They have identified some essential factors that account for high levels of deprivation and vulnerability among widows of India. These include limited freedom to remarry, insecure property rights, and social restrictions on living arrangements, restricted employment opportunities, and lack of social support. They highlighted the social risk and legal hurdles widows face when they try to secure their property rights. There is persistence of negative attitude to women in general. It is right to give attention to widowhood as a particular cause of deprivation. . But this does not mean that action has to take the form of working for and with widows in isolation from other women. They argue that there is intimate links between the predicament of widows and a wide range of patriarchal institutions such as patrilineal inheritance, patrilocal residence and gender division of labour. The cause of widows must be seen as an integral part of the broader battle against gender inequalities.

Krishnaraj (2001) contends that women's subjugation seemed inextricably tied to their economic status. Gender issues were not reflected in the mainstream Economics. Economics as a discipline lacks even a fringe field devoted to the study of women. It is predominantly male dominated. This myopia is inherent in any patriarchal organization and creation of knowledge. Entry of Amartya Sen and Becker into the field of gender studies enlarged the credibility of feminist economist among the mainstream practitioners. Now women have got visibility only, but not power. Knowledge will spur conscience of the gatekeepers of the economic discipline. Feminist economics has a coherent set of ideas that can be used as a platform for examination of the background assumptions in Economics.

Equal access is desirable for several reasons: women and other marginalized groups have important skills and experience that can enrich the development process Dupar and Badenoch(2002). Access to decision making is itself empowering for these groups and provides great social benefits. Gilling et al (2001) remark that there is an emerging consensus that effective poverty reduction requires action on a range of broad ,inter-linked fronts and four distinct areas: First, action is needed to increase the income and expenditure of the poor .Second, action is necessary to improve the access by the poor to assets, services and facilities. Third, it is necessary to empower the poor enabling their participation in political and social processes. Fourth, It is important to reduce vulnerability by addressing chronic insecurity both at individual and meso level

Dorward et al (2003) focus on an important gap in conceptualization and emphasise on markets and their roles in poverty reduction. In many poorer rural areas, increasing productivity of farm activities will have greater potential for stimulating poverty-reducing growth, whereas increased productivity of non-farm activities will play a more prominent role in supporting secondary activities. Mathur (2000) examines the agricultural development and employment scenario in rural areas. He analyses the growth of rural non farm sector and self employment opportunities. He opines that overwhelming majority of village women is not apparently unemployed but are engaged for a major part of their time in some activity ,albeit, at very low levels of productivity and earnings.

Urban employment has grown at the 4 percent while rural employment has grown at 1.7 percent during 1972-88. The rate of growth of employment is much less than the rate of growth of labour force. Talukadar (2000) holds that employment situation of India is marred by a number of ugly marks. Relative share of male and female in total employment has not changed much over the decades. It has remained 2:1. He has examined the contributions of rural industrialization program, wage employment schemes and other initiatives of the government to employment generation for villages.Saikia (2001) examines the role of women in crop production and allied activities in rural Assam of India. She considers many activities that are often not counted as economically productive such as time spent in processing food and care of animals. She attempts to quantify the involvement of women in decision making process both with in and outside the household and examines the extent to which such involvement varies between female –headed and male-headed households.

Patriarchy is very strong among high caste household. The most important factor affecting women autonomy is social prestige associated with higher caste Hindu families. Chattopadhaya and Seddon (2002) hold that women take advantage of their increasing access to education to increasing their autonomy. In spite of being an essential economic contributor, there are social constraints, which work against the women to improve her status and position within the household. When a women is more or as well educated than her husband she tends to be better positioned than otherwise. (Chattopadhaya and Seddon 2002 : 67) Female labour who work and earn do not automatically enjoy some rights .It is again dependent on caste hierarchy. A variety of cultural and socio psychological factors determine her autonomy.

Knowledge of local people is an enabling component of development. Kolawole (2001) argues that local or indigenous knowledge is essential for rural development. He provides the conceptual framework to distinguish between the various knowledge systems currently in use. He argues that western world must respect the cultural values of indigenous knowledge and rights of indigenous people. Ellis (1999) in his paper examines livelihood diversification as a survival strategy of rural households in developing countries. Although still of central importance, farming on its own is increasingly unable to provide a sufficient means of survival in rural areas. The study aims at: first, raising the awareness of livelihood diversification in approaches to rural development, second, considering the interaction among diversification and poverty farm productivity natural resource management and gender relations in rural areas and finally, advancing the policy understanding of diverse rural livelihoods. He analyses the positive and negative effects of diversification. Bebbington (1993) begins with discussion on sustainability and then develop with a case study based on a field work of Ecuadorian Andean region. He investigates the way in which peasants construct their own concepts of desirable livelihoods. He holds that any strategy of sustainable development must seek to satisfy the livelihood goals of the rural poor and to reconstruct the regional political economy is such a way as to facilitate the satisfaction of these goalsThe peasants seek first and foremost to sustain their livelihoods, which are a composite of agrarian activities, off-farm employment and general social conditions (Bebbington : 34)

Hapke et al (2004) in their article examine how gender ideologies differentially inform men and women's work life course in the fishing economy of southern India. Drawing on interviews conducted with fish traders in Trivandrum of India in1993 and 1999 they construct economic life histories for men and women traders. They use these data to illustrate how gender creates different patterns of paid work for men and women throughout their life courses .They analyze how men and women formulate livelihood strategies differently as a result of that differential pattern. The compulsions of commercialization both reflect and reward masculine norms of work and economy. To the extent that women are not able to conform bears directly on their long term ability to earn a livelihood. They conclude that gendering livelihood strategies is not a homogeneous process affecting all women in exactly the same way. Rather at different points in the life course, women's access to assets may change. Thus age and stage in work life course are significant factors shaping livelihood options.

The last two decades of the 20th century stand out as a period of momentous change for sub Saharan African economies. Amidst high levels of material uncertainty and risk, rural population has become more occupationally flexible, spatially mobile and increasingly dependent on non –agricultural income generating activities(Bryceson 2000: 11) He synthesizes the findings and main policy implications of his empirical study on rural livelihoods. He concludes that diversification is higher and takes many different forms including migration among men and sale of home-making skills among women. Diversification offers many opportunities but also brings high levels of financial and personal risks and threatens traditional agrarian and family values. The policy must promote human capital, equipping people with skills to work in new environments and continue the search for appropriate low cost ways of enhancing agricultural productivity

1.4. GENDER AND POVERTY

The gender division of labour within the rural household has remained culturally stubborn. Women as a class are oppressed and subdued by the hegemony of social patriarchy. Economic growth has failed to improve the situation either. Rather technology and labour market imperfections have accentuated the concentration of women in domestic works with non-market roles and activities, generating a new process of 'housewifisation', not 'feminization of jobs' in the rural sector. Educated women are employable but not employed. Although gender empowerment has been a buzzword in development circles, the concept r is more intriguing. Gender concerns and discourses survive within the development bureaucracies dominated by men. It is easier for them to ring-fence gender issues as a problem of poverty and to argue against 'feminization of poverty' than to admit the gender disadvantage which crosses the boundaries of class and ethnicity. Since the beginning of planned development, women have been viewed as a deprived section requiring welfare measures. Amarty Sen (1981) argues that the achievement of India in eliminating famines is far from negligible. Dreze say that India has an effective relief system. Food production is endangered because of the damage to the environment .Sen argues that Land degradation, water scarcity and growing vulnerability of economic stress are real threats to food security. The danger is that we treat hunger as the result of underdevelopment. It is wrong notion. Hungry children become disadvantaged adults tomorrow. It perpetuates the state of underdevelopment. The chance for the change begins and ends with the people on the ground Therefore there is need for appropriate mix of resources, food, water, land, credit, training, market and technology in order to create enabling condition for the poor people. Sen maintains that maximizing human capability is crucially bound up with the existence of democratic rights and freedoms(Sen,1981: 4) .Public security an dwell being and protection against starvation is closely bound up with the existence of electoral democracy and political freedoms necessary to make this operational.

Poverty reduction is the bench mark against which success of development institutions must be measured. Bob Currie(2000) in his book based on the village level information collected d from Kalahandi, Kashipur, Nawapara remarks that the standard prescription for growth have not ended poverty or hunger any where. He asserts that hunger and starvation persisted in KBK districts despite large sums are spent in various government programs. He argues that there is the need to give attention to a broader range of public action that may be adopted by citizens to create pressures for better policy administration. Government. can not afford to neglect public need in a liberal electoral democracy(Curies : 178) The ongoing poverty alleviation programes of the government do not attack the hunger at its roots, Rather they tend to polarize the society by concentrating income in the hands of few and narrowing the social and economic opportunities for the poor.

The basic underlying causes of poverty are common across the states. .Kumar (1997) in her book examines the impact of economic growth from 1960 to 1995 and compares the pre and post green revolution period. It is a macro study and it does not consider the spatial variations in poverty and its diverse causes across the states. She examines the trend of agricultural wage rates, terms of trade, land tenurial system, cost of cultivation, food subsidy, and non farm activities over the period. She examines the distributional impact of growth in the framework of prevailing institutional and structural characteristics of the Indian economy with view to having a better understanding of the underlying causes of poverty in the country and explores ways of reducing the incidence of poverty in villages. Bhalla G et al (2003) project the likely scenarios regarding the employment and income growth in agriculture and non-agriculture in rural and urban areas under various assumptions about sectoral growth rates and employment elasticities. It is evident that India faces problems of generating enough employment in the years ahead to keep pace with the growth in the labour force as also in raising wages and productivity of workers. Against this backdrop authors consider possible strategies for increasing employment significantly reducing rural and urban poverty.

The inequality at home is matched by inequality in

the public spheres. Poor women in certain caste and occupation-based jobs remain in traditional fields of employment. Karlekar (1995) in her paper reflects her experience with the field work over the last 20-odd years. When traditional jobs become unavailable due to number of factors, women are forced to seek employment in other areas, which may have no relationship with their original experience and expertise. Women have a marginal role in family decision making; they are primarily responsible for keeping the hearth going. They are occasionally consulted on marriage negotiations but not on any financial matters. (Kerlekar, 1995: 9) According to her growing industrialization and cut throat market economy suits and reinforces the image of the female home makers par excellence. She finds that her perceptions of women and of what is of concern to them have changed radically. By asking the unaskables, with her intellectual baggage, her perception and sensitivity to a plurality of voices has sharpened. She probes beneath the surface. She traces developments in social theory, especially the emergence of women studies and post modernism over the period and links these to changes in her own orientation and work.

The millennium development Goals (MDG) is to eradicate poverty and hunger and promote gender equality and empower women by 2015. He says the developing countries need to continue to improve their policies and the way they are implemented, without grater impetus; there is a serious risk that many countries will fall far short on many of the MDGs (Mark Baird, 2003). Dewan(1996) focuses on gender issues in economic theory. She attempts at analyzing women's exploitation and oppression and on that basis evolving a theoretical perspective has, because of their interdisciplinary approach, tended to isolate women's studies as a new social science. As a result existing disciplines have benefited little from the new perspective of women studies.

The differential social evaluation of the sex roles, the male-orientation in running households coupled with rural poverty and household poverty enmesh in narrowing choices open to women heads of households.Lingam (1994) classifies the women headed households of Godavari district of Andhra Pradesh. She highlights the structural constraints faced by women in their status as household heads with low literacy levels, low asset holdings, lower productivity of land, lesser access to avenues of income-earning and governmental help and the declining kinship support system. Bandopadhayay(2000) in his article on gender and governance says that India's response to the oppression of women can be described as hypocritical at its worst and schizophrenic at its best. Giving the state the benefit of doubt he analyzes the schizophrenic response. He argues that with the present irrational order, which endorses an antagonistic contradiction, women suffer greater subordination and deprivation both at home and in society.

There is real progress in reducing poverty in recent years in China and India argues that both attacking poverty and globalization were right: poverty rose a little from 1987 to 1998 but fell substantially from 1980 to 1998 (Deaton, 2002) Michel C (1997) in his book analyses the impact macro economic reforms on global poverty He highlights on the situation of Sub Saharan Africa, economic genocide of Rwanda, Somalia, Bangladesh, Vietnam, Brazil, Peru Bolivia, Yogosliovia, .He focuses on the process of third worldization of the Russian federation and other countries. He argues that there is worldwide process of overproduction but unemployment and dramatic contraction of purchasing power of people. The global economic system is thus characterized by two contradictory forces: the consolidation of cheap labour economy on the one hand and the search for new consumer markets on the other. Unfortunately the former undermines the latter in the long run. It generates social apartheid and undermines the rights of women. It is a powerful process, which is conducive to globalization of poverty, which ultimately undermines human livelihood and destroys civil society in the south

Meheta et al (2000) contends that reduction in poverty in India is a myth. They argue that poverty alleviation cannot work unless we know the poor. Therefore the planning Commission must undertake the review of the methodology of poverty estimates. The definition adopted by the government at present has conceptual problem and therefore poverty is consequently underestimated. The state should use that statistics to ascertain the objective reality but it should not use it to camouflage the real state of affairs. By only admitting the existence and severity of the problem the state can give the proper priority that the problem deserves.

1.5. GENDER INEQUALITY

No country can claim to achieve development with high degree of social malfunctiong. No society can achieve prosperity with our gender equality. The need to integrate women into development, was internationally proclaimed in 1995 Beijing conference. Human development Report in the same year focused upon gender disparity highlighting that women receive unequal treatment all over the world .Two new indices were floated in this report, the Gender related Development Index (GDI) and Gender Empowerment Measure (GEM). These indices are widely used by social scientist to measure the status of women in different countries of the world. Saradamoni (1994) in his survey of socio economic changes in Kerala focuses on the situation of women. Kerala has acquired the status of a model which has succeeded in raising the physical quality of life people even with a relatively low per capita income Social movement has not only accelerated changes, but instilled in average Keralite a new sense of individual freedom and dignity. The oppressed classes, particularly the women among them, are very keen that their children should not experience a life of humiliation, want and uncertainty, which was their lot. Mothers strongly believe that few years of schooling would be helpful in the long run. They do not resent when their daughters do not learn any of the traditional skills. The customary restraint against female education has practically disappeared in Kerala. There any job is equated with office jobs, because people realize that such jobs alone can free them from workless ness and insecurity. But according to Jeffrey, Kerala is no model. But it has given lessons to follow and rethink. Kerala has the essential ingredients of what we have always believed necessary for women's' emancipation viz Education, employment,, right to property, freedom to vote etc. It is not that Kerala has become a model, but it has accepted and even internalized others as model. It has happened mainly because the educated, politically alive, yet unemployed people are receptive to new ideas and styles to which they are exposed more and more. They don not cling to tradition as in the rest of India. They contend that Kerala with its progressive politics, rational talk and readiness to adopt changes is still bound by hierarchical ideology. The present day consumerism has created an unhealthy individualism coupled with an urge to mint money (Saradamoni, 1994:27). This has given way to indifference and disrespects inside and out side the home. There is general apathy and cynicism prevailing in the state. There is no feminist consciousness or movement in the state to raise women above that. There is hidden political agenda beneath the rhetoric of legal rights of women in India. She Parasar (1994) explores the interaction of gender concerns with political constraints, which acts upon the state while venturing into reforms in the realm of family laws. Several feminist theories may have relevance in societies wherein women have already gained formal equal rights and opportunities, but in India where women face severe legal discrimination, these theories are inadequate. Tracing legislative history she addresses two crucial issues: (1) how the state has justified its discrepant conduct in reforming religious personal laws of different communities and (2) why the state after accepting the principle of equality of sex has failed to incorporate the constitutional promise of equality into the provisions of personal laws .She says that adopting a paternalistic approach and projecting the equality of sex and uniformity in Hindu law as an instrument of political development rather than as a means of ensuring legal equality per se (Parasar 1994: 3) According to her the state had a political motive for repeatedly portraying itself as pro- women.

The heinous practice of female foeticide (FF) is widespread in several Indian states, which boast of a better record of reducing gender inequality. Athreya and Chukanth (2000) condemn These include three southern states (excluding Kerala) and Maharastra. FF is emerging ass a disturbing new phenomenon. It has strong social roots and social sanction in many states. They say that eradication of this practice is not on the agenda of the central or state governments. Even the major political parties do not reflect any gender sensitivity in our society and polity. However in Tamil Nadu over last four years, a serious government effort is on to address the issue.. They highlight the social mobilization in Dharmapuri district of Tamil Nadu. But there is no room for complacency.

The discrimination against women cuts across castes and class. Since the beginning of planned development, women have been vied as a deprived section requiring welfare measures. Indian culture and social ethos have to a large extent been influenced by a patriarchal value system. Given the cultural and social background, whether 73rd amendment off the constitution would be able bring about a significant change in the exiting situation leading to empowerment of women is still an open question. As a result of deeply entrenched social attitudes and practices, women by and large have not been independent decision makers in the country. Their decisions in most cases have been influenced by the wishes and dictates of the male family members. They are always guided by patriarchal social system and therefore are discriminated against in terms of food and health care and education. She hold that if reservation for women in Panchayat Raj Institutions can ensure their empowerment in real terms, social, economic and political conditions which facilitate their participation should be created. Women have to cross many hurdles like archaic bureaucratic practice and administrative insensitivity, secrecy syndrome of the officialdom before becoming the effective partner in the decision making process (Mohanty, 1995).

The structural reforms would have diverse impact on gender dimension. A futuristic nightmare is visualized for women where widespread unemployment will lead to economic insecurity and an increase in crime, where cuts in government spending and employment would mean worsening health services, lesser access to education and deterioration in civic services (Sonpar and Kapur ,2001). The prevalence of mental distress and abuse and violence are important indicators of the well being of a community and are significantly differentiated by gender. The socio economic changes wrought by structural reforms have the potential to disrupt exiting notions of gender in ways that could be threatening demoralizing and oppressive for women. Some of these factors especially those that concern gender ideology may indeed are difficult to measure quantitatively.

Though the need to integrate women into development has been universally recognized the indices to reflect gender disparity are not free from complications. Rustagi (2000) by utilizing secondary data she tries to identify gender backward districts among 15 major Indian states using 13 gender sensitive indicators. In her study, levels of development as well as gender differences in varied spheres such as demographic, educational, health-related, socio-cultural and economic have been taken into consideration(Rustagi, 2000: 5)These diverse aspects shed light on the extent of gender development at the state and district levels.

1.6. INDIAN WOMAN HOOD

An antinomy apparently contradicts claims that arise from a common assumption. The notion of "virtuous woman" which occupies the popular Indian imagination refers to an antinomy. The myth grafts the notion of modesty on "woman" to thereby create an antinomy of domestic loyalty and public shame, adulation and abuse. Accordingly, author highlights the antinomy of worship and abuse in the popular Indian myth of the virtuous woman Since the myth of a devoted wife reinforces the image of women as naturally domestic. This study also explores the ground for reforming and demystifying the notion.

The "virtuous woman" freezes the term loyalty, which suggest patriarchy. The virtuous woman is a myth where the woman embodies a solid shape of sacrifice, a "use-value" for patriarchal economy. It equates virtue (good), domestic space, loyalty to the man. The myth of 'pativrata' continues to enduringly govern Indian womanhood [Chakravarti 1985:48-49]. It endorses the "popular sexist attitude that 'good women stay at home'. It implies ," women who choose to step out from the safety of their homes are 'molestable' as they provoke uncontrollable male lust..." [Agnes 2008]. There are rising instances of increasing sex violence,domestic violence, crimes against women, whose material implications are physical injury, social stigma and the lack of justice.

The demarcation into mutually exclusive categories of mind and body results in loss of "personhood", loss of control and autonomy of the woman.Women live in constant threat of violence; are discriminated against and exploited, are denied the right to spatial mobility, right to make informed choices over their bodies and sexuality. Societal control over and regulation of these spaces renders them powerless.The dichotomy between their mental and physical selves and non-recognition of women's emotional, mental, psychological, spiritual and physical expressions persists irrespective of regional locations and has led to a restriction of spaces.

Thus all these studies indicate that the issues pertaining to women development are very complex. The dynamics of gender in India is very intricate. The whole host of economic and social structures and processes that reinforce patriarchy, devalue and commodify women and promote such gender disparity. In India there is very little critical analysis on impact of technology on women ,impact of education on women, impact of market on women, impact of privatization process on women, etc. Policy-oriented and action-oriented research on women is scarce and scattered. All studies and reports have only remained as a source of data, which endorses the passivity of the state. Effective policy design requires an effective understanding of the gender issues within a broad social framework. Gender equality is the most significant factor that determines the social transformation. The prosperity of the country depends on the social development which comes through mainstreaming gender. Real development has to be gender-neutral.

REFERENCES

1. Mill J S (1879) The Subjugation of Women, reprinted in *Essays on Sex Equality* (ed) Alice Rossi. Chicago University Press. Chicago.
2. Webb Sydney(1891) The Alleged Difference in the Wages paid to Men and Women for similar work, *Economic Journal*, Vol.1(4)
3. Marshall Alfred(1907) The Social Possibilities of Economic Chivalry, *Economic Journal,*17 March,7-29
4. Pigou A C(1952) Men's and Women's Wages, reprinted in *Essays in Economics,* Macmillan ,London.
5. Sen Amartya(1995)Gender inequality and theories of Justice, in *Women,Culture and Development* (ed) Martha Nussbaum and Jonathan Glover, Clarendon press, London.
6. Becker Garry (1971)*Economics of Discrimination*, University of Chicago press, Chicago
7. Waehrer HY (1977) An economic perspective in Glazer N and HY Waehrer (eds) *Woman in a man-made world*, Rand Mcnally, Chicago..
8. Becker Garry,op.cit.
9. Maden JF(1973) *The Economics of Sex Discrimination*, Lexington, Massachusetts.
12. Hirway and Mahadevia (1996) op cit.
13. Parental acquiscence and even encouragement of the tragic situations is found in traditional values and social attitude.
14. Dube Leela (1981) The Economic Role of children in India. Methodological issues, in Garry Rodger and Guy Standing (ed) *Child work, Poverty and Underdevelopment*, ILO, Geneva, ch.7,p,184.
15. Bardhan Kalpan (1985) Women's work, welfare and status, Forces of tradition and change in India, *EPW*, Vol..XX(51-52), Dec. 21-28
16. Informal sector refers to dualism of Boeke and Arthur Lewis (1954) and Fei Rani's (1964). The onerous existence led by sizeable group in the lower echelons of the urban economy is partly due to stagnation, The contrast refers less to the actual labour performance and more on the context within which people work. This dualism stresses not on the nature of the employment but

on the mode of production. See Mazumdar D (1976) The urban informal sector, *World Development* , Vol 4, pp.555-79. Also see :Hart JK (1973) Informal Income opportunities and urban employment in Ghana, *JL of Modern African studies*, vol.11. pp.61-89. Dasgupta B (1973) Calcutta's informal sector, *IDS Bulletine*, vol.5 (2-3) pp.53-75.

17. Breman Jan (1985) A dualistic labour system : a critique of the informal sector concept in Ray Bromley (ed*) Planning for Small enterprises in third world cities*, Pergamon Press. Oxford, Also see- Joshi Heather (1980).The informal urban Economy, *EPW,* Vol xv(13) March. ; Papola T S (1980) *Informal sector in a developing Economy*, pub, Delhi.
18. The exhaustive review of relevant literatures is done in the succeeding chapter.
19. Mincer Jacob (1974) Schooling,Experience and earnings, NBER,New York
20. MazumdarD(1978) Labour market segmentation and determinants of Earnings,WB SWP.278
21. Mohan R (1981) Determinants of labour earnings indevelopibng countries,WB SWP. 498.

2

Growth and Equity

The symptoms of the present economic crisis of India are basically attributable to structural deficiencies and rigidities of the development process that has an inherent tendency to generate macro economic imbalances which have jeopardised the growth process. It is also true that plethora or direct controls over investment, production, prices, imports, foreign capital and even exports have played havoc with the industrial efficiency and therefore, with the process of sustainable development. Rigidity and regulation breeds corruption, which is the biggest, most pervasive and corrosive problem of India. It weakens the links between policy decisions and their implementation. The real problem does not lie anywhere other than "economic rigidity and non-accountability." India has not yet achieved the flexibility in the domestic economic system in order to achieve growth sustainability

The notion of sustainable development can be regarded as a result of the need to solve a potential and/or actual conflict between growth and conservation, with a particular view on efficiency and equity, now and in the future. It recognises the goal of the survival of human species, of the realisation of unacceptable quality of life for each individual in present and future generations, and of a wise management of natural resources and ecosystems, with the help of a broader economic system. Sustainable development highlights the long-term doomsday scenario and puts emphasis on intergenerational equity, economic-ecological integration and regional scale. It shows a compassionate concern for the posterity. It contends that environment and growth are not contradictory. A sound resource base is a prerequisite for sustainable development, which is defined as the progress that seeks to meet the needs and aspirations of the present generation without compromising the ability of future generations to meet their requirements. It reconciles the need for conservation with the need for development at one stroke. It integrates the imperatives of developmentalism and environmentalism. Sustain ability implies at least the maintenance of the level of wellbeing so that it improves the quality of life, but never allows a regression on through time.

But around the globe throughout the history most modern human institutions have evolved in the ways that are at best oblivious and at worst positively hostile to the health of environment. Man's obsession with economic development till today continues to commit two fallacies: (1) It considers the man kind alone and ignores the interdependent system and (2) It treats environment as a commodity.

2.1. FREE MARKETISM

The policy of free marketism has now become a global phenomenon and order of the day. It is the shock therapy of the World Bank. Practically all over the world (except Cuba, North Korea, Myanmar etc.) there is a move towards free market not only in domestic economic activities, but also in foreign economic transactions. This world wide liberalisation and globalisation programme owes its origin to several factors: (1) the external debt crisis in many developing countries, (2) excessive fiscal improvidence and profligacy of developing countries, which resulted in unmanageable foreign exchange deficit, (3) disenchantment with the system of central planning, corruption and inefficiency in developing countries, (4) public disgust with the operations of welfare state in industrialised countries, which led to the rise of Reaganism and Thatcherism, (5) the collapse of socialist regimes in Eastern Europe, and (6) finally, the spectacular growth of income and standard of living of East and South-East Asian countries through market and trade.

It is interesting to note that, at this juncture, there is convergence of views of both North and South. FBM now holds the centre-stage of attention of both groups of economists of advanced, industrial countries and developing countries. The policy of 'free market mechanism' has been proclaimed as the benign means of relieving the West from 'recession' and developing world *from* 'stagnation.' Ardent votaries of this policy advocate as a "Rules of Thumb" for a blind pursuit, which instead of producing desirable effects may result in disastrous consequences for the developing countries (Hossain 1993). Because free marketism may be a necessary condition but not a sufficient condition for the resumption and reignition of economic growth. At best, economic growth may be an assured product of FBM but not sustainable growth. Above all, it is an accepted fact that even sustainable economic growth does not necessarily lead to 'development' in backward economics. Economic indices and social indices are incompatible and inconsistent. Therefore one has to have an uneasy feeling as to the efficacy of this doctrine of shock therapy. It is an experimental path with different institutional framework and operational rules. It is based on myopic and erroneous premises. It is still hooked on to the theory of 'trickle down effect.' High rate of economic growth is believed to automatically solve all other critical issues like unemployment, inequality, poverty and rural development. It is purportedly ordained with the ideology of 'laissez faire,' where even Adam Smith did not contend an undiluted free marketism. Even Smith was advocating for invisible hand (marketisation) subject to the laws of the state and moral codes of the society. Thus, SAP is likely to fail because it is based on naive illusions of high-tech, which is never defined and ignores the fundamental factor of unequal development. There are many complex facets, and hypocrisy and the failure to comprehend it is likely to result in wrong kind of globalisation.

The identical policy reforms accepted as the 'rules of thumb' and applied indiscriminately, is very unwarranted. The policy of devaluation and monetary tightness, for instance, has proved to be appropriate for some Countries and very harmful for some others. The socio-economic impact of SAP is not uniform among social groups, regions and countries. In industrial countries it has raised labour productivity, but in the process it has accentuated the unemployment rate. It has also succeeded in lowering the inflation rate and fiscal deficit. However, so far there is no sign of an improvement in the overall growth rate of output and income in some countries. On the contrary, income disparity among households and regions have tended to rise. In East and South-East Asia it has been successful and has raised the average standard of living of people. On the other hand, the African economics, particularly the Sub-Saharan region, are undergoing the economic retrogression (i.e., rise in poverty, unemployment, malnutrition, disease and infant mortality). In countries of Latin America, there is mixed experience. But in both African and Latin America the liberalisation process has shifted the labour from the organised to the informal sector where the wage rate is very low and social security is absent. Therefore, the impact and efficacy of the current worldwide movement towards market-induced strategies, discarding the old ideologies can not be understood by clubbing all these countries together. One need to distinguish among four groups of countries: (1) Industrially advanced countries, (2) Newly industrialised countries, (3) Erstwhile centrally planned command economies, and (4) Developing economies of the South. The level of development and characteristics of these countries widely differ. With unfettered openness, scrambling to embrace the market is common for all but the driving forces are different for each. The standard FBM-prescriptions are largely meant only for an overheated industrial economy in order to (i) reduce investment demand at home (ii) make exports competitive, and (iii) attract foreign fund to ease BOP Situations. Therefore, SAP has produced desirable results where the preconditions like good infrastructure, low population growth, growth of human capital, high saving and investment rates committed Bureaucracy, improved work culture, general thrust on productivity, efficiency, and discipline are conducive. Where these conditions are not satisfied it results in inequity with or without growth. Even in successful cases, regional disparity has widened, especially in large economies like, China, Brazil and Indonesia.

2.2. REALITIES OF FRIENDLY MARKETS

Let us put an insight into the role and functioning of the global market. In many countries, markets are neither free nor efficient nor equitable. Markets are never friendly to the poor, to the weak and vulnerable, either nationally or internationally. The markets are handmaidens of powerful interest groups and they are greatly affected by the prevailing distribution of income. Markets can not become neutral or competitive in all situations, unless the playing ground is made more even and playable to begin with. Majority is going to fall outside the marketplace because they do not have enough education, health and nutrition to compete on any footing.

Globalisation of Market unfortunately is not friendly to poor nations or poor people. Let us look at some of the dramatic facts that we derive from the Human Development Report about the functioning of global market.

1. The poorest 20% of the world's population receive only 0.2% of the global commercial credit, 1% of the world trade and 2.7% of the global foreign private investment.
2. The real income disparity between the top 20% and bottom 20% of the I world's population has exploded to 150 times by 1990-more than twice the level of 1960 as a result of working of the global market.
3. The indebted countries of Latin America have paid 4 times higher real interest rates in 1980 compared to the industrial countries (17% compared with 4%) because of the major fall in their commodity prices.
4. The share of Sub-Saharan Africa in global trade markets has declined from I 3.8% in 1970 to 1 % in 1989. in spite of many trade concession.
5. The global capital market has worked in such a fashion in the 1980s that the poor nations started transferring $50 billion per annum of net resources to the rich nations every year.
6. The world commodity market has functioned in such a manner that primary commodity prices (except oil) have declined to their lowest levels since great depression. Sub-Saharan Africa alone lost more than $50 billion in export earnings between 1986 and 1990 because of depressed commodity prices.
7. Above all, all developing countries are being denied at least US $500 billion of economic opportunities in

the global markets every year because of trade restrictions, immigration controls and uneven capital flows. This is about ten times more than the amount of annual foreign assistance they receive.

8. With the adherence of FB model 24 countries have become losers, out of which 17 are in Sub-Saharan Africa, 5 in Latin America and 2 in Middle East. The growth rate of real *per* capita GDP estimated in 1991 (estimated *for* the economies in the lowest quintile of growth) during 1965-85 are shown in the part thesis corresponding to each country. Afghanistan (-.003), Angola (.028), Argentina (0.001), Benin (-0.004), Central African Rep (-.004), Chad(-.016), Gambia (-.010), Ghana (-.012), Guinea (.000), Guyana (-.005), Kuwait(-.o65),' Liberia (-.008), Madagascar (-.018), Mauritania (-.002), Mozambique (-.029), Nicargua (-.018), Nigeria (-.002), P. New Guinea (.000), Peru (.001), Sengel (-.004), Sirra Leona (-.008), Sudan (.002), Zaire (-.011) and Zambia (-.022).

Thus, we observed that the benefits of the global market have been surreptitiously hijacked by the rich always. It is more comfortable to accept the reality that it is almost impossible to redistribute income and asset more equitably. There are many practical problems, there are several political limits. But we can find no difficulty in distributing knowledge and skill equitably among the countries. It is a tremendous leveling *force* to enable people to compete in the market. That is why unless there is a tremendous investment in human capital formation in developing countries, the market shall continue to work inefficiently and inequitably.

2.3. REAL ISSUES

Economic reforms are guided by rules of thumb. The under lying general equilibrium model of the economy *for* which these standard rules, apply is an unrealistic portrayal of most of the developing countries. The model does not seem to address the complex economic structures in developing economies. The model holds good only under very restrictive, assumptions, perhaps only *for* small economies and not *for* large ones. It lacks theoretical support and empirical evidence. There are examples of success and failure of both orthodox and heterodox policy initiatives. Developing countries with different historical contexts and institutional set up, varying lines of casualty in their economic systems require different approaches to stabilisation and structural reforms. Be this as it may, factors such as the structural reforms. Be that as it may, factors such as the structure of the existing capital stock, size of population and natural resource endowments put somewhat flexible boundary conditions on policies aimed at raising productive efficiency, but a general solution is non-existent.

With the ongoing process of globalisation and liberalisation the following six pertinent questions may be raised in the context of Indian economy. Can the policy of free marketism

(a) reduce regional inequality?

(b) reduce income inequality?

(c) reduce rural urban disparity?

(d) mitigate gender inequality?

(e) solve unemployment crisis?

(f) ensure inter generational equity?

2.4. REGIONAL INEQUALITY

The protagonists of economic reforms believe that the agriculture can work as the biggest safety net in the process of adjustment by softening the rigorous of inflation as well as by raising income and employment for the poorer sections of the population. It is misconceived. It is true that a measure of liberalisation is necessary at this present stage, where further growth of the organised parts of the economy would be left to the markets; but unfortunately a large part of the economy particularly the agricultural sector still remains unorganised and backward. This vast unorganised sector can not be integrated automatically with the mainstream of market-led economy. The problems and constraints associated with the agricultural sector of Indian economy would further worsen with the new economic policy. The root of this incompatibility lies in the growth urban bias and rural neglect (rural-urban dualism).

There is a misconception that the agriculture sector as a whole is a heavily subsidised and pampered sector. When we meaningfully divide the agricultural sector into three sub sectors; (1) Green Revolution (GR) Sector, (2) Non-Green Revolution (NGR) Sector, and (3) Agro Based (AB) Sector, one can easily perceive, the impact of new economic reforms. It is understood that the activities of the AB sector are likely to be of considerable help in increasing exports, creating skill- based opportunities and technological up-gradation in farming. But as regards policies, this sub-sector primarily needs a level playing field like other industries and a legal-cum-regulatory regime, which is completely non-existent.

Green revolution areas have made considerable progress towards modernisation and market linkages. But the major part of the agricultural sector still remained 'non-green.' A sharp contrast has emerged during the planning era, among the GR and NGR areas in terms of rise in production, improvement in the yields and extension of irrigation facilities. The contrast is attributable to a number of factors including soil, climate etc, but the most important factor has been pronounced policy bias towards GR areas (where production has increased by more than 9-fold and its yield has increased by 4-fold). The growth in wheat and rice crop have benefited most from the supportive policies for adoption of new technologies, intensified use of modern technologies inputs and increased availability of dependable irrigation. But as regards the coarse cereals and pulses there is lack of policy support. They are neglected by the policy-makers as well as by the market, as the demand for them is very weak. There are number of institutional barriers inhibiting agricultural growth in NGR areas: Eastern India, dry land areas in central, western and southern parts of India. Fallow and wasteland constitute more than 20% of the total land of these regions.

The NGR sector, so far has received meagre policy support excepting relief and assistance programmes. This subsector usually attracts attention only during the period of distress. Both the endogenous impulses for growth and external forces bringing beneficial changes have been very weak in the areas. With the new economic reforms, the isolation of this sector is likely to be more pronounced and its vulnerability to external events is likely to rise. On the contrary, these areas are likely to be more responsive to all development interventions. These regions need major reforms in infrastructure, markets, credit and cooperatives. Once these preconditions for steady growth are established it would be easier to tackle other problems. They need a wide spectrum of policy regime comprising anti-poverty programmes, provision of infrastructure, improvements in markets and institutions, various schemes of input supply and above all, supportive macro economic policies. The task of developing these areas is to build up a society but not merely investing in the sector of an economy. Thus the withdrawal of the role of government will imply the destruction of the unorganised part of the economy and vulnerable section of the society.

2.5. INCOME INEQUALITY

According to Kuznetsian conjecture the inequality reduces after the industrial development. According to Kuznets when historical data on inequality(such Gini Coefficient) is plotted in the vertical axis in association with average per capita income in the horizontal axis ,the relationship would be curved in an inverted U-shape with an initial phase of rising inequality succeeded by a phase of diminishing inequality. The figure depicts a smooth bell shape with a peak a per capita GNP around $US,2000 to US 3000. When low income countries have to experience rising inequality in the early phase of industrialisation, social tension is likely to loom large, endangering political stability. Therefore an important agenda in the market-oriented transition economy is to prevent inequality from rising too sharply or to prepare a safety net of social security for those people who might drop down to poverty.

It is more reasonable to treat inequality as the variation among socio-demographic groups rather than over administrative units. Rural urban disparity, gender disparity or disparity between rich and poor are examples of more meaningful from analytical view point. The fact of gross inequalities is very much evident from several estimates. Very little is available in a time series. Nevertheless estimates made from time to time leaves no doubt about the existence of large inequalities in India. It is seen from table –2.1 that in 1994, 20 percent of the households at the lowest rung of the income ladder receive only 9.2 percent of the national income. At the other end 20 percent of households at the highest rung enjoy as much as 39.3 percent of the national income.. If one takes up the lowest 10 percent of the households at the lower end and highest 10 percent at the upper end the fact of inequality is more glaring with the lowest getting as little as 4.1 percent and the highest getting as much as 25 percent of the national income. The trend and magnitude of inequality can be perceived over the years by the data given below.

Table 2.1. Income Inequality

Year	*Bottom 20 %*	*Top 20 %*
1955-56	34(bottom 10%)	9.6(top 25%)
1975-76	49.4	7
1989-90	41.3	8.8
1992-93	42.6	8.5
1993-94	39.3	9.2

The New Economic Policy, which has been designed in the tune of SAP, overlooks various social objectives such as eradication of poverty, greater emphasis on public sector, faster expansion of basic and key goods, prevention of concentration of economic power in private hands, regional balance and promotion of small industries and *khadi* and village Industries etc. It rather runs counter to all these objectives.

At this stage of industrial development in India at least one can not afford to:

(i) forget that there are many supply side bottlenecks; and

(ii) regard distribution merely as an offshoot of the development process.

All strategies for economic development and policies for combating backwardness, poverty, unemployment, inequality, stagnation etc. are constantly being distorted by the new political and bureaucratic practice. It is a kind of trial and error method having no theoretical foundation nor empirical evidence. It is very difficulty to achieve rapid industrial development with existing supply side constraints, which have to be removed by lone; term deliberate planning. The existing resources can not be readily converted into foreign exchange simply by fiscal restraints and sound exchange rate policy. One can not throw the body with the bath water with the excitement about the new economic thinking. On the contrary a society as prismatic and unequal as India's simply cannot afford to regard distribution merely as an offshoot of development process. The development process has to have a very clear accent on raising the productivity of all classes and particularly of the weaker and poorer sections of the society.

Simultaneous attempts towards stabilisation and economic liberalisation may lead neither to macro economic stability nor to the restoration of growth sustainability. 'Trickle down effect' of SAP shall be more than neutralised by corruption, bureaucratisation, unemployment, industrial unrest and low productivity. These problems can not be handled by 'safety nets,' Draconic and abrupt removal of protection is likely to spell disaster for many large scale and small-scale industries. The industrial sector of the economy is likely to drift into stagnation with low industrial growth and high inflation, which will further aggravate the poverty profile of the economy. Unsuccessful fiscal compression is likely to create 'doublesqueeze' and fail to yield the expected reduction in government's fiscal deficit. It will produce; (i) joblessness in the industrial sector; and (ii) price rise of essential goods. Therefore, SAP is likely to lead to continued stagnation rather than a meaningful structural adjustment. It will fail to bring the majority of rural poor into the vortex of economic development.

2.6. UNEMPLOYMENT PROBLEM

As an answer to the third question raised above it can be said here that the large scale centralised approach with its heavy emphasis on capital-intensive industrialisation shall take most of the investible capital. This approach has never raised the volume employment and has never served the poor. The type of industrialisation that the (NEP) contemplates is not going to be of any benefit to the rural poor. Industrial growth and employment are not related to each other. During 1983-88, Planning Commission of India itself admitted that highest growth rate is associated with lowest growth of employment. SAP and NEP are not stunned to increasing employment in the small-scale sector. At the most, it may generate very few job opportunities, for highly skilled people. Industries shall require labour which can not be supplied by the village poor. It produces the goods which they do not consume. Hence the industrial activity is mostly labour- displacing. All types of ancilliary industries are likely to be preempted and a type of vicious process of reindustrialisation is likely to set in.

Globalisation seeks ostensibly for creating more space for private enterprises. But attractive market incentives for capital formation is only a necessary but not sufficient condition for resumption of private investment and industrial development. All efforts are misguided to promote the growth of 'finance capital' and 'portfolio investment' at the cost of industrial capital and at the cost of investment in agriculture and infrastructure. Promotion of 'finance capital' is likely to shore up speculative activities rather than sustained industrialisation. Therefore, SAP is unlikely to bring neither 'allocative efficiency' nor 'productive efficiency.' There is no theoretical support or empirical evidence as to the effect of liberalisation on economic growth. At the most, Indian market may remain as a captive market for the recession-ridden countries. Market forces may fail to unleash forces for growth and at the most it tends to generate low-income activities horizontally.

The unbridled entry of MNCs now enjoy complete administrative, bureaucratic and political patronage in India. It is a deadly alliance which tends to drag India into a neo-colonial dependency. Acceptance of globalisation slogan is pushing the economy headlong into a set or policies which is in a way irreversible. By giving primacy to the role of MNCs in the bid to attract foreign investment all considerations of investment for the economy in terms of satisfaction of mass needs and self-reliant growth have been extinguished. This fits perfectly well with art investment pattern and production structure to sub serve a social milieu and life style which has no relevance for the broad mass of the people and at the same time impedes the progress towards economic self-reliance. Globalisation without adequate preparedness would be tantamount to opening up the Indian Economy to unfair competition. The adjustment programme is likely to be countered productive. There is no dearth or example of countries, following' the path of structural readjustment, have all suffered substantial deterioration in the terms of trade. The outcome of SAP has ranged from moderately successful to disastrous. One should not feel excited with the examples of Eastern Tigers. The success of South Korea, Taiwan, Singapore, it should be remembered, to a large extent is attributable to the role of the state, which developed the necessary infrastructure, human resources, and intervened in the process of resource allocation so as to achieve overall development. Newly industrial countries are the most indebted countries of the Third world (Amin, 1995). They are the real peripheries of enclave market of the developed world. On the other hand one should observe the deadly consequence of FBM with Argentina, Bolivia, Peru, Morocco, Syria, Venezuela, Brazil, Mexico and many other African and Latin American Countries. Growth of GDP in 1992 of Brazil, Peru, Ivory Coast and Mexico are -0.9, -2.8, -0.3, 2.6 respectively. Inflation rates in 1992 over the previous year in Brazil, Peru, Turkey, are 1008%, 74%, 70% and 69% respectively. Real wage has fallen (1984=100) to 76.2, 72.6,

70.5, 87.9 respectively in Argentina, Brazil, Peru, Tanzania. Thus, the adjustment with human face is another fanciful rhetoric to cajole people at large.

2.7. GENDER INEQUALITY

The division of labour by gender within the household of developing countries is stubbornly cultural. Women as a class are oppressed and subdued by the hegemony of social patriarchy. The gender inequality is very sharp with the rural households. Since the employment options available to the rural women are severely limited and since the opportunities for skill acquisition and job mobility are more limited for the rural female than the male, the work for women has come to mean back-breaking toil, endless drudgery and humiliation. High work force participation for the poor female in the rural areas means the relentless weariness of too heavy workloads and the deprivation of childhood care and schooling for their children (particularly for the girl-child) The dividing line between productive work and domestic work is not only arbitrary but also tends to under estimate the women's contribution to domestic work. The rural woman as a class is saddled with 'triple burden.' If one takes into account the unpaid word, in these countries, women in poor households work much longer hours and have no or less leisure time than their male counterparts. The votaries of SAP argue that now there is a trend of continued feminisation of employment in all developing countries. It does not reflect the sign of progress or prosperity. It does not imply the success of free market policy or emergence of new technological break-through or improvement in the efficiency of the secondary sector either. But there are two major reasons which have led to the feminisation of work: (i) the structural shift of employment from manufacturing to service sector activities in these countries, and (ii) the incidence of poverty (economic strain on households inflicted by the double squeeze) and the question of survival.

The present economic reforms, particularly in the Third world countries are likely to promote (1) highly sophisticated technology and (2) create imperfections in the rural factor (particularly labour) market. These two factors tend to continuously displace the female workers from high productive activities to low productive activities. It is tending to accentuate the concentration of women in domestic works and non-market roles and activities. The globalisation of prices (not income) is likely to spell further economic strain on women, in term of work burden and curtailment of family expenditures. Therefore, feminisation of work is likely to result in feminisation of poverty and promote the process of housewifisation further.

2.8. INTERGENERATIONAL EQUITY

Intergenerational equity is implied by the global concern for environmental crisis. The success of free marketisation policy is wholly misconceived from the environmental point of view. It is in fact tending to generate industrialisation process which is not environmental-friendly. No matter, what type of SAP is adopted, the process of extraction, mining and rapid large scale industrialisation is certainly going to pose problems of environmental degradation. Historically economic expansion has led to the reckless exploitation of natural resources with little or no concern for their renewal. Therefore, one point is very clear, that is, 'developmentalism' and 'environmentalism' are incompatible and conflictual to each other. It is an obvious thing that the system which is market-friendly can never be environment friendly. Therefore, in the context of 'free marketism' the concept of environment-friendly development is a myth.

Unfortunately, the concern for environment has emerged from the Western world (after their free riding), from where the incessant urge for developmentalism has manifested. The advocates of developmentalism are very optimistic. They hold that exhaustion of natural resources and environmental crisis simply an event but not at all a disaster. Protagonists of SAP propose market as solutions to ecological crisis. Globalisation shall enhance the exploitation of natural resources with high capital investment, which helps in conservation of resources. They argue that modern scientific development shall take care of depletion and degradation of natural resources. On the contrary the votaries of environmentalism contend that as population tends to surge ahead, the world is heading towards a catastrophe. The natural resources and the environment which is already burdened by the present population growth will simply collapse under the weight of the demand and pressure of future population growth. But in reality the environmental crisis is neither as grim as the pessimists believe nor as rosy as the optimists claim. The most plausible outcome is that we are feeding ourselves at the cost of our children and grand children. The over-ploughing, over pumping intensified use of al! natural resources, in an attempt to survive is possible, only in the short run. But in the long run the dietary intake will creep in, food availability shall fluctuate, crop shall become more vulnerable to pests, weather will fluctuate. And the fact remains that the atmospheric concentration of carbon dioxide has increased by 25% over the past century and oxygen is not growing at double that rate. The ozone is becoming depleted. There is rapid increase in green house effect and global warming. Flotillas of garbage ride the currents of every ocean. Acid rain is killing lakes of every continent. Dozen of species become extinct every month as a result of the expansion of deserts in one hemisphere and denudation of forests in another hemisphere.

It is true that many types of equipment and preventive measures are available which can mitigate the adverse effects of the industrial process on environment. But these processes and equipment are very expensive and frequently not even available to developing countries. This problem has further worsened because knowledge is being treated as a private property in the new patent regime. Modernisation and upgradation of traditional methods of production are often environment-friendly. But it can be achieved only under a regulated regime. Modern science makes it possible through decentralised production processes which are necessarily environment-friendly. But it itself is a function of knowledge. Without globalisation of knowledge and scientific development, the ongoing SAP can only lead to further intensification of the harnessment of natural resources and deterioration of the environmental standards. With the extension of the domain of patentability the contemplated SAP shall lead to globalisation of ignorance but not globalisation of scientific discoveries. Free dissemination of knowledge which today reposes with the developed countries is an essential prerequisite for ensuring environment-friendly development. The ground reality is that the developing countries are now at the stage of underdevelopment. Their intervention and harnessment of environmental resources is likely to be more in the future. As their income level has remained very low, they can not afford to pay attention to the quality of life, the condition of the habitat and imbalance in the ecosystem of themselves nor for their posterity. When the billions of poor people in developing countries can not be denied of their basic requirement for their survival in an era of mass consumption, the consequences of this seems to be very dismal for the whole world in the shape of environmental degradation. The pattern of production and consumption which would be environment-friendly necessarily calls for regulation, government intervention and planning. It can never emerge from the interplay of market forces. The free play of market forces especially in an economic system with a highly iniquitous distribution of income and wealth can not bring about an environment-friendly pattern of development.

The contemplated Economic Growth, in the SAP tends to cause over exploitation of natural resources. Because it is a fact that all capital intensive technologies are energy intensive, if not pollution intensive. The multinational businessmen tend to be oblivious of the consequences to the society, in their scrambling for profit maximisation. Therefore, it is a obvious thing that they never adopt environmentally sound business practices, which reduce emissions, prevent' wastes, consume energy and natural resources. Scarcity of natural resources shall ultimately lead to crisis of survival for all living being. Growth of market can not solve the very crisis it creates. Natural resources can be converted into cash but cash can never be converted into nature's ecological processes. Those who offer market solutions, to environmental crisis limit their thinking. horizon to the market only. They look forward for inventions of substitutes and to the commercial function of natural resources as commodities and raw materials. However, in natures' economy, the currency is not money but life (both of human and other living species). The increased availability of financial resources cannot regenerate the life lost in the nature through ecological destruction. It is a fact that the economic growth based on unsustainable resource-use can not continue indefinitely. It has a built-in-doom. It endangers the carrying capacity of the planet and despoils the life support system. Therefore, the government has a positive role to curb all pollution- intensive activities and energy-intensive activities. It has to encourage energy efficiency and waste minimisation and develop flexible, cost-effective regulatory programmes. Healthy economy and healthy environment do not go together. Thus, if we want to have an environment-friendly pattern of development but not just talk about doing so, state intervention is inescapable. The extent that SAP is attuned to globalisation of the economy and reliance on marketisation one can neither think of simple development in general nor environment-friendly development in particular.

Thus, the answers to above six issues are consistently negative. The transition for the economy as backward as Indian Economy, which suffers from: rigidities in various fronts, macro economic instability and imbalances, non-accountability, bureaucratism and corruption at all levels is likely to only foster the interest of modern capitalism. Therefore, the future implications of economic reforms are dismal in terms of the real issues of equity in developing countries. We are putting the cart before the horse. Development after a point generates and reinforces the need for globalisation but not vice versa. Globalisation without development is likely to lead to the ossification of the structure of underdevelopment. The policy of globalisation for India is premature and misconceived rather than wrong. There are many inherent contradictions, illusions, irrelevance and hypocrisy in the new economic model. It is based on wrong and myopic premises. It does not address the real questions that affect the Indian economy. It puts over emphasis on efficiency and modern industrial sector at the cost of rural sector (Where majority ekes out their living) and equity aspects.

One must always remember one simple thing that the salvation of the developing economy as vast and diverse as India's, lies only in the transformation and revitalisation of its rural economy, which requires extensive role of the public sector and which makes the role of the state inescapable. One's sense of idealism is in direct proportion to one's distance from the real scenario. Even the best judgment of the rich and the best model of the Harvard, Oxford, Yale and Washington can not always reflect and accommodate the harsh realities, potentials and priorities of the majority of the population of the developing world.

2.9. LOOKING AHEAD

The symptoms of the present economic crisis of India are basically attributable to structural deficiencies and rigidities of the development process that has an inherent tendency to generate macro economic imbalances which have jeopardised the growth process. It is also true that plethora or direct controls over investment production, prices, imports, foreign capital and even exports have played havoc with the industrial efficiency and therefore, with the process of economic development. Rigidity and regulation breeds corruption, which is the biggest, most pervasive and corrosive problem of India. It weakens the links between policy decisions and their implementation. The real problem does not lie anywhere other then "economic rigidity and non-accountability." India has not yet achieved that flexibility in the domestic economic system in order to reap the benefits of the internationalisation process.

Thus, many developing countries of the world including India, instead of mindlessly marching with the new economic reforms, requires a type of structural reforms, before opening up its economy to the competitive regime, which should have ensured:

(i) Higher standard of living to the village people,

(ii) Production for mass-consumption,

(iii) Organisational and institutional reforms,

(iv) Bureaucratic and political reforms,

(v) Educational reforms and effective programme for skilling, and

(vi) Use of labour-intensive technology.

On proper diagnosis, Indian economy is carelessly marching on a 'knife-edge balance' with great risk and uncertainty. Hence, at this juncture India instead of following the new path must adopt a policy of decentralism in order to ensure intra-generational equity and Ecosystem approach in order to achieve sustainable growth and intergenerational equity and gender equity.

REFERENCES

1. Barbier E.B., (1989), *Economics, Natural Resources Scarcity and Development* Earth Scan, London.
2. Borelli Peter, (1983), *Cross Roads: Environmental Priorities for the Future,* Island Press.
3. Brown L.R., (1981), *Building a Sustainable Society,* WW Norton, New York.
4. Brown L.R., et al., (1993), *The State of the World,* Report of the World Watch Institute on Progress towards a Sustainable Society.
5. Das Kumar (1988) Ecosystem Approach, *Indian Journal of Regional Science* Vol. xx 0).
6. ————*(1990)* Intergenerational Approach for Sustainable Development, *Proccedings of 11th International Seminar on Environmental Impact Assessment, held at University of Aberdeen,* August.
7. ———(1993) *Environment and Development Conundrum,* Discovery Publishing House, New Delhi.
8. Hekstra G.P., (1989) *Global Warming and Rising Sea Levels,* The Ecologist Vol. (19(1).
9. Hussain M., (1994) *Sustainable Development,* RPH Publishing, New Delhi (ed).
10. Kothari R., (1982) *Environment and Development in Asia and the Pacific: Experiences and Prospects,* UNEP.
11. Nijkamp P., et al. (1993) Dynamic Modeling for Sustainable Development, *Revue European Des Sociales. Science,* Vol. XXXI, (96).

12. Pearce P.W., and Atkinson G (1992) *Measuring Sustainable Development,* CRERGE, University College of London.

13. Redclift M (1987) *Sustainable Development,* Methuen, London.

14. Smith RL (1976) *The Ecology of Man, Harper and Row,* London (ed).

15. Smith WR (1982) *Energy from Forest Biomass,* Academic Press, New York (ed).

16. Tobia MK (1984) *Sustainable Development,* Butterworths, London.

17. Vandana Shiva and J. Bandopadhay (1988) *Political Economy of Ecological* Movements, *Economic and Political Weekly,* Vol. xxiii (24) June.

18. WECD (1987) *Our Common Future,* Oxford Univ. Press, Oxford.

3
Globalization and Neohousewifization

Globalization is a global economic movement of economic integration. Its impact has become all pervasive. All sectors of developing countries seem to be vibrating with economic buoyancy. It has generated an atmosphere of over optimism of instant economic growth. There is expansion of trade, investment, market, and increase in GNP, productivity, per capita income, profit, efficiency, salary etc. Life styles of metro people in developing countries have become more attractive , comfortable and fashionable than ever before. Globalisation is an extremely powerful ideology being projected as having no alternative.[1] It is being regarded substantively as the growing interdependence and interconnectedness of the world that is the part of the logic of modernity We are made to believe that it creates unprecedented new opportunities for sustainable development and poverty reduction. But in fact globalisation poses a great threat to employment, women and livelihood of the vulnerable section. It entails the greatest moral challenge facing our generation.

3.1. GLOBALIZATION PROCESS

The supra national movement of economic reforms

is aiming at export-led growth. The faceless capital has increased enormously while labour has declined. Making globalisation work for the poor is almost an oxymoron. Globalisation to a great extent a euphemism for American imperialism. Market is never friendly to the poor nor backward regions. The benefit of the market driven growth will not automatically reach the poor people.[2] Recent data given both by NSS and NCAER on poverty suggest that there is rise in rural poverty ratios in India since economic reforms. The undoubted increase in economic growth has not trickled down to the poor people. [3] A futuristic nightmare is visualised for women where widespread unemployment will lead to economic insecurity and an increase in crime, where cuts in Govt spending and employment would mean worsening health services. lesser access to education and deterioration in civic services. As jobs disappear and cost of living rises, women will be forced to seek employment in insecure poorly paid jobs .Since gender relations at the household level governing the sexual division of labour tend to remain rigidly in place women will be forced to give up their education or prospects for gainful employment in order to help their mothers with household maintenance. Rising food prices will mean poorer nutrition ,especially for female members of the family

1. Even Professor Amartya Sen has remarked like this in his recent lecture delivered at Mumbai in Feb 2001
2. Harris John (2001), Globalisation and World's Poor, *EPW*, June 9,
3. Lal Deepak et al, Economic Reforms and Poverty Alleviation, EPW, March 2001.

Thus economic reforms, by ignoring the crucial structural aspects of gender, interact with the existing gender asymmetries to affect women in negative ways. They argue that prevalence of mental distress and abuse and violence are important indicators of the well being of a community and are significantly differentiated by gender. The socio economic changes wrought by structural reforms have the potential to disrupt exiting notions of gender in ways that could be threatening demoralising and oppressive for women.. Some of these factors especially those that concern gender ideology may indeed be difficult to measure quantitatively.

Globalisation process has three cardinal aims:

1) Modernisation.
2) Marketisation
3) Multinationalisastion

The post liberalisation period has marked a distinct upturn of the growth trajectory .The urban sector is growing impressively very fast . The growth rate in service sector and IT sector of India has become very impressive But with the euphoria of globalization and 'high-tech civilization', the concern for the people or social development is dismissed as an obsession of egalitarian romantics. It is associated with the power movement of industrial darwinsm ,which entails the disastrious trend of marginalization process. It generates a powerful bypass system which manifests in over exploitation of labour, and other productive resources. It is intensifying the process of casualisation of jobs and informalisation of business. Because it pursues merely pro-business strategy in the garb of pro-market policy. In this process the female suffers the most. It bypasses the woman. Globalisation overlooks various social objectives such as gender inequality and women empowerment.

3.2. GENDER EMPOWERMENT

Although gender empowerment has been a buzzword in development circles, the concept has been used in so many different ways by different agents that it remains ambiguous. The concern for gender empowerment has become as louder as the excitement generated by globalization. Conceptualising power and gender adequately entails understanding its multi dimensional nature, the complex ways in which women experience subordination and the ways in which they negotiate or manage this state of affairs. The highest gender gap is noticed in backward states like Rajstan followed by UP, Bihar, MP and Orissa. The dividing line between productive work and domestic work is not only arbitrary but also tends to underestimate the women's contribution to domestic work. The women as a class is saddled with 'multiple burden'. The family decisions in most cases have been influenced by the wishes and dictates of the male family members. They are always guided by patriarchal social system and therefore are discriminated against in terms of food, work load and health care and education.

Human Development (HDI) is a measure of overall levels of human development in the society and does not measure the gender disparities that exist. and GDI is also measured by many organization. But they are statistical averages, which conceals the reality of Indian society.

Table 3.1 : HDI and GDI

Countries	*GDI*	*HDI-GDI*
India	.553(105)	-1
China	.715(76)	3
USA	.932(4)	2
UK	.920(12)	2

Source: Human Development Report , UNDP ,different Years

GDI= Gender Development Index,

Data given in Table 3.1 reveals the gender inequality across the countries. In terms of Gender Development Index India's rank is 105 among 162 countries The second column indicates the difference between the ranks of HDI and GDI. It is negative for India. It implies that there is gender inequality in these countries. Female Literacy Rate in India is only 44, while it is 75 % in China.

India, particularly Orissa is a mosaic of many paradoxes and contradictions. One such paradox is the gender inequality. The land which worships the woman most , has the highest violence against women and bride burning cases . The capital intensive technology has rather trivialised the gender issue. The whole host of economic and social structures and processes that reinforce patriarchy, devalue and commodify women. Horrendous phenomena as dowry in Orissa has been increasing. It transcends the rural urban dichotomy. Its incidence cuts across all caste and class boundaries . The cases of bride burning has increased. Child marriage practice still prevails. Drop out rates in the schools for girls has been increasing. Practice of girl child labour has been increasing. Selling of girl child has increased. Rape case has been increased. The female foeticide is a serious menace in Orissa. In fact prenatal Diagnostic Centres have become sex determination clinics. It is sheer hypocrisy that the so called modern civilisation with its pretensions to high thinking considers that to be born as a girl is a crime and burden .

After so much technological advancement, women continue to perform their drudgery- ridden traditional jobs. The working condition of employment in the urban informal sector is becoming worse. There is lack of training, job insecurity, health hazards, low wages, longer working hours, intensive supervision and contractual tasks etc, irregular salary and absence of social security benefits etc This entails heavy exploitation of women workers. Sometimes young girls are pressurized by the family to work in factories or offices. Sometimes they choose 'bad jobs 'on their own in the face of strong parental oppositions. They see their job as a route to escape and find personal liberation. Employers take the advantage of their psychological/economic insecurity. Social dynamics so operate in side the house that even working women are not happy either.

3.3. FEMINIZATION OF JOB

India is a mosaic of paradoxes and contradictions. One such paradox is the gender inequality. The nation which has been preaching the messages of love, equality and compassion for centuries, ironically, has the deplorable socio economic status for women even today . The realities are worse than the scenario that is published in reports and newspapers. Some scholars dismiss the problem of gender-disparity as a 'non-issue' by invoking the economistic theoretical explanation of a 'dual economy'. Ironically they also contribute to either the notion of 'feminization of jobs' or 'feminization of poverty'. Almost all Indian studies on gender have tended to overstress the personal and under stress the societal consequences of gender asymmetries .

The votaries of structural adjustment programme argue that now there is a trend of continued "feminisation of employment" in all developing countries. It seems to be a myth. It does not reflect the sign of progress or prosperity. It does not imply the success of economic reforms or emergence of new technological breakthroughs either. But there are two major reasons which make us believe the feminisation of work:

(1) The structural shift of employment from manufacturing to service sector activities in these countries and

(2) the incidence of poverty(economic strain on the household inflicted by double squeeze) and question

of survival.

The contemplated industrial growth is tending to generate a process of jobless growth. Now while every country of the world is characterised by joblessness, women as class had to bear a much heavier burden of unemployment over the past two decades. It is observed that unemployment among women has increased in almost all countries even under reforms regime.On the contrary, the present economic reforms, particularly in India are likely to :

(1) Promote highly sophisticated technology (so called High -Tech) and

(2) Create imperfections in the rural factor (particularly labour) market.

These two factors tend to continuously displace the female workers from high productive activities to low productive activities. It is tending to accentuate the concentration of women in domestic works and non-market roles and activities.

The urban centers are flourishing with economic activities with large surplus adult men, who leave their wife and children in the villages to take care of their grand parents and property. The propensity to marry among educated Indian urbanite has been falling. So prostitution is flourishing in the urban society. But the same man blames the women as prostitutes. Man makes them either 'good mother' or 'bad prostitutes' in the society. Both represent cultural prejudices against women. Both 'chaste wife' and 'worst prostitute' mirror each other. [18] These are masculine articulations. The first one connotes life long sexual slavery to one man, while the other sells herself to several men. In either case femininity is condemned to servitude to malekind.

3.4. CASUALISATION OF JOBS

An economy which sharply aims at export oriented production and multinational investment is hardly likely to generate jobs for the women and other vulnerable sections of the society. There is inherent male bias in the formulation of macro adjustment policies. It is creating a system which is ultimately as centralised and undemocratic as any that can be imposed by the meddlesome bureaucracy. The main thrust of globalisation measures is greater commodification of all aspects of everyday life and work. With the LPG policy the jobs in the formal sector are continuously reduced and jobs in the informal sector have been increasing. The LPG model is tending to generate a vicious TRAP involving jobs like Tailoring, tutoring, Receptionists, producing Achar and Papad and agarbati working in beauty Parlour. All these jobs are visible and no doubt make the females more active and smart. But most of these jobs , belong to the inside spheres and semi domestic sectors. The best job in the entire set is perhaps the receptionist, which is unfortunately based upon the candidate's beauty smartness but not on her intelligence,or skill or experience. Rest of the jobs are low paid and under paid categories. Most of these belong to the informal sector, which is unregistered, and unprotected, subject to all types of exploitation and intimidation.. It is unfortunate that greater availability and casualisation of these jobs makes us believe in the feminisation of jobs. Moreover these jobs are available to the upper and better off section of the women. Market forces undervalues everything which is not directly calculable. The globalisation of prices (and not income) and nationalisation of poverty are likely to spell further economic strain on women, in term of work burden and curtailment of family expenditures. Therefore feminisation of work is likely to result in feminisation of poverty and promote the process of neo housewifisation.

With the confluence of economic growth and high-tech industrialisation the caste-class-specific gender bias against the women is likely to remain more pronounced in all backward regions like Orissa, MP, Bihar. Because market is never friendly neither to the weak, unskilled, illiterate, ignorant, vulnerable people nor to backward resource- poor regions.

3.5. GENDER DISCRIMINATION

Economists contribute a little insight into the social dynamics of gender discrimination. The employers feels as if employing female worker unduly adds to the cost. This cost (or disutility)is reflected in the discrimination coefficient (d) measured in monetary units. The cost of employing a male labour is the prevailing wage rate. But the 'perceived cost' of employing the female worker is her wage plus the d involved in employer's prejudice. The employer will have no preference between male and female when the cost per worker is the same

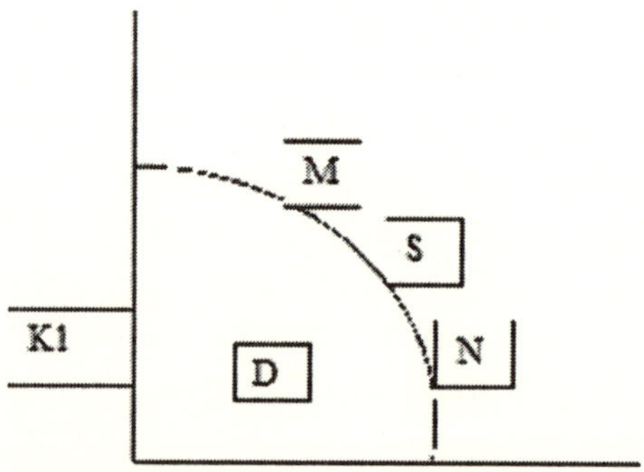

$w_m = w_f + d$

In this situation he will be indifferent

But he hires more male workers if w_m is closer to w_f

i.e., $w_m - w_f < d$

He hires only female worker if wf is sufficiently lower than w_m

i.e., $w_m - w_f > d$

The discrimination coefficient(d) determines the gap between two wages Economists however justify all wage differentials in terms of productivity differential. Higher marginal productivity deserves higher wages in the labour market. If the male has higher productivity then paying higher wage according to productivity differential is justified.

It does not amounts to gender discrimination.

If $d = MP_m - MP_f$ (no gender discrimination)

If $d > MP_m - MP_f$ (gender discrimination persists)

The gender discrimination in the labour market can be of four types:

Lower wage for female workers

Employment discrimination

Occupational segregation

Human capital discrimination

All these discriminations impose costs on women labour. The discriminator enjoys the direct benefits and male worker enjoys the indirect benefit. But discrimination does more than simply transferring benefits from woman to employer or woman to man. Gender discrimination actually reduces the economy's output and income like any other artificial barrier to free competition. It decreases the economic efficiency and reduces production. Effects of gender discrimination can be depicted as a point inside the economy's production possibility curve such as D, where the economy attains K_1 of capital goods and C_1 of consumer goods. D is less desirable combination than M, N,or S on the PPC. The cost of discrimination to society is the sacrificed output. By preventing the economy from achieving productive efficiency gender discrimination reduces the nation's real output ,employment and income. Elimination of this kind of discrimination will equalize the wage rates and result in the net increase in the GDP.

3.6. NEO HOUSEWIFISATION PROCESS

Independence in all countries has brought radical changes in the traditional hierarchy for men but much less for women in Orissa. For example, modernization of agriculture resulted in mechanization ,which had reduced the work burden of male . But women of families. Advocates of globalization argue that there is feminization of jobs by looking at the rising Orissa continue to perform their drudgery- ridden traditional hand operated tasks unless their family income is sufficient to shift some work to another women from less well-off work participation rate among females. But it does not solve the problem of gender inequality in Orissa. The ergonomics and working condition of employment in the urban informal sector is becoming worse. There is lack of training, job insecurity, health hazards, low wages, longer working hours, intensive supervision and contractual tasks etc, irregular salary and absence of social security benefits . This entails heavy exploitation of women workers of Orissa. Sometimes young girls are pressurized by the family to work in factories or offices. Sometimes they choose 'bad jobs' on their own in the face of strong parental oppositions. They see their job as a route to escape and find personal liberation. Employers take the advantage of their psychological/economic insecurity. Social dynamics so operate in side the house that even working women are not happy either. Given the opportunity they prefer to leave the job and remain as idle mothers. Some of them even cherish the 'comfort and care' of the husband for their non working wives.

Backward countries has more gender inequality and

high growth of consumerism.

There is neither allocative efficiency nor productive efficiency. All modernisation measures in the backward society ensures stunted economic growth. It goes from D to N and then to T point. But the production possibility curve of advanced society, after technological advancement, jumps forward from B to R which implies higher economic growth. Gender neutral society is always more conducive to economic development and meaningful prosperity

The ergonomics and conditions of different types of employment for women in the private sector is very worse. There is lack of training, job insecurity, health hazards, low-irregular wages, longer working hours, intensive supervision and contractual tasks etc . This entails heavy exploitation of women workers. Sometimes young girls are pressurized by the family to work in factories or offices. Sometimes they choose 'bad jobs' on their own in the face of strong parental oppositions. They see their job as a route to escape poverty and find personal liberation. Employers take the advantage of their psychological/economic insecurity. On the contrary, social dynamics so operate in side the house that even working women are not happy either. Given the opportunity they prefer to leave the job and remain as idle mothers too.

Employment of Women in UDCs intensifies further gender subordination. Industrialization is a process which marginalized women in the sense of excluding them from various industrial employments due to lack of skills which industries warrant . Women remain at the bottom of labour market hierarchy. Since men are the decision makers both in family and labour market , better educated and trained than female they draw more benefit from the industrialization process (involving increasing specialization of labour) than women. But when we analyse the ergonomics,we notice that women have always replaced men under the condition of flexible and deregulated employment. Industry depends on the conversion of all industrial employment to the informal condition endured by female labour, who is more acquiescent and. There is increased erosion of 'workers right' in the industrial management. There are 3 clear tendencies noticed with industrialization :

- intensification of gender subordination
- decomposition of existing forms of gender subordination
- recomposition of new from of gender subordination

Till today the society has failed to reconstruct the model of man as a 'standard worker' . We have not succeeded to construct the neutral model of a worker. We always revert to the comparison with man workers regarding wage, working hours, retrenchment, productivity and so on. Thus women subordination persists always in the labour market. They are getting unskilled jobs because women considered as inferior bearers of labour..

Economists see women's poverty as the consequence of underdevelopment rather than subordination. They myopically prescribe anti-poverty approach or efficiency approach. They collapse all forms of disadvantage and deprivation into poverty. That approach believes that women are victims of development. Thus Gender issue can never be approached with poverty reduction policies. Gender concern exists with in the development bureaucracies which deny the otherness of the poor and direct the attention to the gendered character of development agencies themselves. Rescuing gender from poverty trap implies that we need poverty-independent gender analyses and policies which recognize that poverty reduction policies are not necessarily appropriate to tackle gender issues because gender subordination is not caused by poverty. But in India, there is a trade off between women's material well being and their autonomy. This situation is not faced by the poorer section. This is one way of looking at the limited degree to which poverty and gender development can be approached synergistically with the same policy instruments. If rising household income has a perverse effect on women's well being then poverty reduction policies even if successful, does not increase women's well being. There is great variations in the degree and manner by which women gain from rising family incomes and poverty reductions. Much depends on the transactions and transfers with in the households. Thus Money is neither necessary nor sufficient condition for transforming gender relations in Indian society. So non financial leverage gained by women from her participative role in the development process is relevant to changing gender relations.

The gender inequality in Orissa has remained very sharp within both rural and urban households. It manifests also in the labour market. Since the employment options available to women are severely limited and since the opportunities for skill acquisition and job mobility are more limited for the female than the male, the work force participation for the female means the relentless weariness of multiple burdens. The economic citizenship has failed to improve the situation either . Both technology and labour market imperfections have been continuously displacing the female workers from high productive activities to low productive activities, through casualisation and contractualisation of jobs. Growing industrialisation and cut throat market economy suits and reinforces the image of the female home makers par excellence. The work participation rate of female is rising in the informal sector only. They are ill-paid but don't leave the job due to increasing unemployment. This need for survival drives the woman to a virtual rape situation. Harassment at work place is real and pervasive. The women have no courage to report due to the fear of further harassment, trauma and re-victimization. Even earning women do not have the freedom to spend or regulate their lives. They are expected to hand over their salary to their husband or in-laws. The problems of managing both the employment situation and the home, and the suspicions about the woman's character continue to make matters worse. The male dominance is all-pervading and there are implicit assumptions that the wife should have a lesser designation at the work place. The gender bias at work expects a woman executive to "look like a woman, behave like a lady, think like a man and work like a donkey".

The gender division of labour within the household of Orissa has remained culturally stubborn, till today . Women as a class are oppressed and subdued by the hegemony of social patriarchy. In Orissa, new labor saving devices have not changed the patterns of life and labor of farming community. State policy treats farm women as consumers, not producers. Farm women perform their field labor under a patriarchal system in which their work "belonged" to male family members. Their household labor remained unaffected by the technological revolution which changed life style of urban women . Ironically, all home appliances and cooking gadgets encourage women to adopt the full-time homemaker role taken by urban housewives.[15] But village women of Orissa prefer their productive roles on and off the farm . The village society of Orissa recognizes farming as a male occupation, so many of women's contributions to modernizing farm life have been ignored or underestimated.

After globalization, it is an obvious trend that percentage of working female in the job market is ever increasing. Girls are really toping the list in different examinations and competitions. There is no doubt about their scholastic attainments. They have excelled in different spheres of life. They have become more career oriented. But what is really their percentage? What has happened to their social status and familial status? The gender division of labour within the household of in India has remained culturally stubborn, till today . Women as a class are oppressed and subdued by the hegemony of social patriarchy. The gender inequality is very sharp within both rural and urban households. It manifests also in labour market. Both technology and labour market imperfections have been continuously displacing the female workers from high productive activities to low productive activities, through casualisation and contractualisation of jobs. Feminization job is really feminization of poverty and "feminization of wrong jobs"

After liberalization there is more concentration of women in domestic works and non-market roles and activities. Each household has two clear roles to play : producing and consuming. The consumption activity has two components:

$$C = C_o + C_h$$

Where C_o means goods and services supplied and consumed from outside the household. And C_h represents goods and services supplied from the household itself. The production activity has two components:

$$P = P_o + P_h$$

Where P_o stands for the goods and services produced for the outside market and P_h means good and services produced for the house. Each household has no control neither over the C_o nor P_o. In the process of marketisation, the purchasing power of the common man is not increasing. The globalisation of prices inflicts economic strain on the family, which ultimately spells further strain on the women only. The economic strain is partially absorbed and neutralised by women by curtailing C_h and raising P_h. It only amounts to spell a heavier pressure on women and housewives. Modernization is generating a TRAP which is not very easily perceptible. T stands for tailoring, tutoring, R stands for jobs like receptionists, A means female engaged in producing Achar and Papad and agarbati and P stands for getting a job in the beauty parlour. All these jobs are visible and no doubt make the females more active. But all these jobs ,except the receptionist, belong to the inside spheres,(outside the house but inside the gate) and semi domestic sectors. Most of these belong to the informal sector, which is unregistered, unrecorded and unprotected, subject to all types of exploitation and intimidation.. It is unfortunate that greater availability of these jobs makes us believe in the feminisation of jobs. There is hyper spread of informal jobs and insecured jobs.There are more exploitative. Therefore feminization job means feminization of poverty only.

The gender relation has not changed much in India, even in towns or cities .It is most oppressive for the rural women. The maledom has created such attitude and aura where the wife (except in very poor households, where there is no margin of choice)feels very satisfied being at home. She is made to enjoy the luxury of sitting idle and taking care of the children. She is made to feel ashamed of working for a wage in the presence of a working husband. She feels good if husband is having enough manliness to keep her as a decorative piece at home as baby-producing machine or care-providing agent. Individually she may not have any compunction. The man-made design is powerful enough to control and suppress her 'feeling of deprivation' or mind to assess her social position as a human-class. Because she is brought up in the culture of altruism. It is also very difficult to find a single lady remorsing with yell and yelp or audacity to face the challenge of any conjugal estrangement. Under cultural pressure woman acts and appears to be happy and jocund. The reduction of number of tasks performed in the family is accompanied by a reduction in the autonomy of the family, which becomes dependent not only on market but on the government and other public institutions. This process has benefited the male and adults, but transformed the housewives to lonely performers of routine manual domestic work confined to the household. Educated working lady in the metros has become smart and free enough comparable to a French lady or any lady of the western society. But it is the travesty of modernity for her . Feminisation of jobs is a myth and education is less meaningful. She has to play several roles of a mother, cook, tutor, tailor, shopper, driver janitor, gardener, home-nurse in addition to attending guests, old parents, patients in hospital, marriage parties and going to bank, children's school, laundry, temple alone. This results only in "neo-housewifization", where the modern lady is saddled with multiple burden . This freedom of movement involving the remote control of the male does not necessarily imply gender equality or women empowerment in backward states.

3.7. ECONOMIC INDEPENDENCE

The concept of "virtuous woman" prevails among all category of woman as before. It freezes the term loyalty, which suggest patriarchy. The virtuous woman is a myth where the woman embodies a solid shape of sacrifice, a "use-value" for patriarchal economy. It equates virtue (good),shyness, domestic space, loyalty to the man. The myth of 'pativrata' continues to enduringly govern Indian womanhood [Chakravarti 1985:48-49]. It endorses the "popular sexist attitude that 'good women stay at home'. The Working ladies do not necessarily enjoy economic freedom. Because the " virtuous woman" is not expected to enjoy any freedom of movement or freedom of thinking or decision making, when male members are present in the family. Economic independence also ultimately becomes a myth for Women in Indian society,unless she herself distinguishes her two identities: womanhood as wife or mother and her personhood as women in the society.

Yet Outside earnings give her:

- a better breakdown position
- a clearer perception of her individuality and well being and
- a higher perceived contribution to the economic status of the family.

The greater economic role for women definitely improves their status within and out side the family. However money is not sufficient condition for transferring gender relations in modern social order in Orissa .

Even today man continues to exercises his subtler control on the family production and reproduction system. It is gradually institutionalized at several spheres: work, culture, customs, religion and education. The socio-religious and cultural influences on the girl child are so strong, both physically and mentally, that even with education and influences from outside, she is not free to think of herself as an individual.

Thus we need a meaningful social transformation, which gives the equal independent human status to women . In Orissa , girls are educationally very successful but socially women are not. With the materialistic success the wife is happy in the market but woman is unhappy in the society. The wife may be happy but the women is not. The real progress should occur when the women become the producers of their own welfare and bounty, not the recipients of charity . Empowerment of women is not a fruit or result to achieve by some mathematical model. It is process not a product, it is to evolve from the society itself but not to be triggered by outside donors or agencies. It can not come from the borrowed ideas and prescription or direction of the malekind. It has to emerge from within,as an intitlement not as an enthrustment.

REFERENCES

1. Agarwal, Bina (1997), 'Bargaining' and Gender Relations: Within and Beyond the Households. *Feminist Economics*. 3(1),1-51.
2. Bandopadhayay, D .(2000) Gender and Governance in India, *Economic Political Weekly*, July 29,
3. Becker, G (1960) An economic Analysis of Fertility in G Becker (ed) Demographic and economic Change in Developed Countries, Princeton University Press. Princeton.
4. Das, Kumar (1990) Paradox of poverty and Planning in India, Economic Quarterly, Vol.25(4),Berlin
5. Das Kumar(2007) Status of Women in Indian Society, Asian Profile, Volume 4(3),pp.234-56
6. Sen, A K (1990) Gender and Cooperative conflicts in Persistent Inequalities: Women and World Development (ed) Irene Tinker Oxford University Press, New York
7. Karlekar ,Malavika (1995), Search for Women Voices, *Economic and Political Weekly* 29th April.

4

Gender Dynamics in Development Process of India

This chapter makes a probe into of persisting gender inequality in India . The researchers blinded by populist sympathy for the poor, easily overlook the social and cultural dynamics which endorses the gender relations of inequality. Economic prosperity does not necessarily imply a healthier unisex society. Higher education or reservations of seats or jobs for women does not ensure gender equality. Higher family cohesiveness or lesser degree of divorce does not imply gender fairness either. It argues that it is not possible or necessary to undergo a gender vertigo to arrive at a transformation of the gender relations. It is not necessary to imitate the western route either. Slow and steady process of social transformation can ensure women liberation only through awareness building

Although gender empowerment has been a buzzword in development circles, the concept has been used in so many different ways by different agents that it remains ambiguous. Conceptualising power and gender adequately entails understanding its multi dimensional nature, the complex ways in which women experience subordination and the ways in which they negotiate or manage this state of affairs. The gender gap in terms of different indices such as life expectancy, literacy and earning have in fact increased from sixties to nineties in south Asia and Sub Saharan Africa. UNDP developed Gender Development Index(GDI) as a tool to capture gender inequality. It notes the inequalities between men and women on the same variables that make up the Human Development Index related to the over all achievements in that society. It includes three variable: health education and income. It has been criticised on the ground that by considering only three variables, it fails to take into account important dimensions such as the quality of community life access to basic amenities and human rights. Important dimensions relevant for women such as safety and security , household allocation of resources, unpaid labour, mobility constraints and on sexual and reproductive freedom by patriarchal ideology do not find any place It is argued that rising incomes may not indicate improved status for women. Education and income may be high, there may still be greater degree of violence against women. In a society there may not be overt gender disparities in provisioning for basic needs, but dowry demand may be showing escalating trend. Recognising the centrality of gender based power imbalances the UNDP has clearly identified the movement towards gender equality as a political process. UNDP's Gender Empowerment Measure (GEM) attempt to reflect women's political participation, their access to professional positions and their earning power. A comparison of GDI and GEM yields interesting results .For example countries like France and Japan are high in GDI but lag far behind on the GEM. Some developing countries like China ,Cuba and Barbados have high GEM ranking than developed countries like Japan, France and Spain. The GEM is also criticised on the ground that it is again based on three variables. It is built on a very narrow conception of empowerment. It does not include legal and human rights nor does it reflect the ways in which cultural constructions of gender identity. Thus in order to assess the impact of structural reforms on women, the conventional parameters used to measure gender disparity is not enough. It is therefore necessary to consider research methodologies that go beyond the quantitative in order to do justice to the complexity of these phenomena.

4.1. GENDER DISCRIMINATION

The development process assume men and women to be abstractly equal ; both making rational choice. Gender is not recognised either as an asymmetry or as a system of power relationships. The mainstream Economics has rather trivialised the gender issue(Becker 1960). At the most it addresses the issue of unequal wages among men and women.. This myopia is inherent in any patriarchal organisation and creation of knowledge. Neo classical economic theory has concentrated more on wage differentials rather than gender segregation, employing mainly models of perfect competition where wages are equal to the values of worker's marginal product. The conclusion of such an analysis is that women's economic situation is a result of tastes and choice of women themselves and of employers etc., acquired through both specialisation of and socialisation by individuals .

The division of labour by gender within the household of in India is stubbornly cultural. Women as a class are oppressed and subdued by the hegemony of social patriarchy. The gender inequality is very sharp within the rural households. Since the employment options available to the rural women are severely limited and since the opportunities for skill acquisition and job mobility are more limited for the rural female than the male, the work force participation for the poor female in the rural areas means the relentless weariness of too heavy work loads and the deprivation of childhood care and schooling for their children (particularly for the girl child).The most serious aspect of gender inequality is the gender gap in literacy level. The highest gender gap is noticed in backward states like Rajstan followed by UP, Bihar, MP and Orissa. The dividing line between productive work and domestic work is not only arbitrary but also tends to underestimate the women's contribution to domestic work. The women as a class is saddled with 'multiple burden'. If one takes into account the unpaid work in India, woman in poor household work much longer hours and have no or less leisure time than their male counterparts. In the age of globalization technology and labour market imperfections have continuously displaced the female workers from high productive activities to low productive activities. It is tending to accentuate the concentration of women in domestic works and non-market roles and activities.

In India since the beginning of planned development, women have been viewed as a deprived section requiring welfare measures. Indian culture and social ethos have to a large extent been influenced by a patriarchal value system. Given the cultural and social background, whether 73rd amendment of the Indian constitution would be able to bring about a significant change in the existing situation leading to empowerment of women is still an open question. As a result of deeply entrenched social attitudes and practices, women by and large have not been independent decision makers in the country. Their decisions in most cases have been influenced by the wishes and dictates of the male family members. They are always guided by patriarchal social system and therefore are discriminated against in terms of food , cloth, housing, health care and education.

4.2. GENDER STEREOTYPES

We find many varieties of social stereotypes regarding women in India. Common remarks regarding single mothers are: 'Women are responsible for separation'. They bring separation by 'behaving badly'. They should suffer for their yobbo . 'She has loose character'. 'The termagant and errant wives should suffer their comeuppance' . So on. But after separation they suffer from predation of men. It is fairly a routine hazard of widows/ divorcee ladies. Normally we accept the justification that 'they have money and they earn'. So they suffer from such predations. But there is gender discrimination in this phenomena. The common notion works in the mind of the man that woman should not have left the man despite all adversity. A woman without man to protect her is potentially available for sex and entertainment of other men. She is a 'product' meant for man's consumption and entertainment. She is of the man, for the man and by the man. Children are grown up in female-headed households suffer from social stigmatization.[3] Common reactions towards lone mothers include imposing isolations through speculative gossips or restricted social contacts. The female neighbors used to be very jealous and comment on any type of household purchases :a jewelry or a cloth etc . They keep distance from lone mothers. It is due to : (i) women themselves are worried about women on their own posing a threat to their marriage (ii) own husband may get suspicious about fraternizing with women who theoretically have more freedom. Solo motherhood is the reflector or rear view mirror for the dynamics of power and dependency. It is largely considered as a social perfidy and recalcitrance. The more difficult and stigmatized solo mother hood is in a society, the greater the barriers against opting out of mental torture of a bad marriage.

The immoral and sexual deviances are linked with

reactions to economic circumstances of lone mothers. The upward mobility of a lone mother evokes suspicion about immoral earnings also. They lead a life of social sympathy. Male has created a social atmosphere where the females themselves used to pity the lone mothers. So genuine economic prosperity of a lone mother has to be concealed in the society. In order to fend off charges of promiscuity and loose morals many lone mothers tend to lead extremely restricted social lives. Many lone mothers have good net work with the neighbors, but they fear they may lose their sympathy if they were to take up with another man. Both social stigma and economic disadvantages are mutually reinforcing against the single mothers. All these manifestations act as powerful deterrents to women's choosing to be free or thinking to be equal to man.

4.3. CULTURAL ARTEFACTS

Women's role, her fertility and her work in the family and society at large are influenced by economic development of the nation. As economic development proceeds family production for its own use declines. Larger share of goods for family consumption is produced outside the family. This brings changes both in the relation of family members to the out side worlds and in the relation between family members themselves. But in India gender discrimination is culturally stubborn. Women used to remain more burdened with family production. Traditional attitude of the villages, despite paean of modernization, prevails every where today . The need for self protection ,security and lineage has still remained as a strong incentive for having a cohesive family. Therefore educated people today (even many doctors) are found to be father of 5-7 daughters due to their 'son preference'. The highest gender gap is noticed in backward states like Rajstan followed by UP, Bihar, MP and Orissa. [4] Children are socialized to accept their present and future roles without any protests. Boys are encouraged to learn to debate, defy and escape from any responsibility, girls are taught to obey and remain docile.

Economic development is creating a gap in skilling process of man and women and endorsing the revolving doors of occupational segregation. 'High-tech' continuously displaces them to all low-skill and low paid jobs with ergonomics of casualisation and flexibalisation. Role of schools is not only to teach intellectual skills and impart knowledge but also to indoctrinate pupils with dominant cultural values. Cultural education for girls is full of traditional prejudices. The early socialization of girls by parents and teachers contribute to the development of 'superiority feeling' in boys and 'inferiority feeling' in girls. Machismo, being all pervasive in educational, political ,economic and social subsystem, is a real maelstrom for Indian society. The Indian mother transmits the notion of correct 'social behavior' of the family to the girls but the boy need not know the name of his own grand father. The girl grows in a vertical relation of obedience and command. All adolescents girls are taught to be mellifluent and skilled in domestic spheres involving all repetitive and irksome jobs. But the male does the concentrated bust of activity in certain season or weeks of the year and enjoys idleness for long period The male adults stroll up and down to the town, to gossip with friends, to loiter in market places. All these bohemian activities are considered befitting manifestations of the male role. But all duties and tasks of the girls are subsumed in their 'social role'.

The Indian family ,being an undifferentiated unit governed by altruism, is the epitome of gender asymmetries. The right to consume any thing in the house is different for women, regardless of economic status.. Any kind of consumption including food is not simply determined by its availability or adequacy. In India, women fast for the welfare of their husband while men do not reciprocate. If at all male is fasting that is for spiritual purposes but female fasts for the auspiciousness of the household collectively. The behavior of women is certainly and commonly bound up with altruism and prioritizing the needs of others. It is the central element in feminine identities. Men eats before women always. Women's eating before the man or male adult of the family is culturally forbidden . Women and girls learn to refuse to take meat, milk, ghee or any rich dishes. They normally eat the residual quantity of food left by the male members. In formal occasions men and women eat separately. Men eat with the guests .Women eat with the girls and small children. Girls learn and follow the mother to maintain social customs. Women never confess that she is hungry or thirsty. It is considered as a non-women etiquette. Man, while eating, refrains himself from talking and expresses gratification. Male enjoys the 'yum yum' monopoly who seems to live to eat . They eat slowly with restraints urging the other male co-diners to eat more and more(even in poor families) and take digestives after eating. Women while serving the food, carry this modesty to the extremes.[5] Even pregnant and lactating mothers do not get right calorie of food. They suffer from anemia, jaundice and several problems of malnourishment. Women are progressively weakened by successive pregnancies. Women is admired for working late into their pregnancies. They are expected to take rest only for 2 weeks after the child birth, during which they are given splendid nutritional food. After 3 -4 weeks the child is tied to the mother's back. So her food consumption is rigidly determined , so too her work load because it is inseparable from her social role.[6] Not eating (or fasting) and telling lies that she is not hungry is considered a positive moral values for women but it is neutral (or negative) for men. Girls are indispensable for domestic activities in each family. Therefore education is a form of consumption from which girls are conspicuously excluded. But son's education is an investment. Thus birth, growth, education or achievement of the girls before marriage is by accident.

4.4. THE INCIDENCE OF DOWRY

The whole host of economic and social structures and processes that reinforce patriarchy, devalue and commodify women and promote such horrendous phenomena as dowry. The problem of dowry in India transcends the rural urban dichotomy. Its incidence cuts across all caste and class boundaries .The prevailing patriarchal myths seeks to situate dowry as a girl's share of parental property or as daughter's life insurance policy secured by her parents at the time of her marriage (Mishra 2000) The structure of acceptance enjoyed by dowry is significant. This explains why some of the victims are not helped by co villagers. Besides, help and sympathy for the victims of dowry blurs gender-based distinction. The attitude of women at the family level and in the official capacity (woman *sarpanch*, woman doctor, woman police, woman BDOs, woman teacher etc) reveals this most unambiguously. Most of dowry deaths and torture are not reported any where ,because of the fear of social stigma or lack of knowledge about or fear of complexity of long legal process., unless the level of terror and violence becomes a threat to the life of the victim or in the event of her death. It is unfortunate that most of the dowry victims have been married off in line with patriarchal notions of responsibility by their parents with out any attempt to educate them or make them stand on their own feet. This is coupled with a general neglect of a girl's education/career moulds victims to a stereotyped role associated with reproduction and 'wifely 'responsibilities .This reduces them to the position of a domestic cows or an unpaid maids, veiling a structure of exploitation associated with household labour. We also notice many attempts to argue for festivals, *like durga puja, laxmi puja and kali puja etc*, where women power is worshiped. Women's sub human status is very often justified by religious fundamentalists by our obsession with our rich tradition. We also draw upon many customs like '*sabitri amabashya*' etc in order to legitimise predatory demands. This coexist with a lumpenised perception which commodifies marriage and converts a sacred act into a materialistic exchange.

But Indians are proud to say that there is love, cohesion,culture, less divorce, and familial harmony inside the house. But this 'pseudo harmony' does not imply a healthy society either . In fact it conceals the disharmony and dominance and represents a conflictual cooperation.[7] The effect of masculinity, which is merely an expression of brute male power with yahoo mentality has not reduced unfortunately in the era of globalization knowledge . Male promiscuity today is being excused, legitimized and celebrated . On the contrary beauty, 'chastity and motherhood' are convenient and elaborate fictions which not only convince the women that they are destined to be subordinates to men but also enabled them to gladly accept that relations of inequality. Average Indian educated male(even some female social researchers) may simply dismiss all these narrations and arguments as non-issue and dub it as exaggeration of western feminism.

4.5. LOOKING FORWARD

Gender empowerment has been a buzzword in development circles of India, but the concept has remained ambiguous. The gender gap in terms of different indices has increased from sixties to nineties in south Asia.Technology and labour market imperfections have continuously displaced the female workers from high productive activities to low productive activities.The preference for women and girls child worker is most common in the unorganised sector because in such jobs it is relatively easy for the employers to circumvent the laws. The schooling of the girls is determined more intricately by factors such as caste, religion, family type and size, occupation, kinship pattern and marriage etc. Marriages of girls without education, lead to second stage of bondage in girl's life. The whole host of economic and social structures and processes that reinforce patriarchy, devalue and commodify women and promote such horrendous phenomena as dowry.

Even today man continues to exercises his ever subtler control on the family production and reproduction system. It is gradually institutionalized at several spheres: work, culture, customs, religion and education. Therefore liberation of women will not be easy or complete without the destruction of neo-patriarchy which has four levels of control: production, reproduction, socialization and sexuality. It is not enough if girls succeed in the educational ladder or if women work participation rate increases in the labour market. The social and economic structures today lock production and reproduction together , which perpetrate male dominance and female submission. The liberation of women can only be achieved if all structures in which women are integrated are transformed simultaneously. A modification of any one of them can be offset by a reinforcement of another, so that a mere permutation of the form of inequality is ultimately achieved. Thus a social transformation, which brings real modernity is warranted for India but not this razzamatazz of consumerism.

Economic development process is never gender-neutral. So any prescription based only on 'household bargaining' model of the economists will be inaccurate for backward states. Poverty can not serve as the proxy for subordination of women. Therefore anti poverty policies can not be expected to necessarily improve the position of women. Until very high level of income reached, the rise in household income aggravates the gender inequality also. Money is neither necessary nor sufficient for transferring existing asymmetric gender relations. Thus Gender issue should never be approached with poverty reduction policies. Because this approach believes that women are victims of misdevelopment. Rescuing gender from poverty trap means we need poverty-independent gender analyses and policies .The gender issue should be delinked both from economics and politics.

REFERENCES

1. Bandopadhayay, D (2000) Gender and Governance in India, *Economic Political Weekly*, July 29,
2. Das Kumar(2007) Status of Women in Indian Society, Asian Profile, Volume 4(3),pp.234-56
3. Sen, A K (1990) Gender and Cooperative conflicts in Persistent Inequalities: Women and World Development (ed) Irene Tinker Oxford University Press, New York
4. Kabeer,Naila (1999) Resources,Agency, Achievements: Reflections on the Measurement of Women's Empowerment. *Development and Change*. 30, PP 435-464
5. Karlekar ,Malavika (1995), Search for Women Voices, *Economic and Political Weekly* 29th April
6. Krishnaraj, M (2001), How Gender Figures in Economic Theorising and Philosophy, *Economic and Political Weekly* ,28 April
7. Lingam,L(1994) Women headed Households: coping with caste, Class and Gender Hierarchies, *Economic and Political Weekly*, March 19.
8. Parasar , Archana (1994), *Women and Family Law Reforms in India*, Sage Pub, Delhi
9. Razavi ,Shahra (1999) Gendered Poverty and Well-being: Introduction. *Development and Change*.30, PP 409-433.

10. Sonpar, S & Ravi Kapur (2001),Non conventional Indicators: Gender disparity under structural Reforms, *Economic and Political Weekly* ,Jan 6

11. Swantz, Marja-Liisa (1995). Embracing Economies of Women: paths to sustainable livelihoods *Development* . (3) , Pp 27-29.

5

Exploitation of Girl Child Workers

This chapter is an abridged version of a larger study on Economic Exploitation of Children in India .The study is based on both secondary and primary data on girl child laboour. It seeks to examine various questions that have not only remained unanswered but also largely remain unasked. It highlights the nature and magnitude of child labour practice in India .It examines the efficacy of the present educational system of India and the socio-economic and demographic characteristics of girl child workers in the informal sector .It identifies the causes and correlates of girl child labour and analyses the pattern of employment and degree of exploitation of girl child labour in various occupations in the unorganised sector of backward regions of India. It studies the plight of girl childworkers and impact of development process on gender discrimination and gender empowerment. It also reviews the political economy of state intervention for the development of girl children and evaluates the existing legal protection and welfare measures . Hence this study is highly imperative to generate an objective understanding and resurrection in the policies on girl child labour in India.

India is a mosaic of paradoxes and contradictions.

One such paradox is the practice of child labour. The country where able bodied adults remain unemployed, the nation which has been preaching the messages of love, equality and compassion for centuries, ironically, has the highest incidence of child abuse and exploitation in the world. The country which has promoted international thinking and efforts in creating a congenial environment for child development, has its own children living in deplorable conditions. The story of exploitation of child labour in India is no less horrifying than Dicken's description. Every morning one is alarmed when the tragic lines hit the newspaper about the brutal realities of working children. The realities are worse than the scenario that is published in reports and newspapers. The child labour is the most pernicious, unethical, illegal, immoral and inhuman practice. Employers always find them cheaper and more productive. According to World Bank report published in the first week of January 2000 there are six crores working children in India including the one and a half crore bonded working children The agricultural and urban informal sectors are notorious for the flagrant violation of child labour laws

5.1. GENESIS OF THE MALADY

The roots of the problem of child labour are hidden in the socio economic environment of India. The uneven character of Indian society which allows rich to be richer and poor to be poorer creates a social environment which favours the employment of child labour [1]. Economic distress of the people in the lower income group creates the basic urge for sending their children to work so that the children at least do not have to share the starvation that the parents suffer. Thus child labour is indeed and economic problem. Economic environment contributes to the child labour market by two forces ; Push forces and pull forces. Push forces represent the supply side. (poverty, inequality, misery, high dependency, starvation, rising prices of essential goods, inadequate and inappropriate schooling facilities etc) and pull forces. Push forces represent the supply side. (poverty, inequality, misery, high dependency, starvation rising prices of essential goods, inadequate and inappropriate schooling facilities etc) and pull forces represent the demand side (assured subsistence, food, shelter, free from family worries, existence of exploitative middle men and employers who are always is search of cheap labour). The main source of child labour are the landless and poor families with meagre income, where lies the paradox of life and death and the necessity to augment the family income at the cost of the future of the society from natural point of view, the future aspiration for the child himself from the individual point of view and future prospects for the household from the familial point of view [2]. Economic distress of the people in the lower-income group has been significantly responsible for the perpetuation of child labour. Children in these families have got only two choices : to work or to starve.

Studies on child labour in India have been conducted both at micro and macro levels. While the former relays on field survey, the latter are based on secondary data. Studies carried on the global scale by international organisation such as ILO, WHO UNICEF, World Bank, bring out the glaring facts about child labour problem in developing countries, Researches have been made on many facets of child population, demographic characteristics, child abuse, exploitation, workforce participation, education, literacy dropout rates, health, nutrition and family planning. From the review of relevant literatures[19] it is observed that most studies on child labour have focused attention almost exclusively on the exploitation of the children as wage labour in the urban industrial sector of third world countries. Some scholars dismiss the problem as a 'non-issue' by invoking the economistic theoretical device of 'dual economy'. Almost all tend to accept child labour as the harsh reality for India under the pretext of poverty and population growth. Every researcher and activists are convinced and take a sympathetic view and remain indifferent about state intervention for banning of child labour. They only advocate for humanising the development process. Many scholars have seldom considered the significant role played by the children in the rural and peri-urban families in their struggle for survival. Main stream Economics and sociological literatures tend to subsume the entire life experience of children under such euphemistic rubrics as "socialisation. Almost all studies have tended to overstress the personal and under stress the societal consequences. This chapter attempts to reveal the real picture.

Social structure of our India is characterised by caste and class hierarchy. Though children of all categories of families are born free and equal by all standards, but thereafter social conditions are created to bring innumerable differences among them.[5] .The comfort of the upper castes. The people of low castes and down-trodden communities, through ages have become rather stagnant and deprived of high aspirations. Lenin, rightly remarked that the poor people have neither the capacity nor willingness to come out of it. Poverty extends to all castes and classes. But in India the child of a very high caste prefers begging to work. They do not accept jobs in socially less dignified pursuits. Under economic compulsion they (high caste people) may have to sell their movable and immovable property, but do not work. Thus evil of child labour has got its roots firmly grounded in the backward society where caste, ethnicity, religious and social taboos, persistent poverty and above all political plurality play important roles in the structure and function of the society.

Indian society is a combination of 'haves' and 'have-nots' literates and illiterates and 'master and servants. Social inequality is reflected in the prevailing education system. Rich and higher caste people consider education an investment ,while the poor peasants, and destitutes have to sell the labour potentials and mortgage the future of their children to supplement their family income and avoid starvation. Educational, religious and all social institutions are controlled by the upper caste and elite group.6 Lower caste and illiterate people were purposefully kept ignorant about the basic rights of human beings. As a result children of the lower strata have had no other option open than to enter into various activities of the informal sector..

5.2. MALDEVELOPMENT IN INDIA

Practice of child labour in India is not a post industrial phenomenon. It is simply the product of misdevelopment process. Its persistence has inverse relation to the level of economic development. Poverty is undeniably the major factor leading to child labour. The perpetuation of child labour is a blot on the conscience of modern society [3]. Orissa being an endemic region with proverbial poverty and unemployment and with the reputation of being a reservoir of cheap labour is important for the study of the problems of child labour. Poverty coupled with rapidly growing population has compounded this problem of child labour [4]. Growing immiserisation of families burdened under big family size, compel the parents to use their children as assets. The number of child labour in Orissa is ever rising . The magnitude of the problem is swelling unabatedly and has acquired dangerous dimensions.

Majority of child labour exist in rural areas engaged in agriculture, animal husbandry and other household industries which has not received much attention from researchers and policy makers. Since it is carried out under the guidance of parents, many consider it as non-exploitative. Many accept it as a part of socialisation process. It is the only means of acquiring the necessary traditional skills required for the survival in the given environment .Such work is believed to develop the self confidence, self-respect and personalities of young workers and prepares them to take up the responsible of family occupations from their elders as they grow. Also many children willingly carry out little jobs with their parents. They do certain works playfully on behalf of their parents, which form a part of socialisation process [5]. But very often it increases and because of poverty, [6] regardless of its causes. The work not only adversely affects his health but also mortgages his whole future. They are treated as small adults. They are treated as machines and ill-treated as asses and donkeys. Some times they work without any remuneration. Sometimes they work under hazardous conditions. In all cases they are the highly neglected and exploited working class.[7]· They are forced to work with their woes denied even the minimal liberties for a human living and are treated mostly as sub- bonded labourers . In some cases parents obtain money from the employers by mortgaging the services of their children and later on the amount of loan with interest is estimated.

5.3. POVERTY SCENARIO

This section makes an attempt to anatomise poverty and its association with child labour problem in the country. In a poor country like India, where a job can mean the difference between living and dying, child labour is a social necessity and that children who work are healthier than who do not. [8]. Direct consequence of poverty is low level of consumption resulting in high death rate , low life expectancy and high infant mortality.[9] Another ill effect of poverty is deterioration in social values and the prevalence of demeaning acts like selling of children for paltry amounts of only ten or fifteen rupees. Although government of India has been planning to remove poverty, development has only resulted in raising the per capita income only.[10] It has not meant social development in the real sense of the word. The indicators of the physical Quality of life (PQL) remain as discouraging as before[11]. Another unhealthy feature of the development process in India is the growing inequality in the distribution of the fruits of progress and prosperity achieved so far. Social development has been further impeded by the diverse character of Indian society resulting for the stranglehold of the caste system and religious bigotry.

Indian elite are proud over the past culture and history. So do our bureaucrats and planners wallowing amidst documents and propaganda containing exciting information over their preparedness to coast into the 21st century. But unfortunately the present economic policy, which is being pursued for last couple of decades by government of India, which continues to be top-down venture, which continues to emphasise on removal of poverty and rural development and at the same time increasingly tending to adopt the policy of free marketism seems to be chauvinistic but hallow and deceptive. The worldwide movement toward laissez faire policy, designed as a shock therapy for the developing countries has created the over enthusiasm of instant change. But unfortunately this strategy, like the previous developmental strategy promises a brighter future through pious policy pronouncements and euphoria of trickle down effect.

After the colonial era, 50 years of planned development efforts have resulted in the persistence of a huge but unproductive primary sector, slender industrial sector and a bloated tertiary sector in the economy. The process of industrialisation continues to be inefficient disarticulated and regionally concentrated in and around few urban conurbations. The process of urbanisation, similarly has been dysfunctional and inequitous. The urban centres continue to be the focal points of the suction mechanism for commodities, income and labour force.[12]. Rural development is paid only a lip service. Political slogans an bureaucratic rhetorics for rural development reveals the ultimate vested interest in maintaining the status quo only. Policy statements of government of India do not really reflect their intentions. Indian democracy provides and illusion of benevolence for concealing the ruthless exploitation of the majority. All public funds and investments go to benefit sections with political visibility and economic stake. On an average 20% of total investment go to 70-80% of the population who live in the villages and urban slums. The development strategy has remained a gamble. The maybe benefits do not trickle down to the rural sector and poor people.

During five plan decades India had adopted : 1) growth oriented strategy, 2) welfare oriented strategy and 3) integrated development strategy and has completed eight five year plans. Industrial scenario of India has passed through three phases (a) Industrial growth with regulation (1950-65) (b) Industrial slowdown (1965-74) and (c) third phase industrial revival without regulation (1974 on wards0. In spite of considerable economic development in terms of higher production, income and employment in different sectors of the economy the problem of poverty persists with same gravity. The welfare approach have had the effect of perpetuating and reinforcing the rural backwardness and dependency.[13].

It is saddening to note that after completion of 8 five years of planning, with several tinkerings in plan techniques, the problem of poverty has remained as grim as ever. The rural sector has been struggling hard to extricate itself from abysmal poverty and squalor. The rural economy has remained closer to the subsistence level and painfully sensitive to the vagaries of nature. Rural people at best enjoy a fragile existence. It is the country, where both "star and dole" culture flourishes. All plans and policies have excessively concentrated on the modern sector at the expense of traditional, rural and informal sector where the majority eke out their living, beautification of metropolies and urban nodes has created concrete jungles, stifling the cry of the rural mass and urban poor into nothingness. The fact that almost all benefits of development gravitate towards the

5.4. GROWTH OF INFORMAL SECTOR

Children by droves are now being employed in the informal sector, which is largely unregistered and unprotected and which escape all government inspection and control in terms of safety regulations, minimum hygiene standards, ventilation requirements etc. The term informal refers to a dichotomy which cuts across all sectors of the economy. Informal sector is a catchword covering a considerable range of economic activities which are frequently included under the all-inclusive term of "self-employment" This refers to the employment of a sort that is very little organised if at all, which is relatively difficult to enumerate and is therefore ignored by official censuses [17] and in which working conditions are rarely covered by legal statutes.

Any description of informal sector is inadequate. Any definition is inaccurate. Lack of a comprehensive empirical base is perhaps the reason for the celerity with which the concept has found acceptance. The lack of proper definition is very often, although not satisfactorily compensated by a somewhat arbitrary listing of these activities which meets the eye of anyone who visits and strolls through the streets of a city in the developing countries like India : Street vendors, newspaper sellers, shoeshine boys stall keepers, household servants, porters, beggars, hawkers, prostitutes, rickshaw pullers etc. Hence the group of small tradesmen the mass of unskilled and loose workers and others with low and irregular income who lead a labourious, semi criminal existence on the margins of the urban economy constitute the "Informal sector".[1.8]

Thus the principal characteristics of the informal sector in India are :-

i) Ease of entry.

ii) Reliance on indigenous source of inputs.

iii) Unregistered family ownership of enterprise

iv) Small scale of operation and low productivity.

v) Labour-intensive and adapted technology.

vi) Skills acquired outside the formal school system,

vii) Unprotected and unrecognised by the government.

In India girl child labour are distributed over various sectors in number of activities. The indicative list is as follows :

Primary sector : Worker and wage-earners in : Cultivation, agricultural labour, weeding , ploughing, tea plantation, animal care/ husbandry sowing, fishing, domestic work, forestry, protecting crops from animals etc.

Secondary Sector : Workers and helpers in : Cottage, handi crafts, household industries, Handloom industries, Hosiary, wool cleaning, small scale manufacturing, foundries, brick-kilns cobblery, dyeing, stone cutting mica cutting, diamond cutting, stiching, embroidery, sewing, pottery, bidi rolling, printing, cloth printing, carpentry, black-smithy, machine parts, wires, mining and quarrying etc.

Tertiary sector : Maids and bartenders in : Hotels, & motels, Dhabas and restaurants, tea stalls, shops mechanical, cinema halls, repairing shops laundries, bus-taxi-cleaners, petrol pumps shoe shine boys, automobile service stations etc.

Self-employed sector : Vendors, Petty producers, hawkers, street traders etc.

Organised sector : Food products, wood products, textile products, gem polishing, brass products, chemical products, mineral products, steel products, fireworks, handloom industries, lock making, etc

The preference for girl child worker is most common in the unorganised sector because in such jobs it is relatively easy for the employers to circumvent the laws prohibiting child labour. It is easy to conceal children during the visit of factory inspector. They overstate the age to make them eligible for employment, they also understate the age of an adult worker, who would qualify for adult wages. The laws in India has proved inefficient to deal with such practices. Indeed one of the problems of legislation prohibiting child labour is that it drives them under ground. In such circumstances, child workers are totally unprotected, they are not covered by any benefits or provided with any facilities, Bare survival is the goal of the majority of these girl child worker. They do not receive any sick leave or indeed any leave at all, are not protected by any on-the job-injury provision Their working conditions are entirely deplorable.

5.5. THE PATRIARCHY

The division of labour by gender within the household of in India is stubbornly cultural. Women as a class are oppressed and subdued by the hegemony of social patriarchy. The gender inequality is very sharp within the rural households. Since the employment options available to the rural women are severely limited and since the opportunities for skill acquisition and job mobility are more limited for the rural female than the male, the work force participation for the poor female in the rural areas means the relentless weariness of too heavy work loads and the deprivation of childhood care and schooling for their children (particularly for the girl child).The most serious aspect of gender inequality is the gender gap in literacy level. The highest gender gap is noticed in backward states like Rajstan followed by UP, Bihar, MP and Orissa. The dividing line between productive work and domestic work is not only arbitrary but also tends to underestimate the women's contribution to domestic work. The women as a class is saddled with 'multiple burden'. If one takes into account the unpaid work in India, woman in poor household work much longer hours and have no or less leisure time than their male counterparts. Technology and labour market imperfections have continuously displaced the female workers from high productive activities to low productive activities. It is tending to accentuate the concentration of women in domestic works and non-market roles and activities.

In India since the beginning of planned development, women have been viewed as a deprived section requiring welfare measures. Indian culture and social ethos have to a large extent been influenced by a patriarchal value system. Given the cultural and social background, whether 73rd amendment of the Indian constitution would be able to bring about a significant change in the existing situation leading to empowerment of women is still an open question. As a result of deeply entrenched social attitudes and practices, women by and large have not been independent decision makers in the country. Their decisions in most cases have been influenced by the wishes and dictates of the male family members. They are always guided by patriarchal social system and therefore are discriminated against in terms of food and health care and education. The whole host of economic and social structures and processes that reinforce patriarchy, devalue and commodify women and promote such horrendous phenomena as dowry.

5.6. FATE OF GIRL CHILD

India is one of the few countries of the world where sex ratio is adverse for females. While 12 million girls are born in India every year almost 50,000 female foetuses are aborted in a year after sex determination. Despite the law against sex determination enacted in 1994,the female foeticide is still a serious menace in the country. In fact prenatal Diagnostic Centres have become sex determination clinics. They have mushroomed all over the country . Thanks to breakthrough in medical sciences. The discovery of amniocentesis is being grossly abused to wash away the female foetus from the womb .It is sheer hypocrisy that the so called modern civilisation with its pretensions to high thinking considers that to be born as a girl is a crime. When a girl child is born generally she is not welcome. In several parts of rural India, a midwife's fee is lower when the new born baby is a girl than of a boy child. The imaginative scheme announced in 50th anniversary of India's independence, giving Rs.500 to the parents of the new born girl only endorse anti-female stereotypes. It only gives an incentives to the parents to keep their daughter alive at least temporarily .It is a fact that in the Indian society and social attitude towards the birth of a girl child is identified with a cause of worry for parents. But every friend and relatives congratulate the parents of the girl saying , "Laxmi (the Goddess of Wealth) has arrived in your home. You are very fortunate" Even though the first year of this decade was celebrated as the international year of girl child, female children continued to get raw deal in India. The infant mortality rate is much higher among girls than boys. There is discrimination against the girls in providing social benefits like health care, education, nutrition etc both at familial level and societal level. No wonder ,the attitude towards girls has not changed over the decades which have seen economic, social and cultural developments in so many spheres of our national life. The irony is that all legislations and programmes meant to protect and ensure their welfare have remained on paper or have been implemented only minimally. Parents of poor families find little meaning in sending girls to schools. To a large extent the deprivation of the girl children is due to the grinding poverty and social factors when even the daily existence for a family is struggle for survival.

Another important problem facing our society is the incidence of child marriage. Child marriage not only deprives girls of health and nutrition but education too. At a time when they are not physically fit to take responsibilities of motherhood they not only face higher risk of pregnancy, but they also face compounded risks related to ill health all through rest of their life. The child marriage Restraint Act if 1978 prevents marriage of the girl below 18 years and makes it a crime. But the practice of child marriage is rampant in UP, Bihar, MP, Rajstan and Orissa Even though the offence is non-cognizable, the police can take the offender into custody. Similar is the fate of dowry Prohibition Act which is practised in its breach rather than in observance. Thus even though a number of Acts and rules have been passed since India's independence for the welfare of the children, they have failed to make any impact on the life of the girl child because of lack of social and cultural support The socio-religious and cultural influences on the girl child are so strong, both physically and mentally, that even with education and influences from outside, she is not free to think of herself as an individual. This is true for the overwhelming majority of girl-children. It is a sad commentary on our society that girls child has remained the most unwanted and ominous.

Mothers get gradually accustomed to all exploitative situations and regards their own status as inferior within the family. They inculcate the same biases in their daughter's psyche ,consequently perpetuating this mode of behaviour in future generations. Early marriages are rampant in every parts of the country except towns and cities. It denies a girl an opportunity for development and increases the risks of getting immature babies and infant and maternal mortality, gynecological complications, repeated pregnancies. As per medical advice a girl needs four to five years for her physical growth after attaining puberty. This is denied when she is married off young and this leads to a vicious cycle. Marriages of girls without education, lead to second stage of bondage in girl's life, a bondage much longer, more terrible, more unbearable, than the years spent at parental home

5.7. THE PROBLEM OF DOWRY

The whole host of economic and social structures and processes that reinforce patriarchy, devalue and commodify women and promote such horrendous phenomena as dowry. The problem of dowry in Orissa transcends the rural urban dichotomy Its incidence cuts across all caste and class boundaries .The prevailing patriarchal myths seeks to situate dowry as a girl's share of parental property or as daughter's life insurance policy secured by her parents at the time of her marriage The structure of acceptance enjoyed by dowry is significant. This explains why some of the victims are not helped by co villagers. Besides, help and sympathy for the victims of dowry blurs gender-based distinction. The attitude of women at the family level and in the official capacity (woman sarpanch, woman doctor, woman police, woman BDOs, woman teacher etc) reveals this most unambiguously. Most of dowry deaths and torture are not reported any where ,because of the fear of social stigma or lack of knowledge about or fear of complexity of long legal process., unless the level of terror and violence becomes a threat to the life of the victim or in the event of her death. It is unfortunate that most of the dowry victims have been married off in line with patriarchal notions of responsibility by their parents with out any attempt to educate them or make them stand on their own feet. This is coupled with a general neglect of a girl's education/ career moulds victims to a stereotyped role associated with reproduction and 'wifely 'responsibilities .This reduces them to the position of a domestic cows or an unpaid maids, veiling a structure of exploitation associated with household labour. We also notice many attempts to argue for festivals, like durga puja, laxmi puja and kali puja etc, where women power is worshiped. Women's sub human status is very often justified by religious fundamentalists by our obsession with our rich tradition. We also draw upon many customs like 'sabitri amabashya' etc in order to legitimise predatory demands. This coexist with a lumpenised perception which commodifies marriage and converts a sacred act into a materialistic exchange.

5.8. PRIMARY EDUCATION SYSTEM

Access to primary education has been formally accepted as a human right for almost half a century. Yet , on the eve of 21 st century only about three quarter of the children of the school going age are able to attend a primary school in the developing world. A large number drop out before reaching class V and there are many other s who never see schools. Although in India a high priority is placed on education in policy statements this has not necessarily ensured adequate resources or covered marginal groups in national programmes. Thus in India with 30 percent of the world's illiterates has female literacy rates much lower than in sub Saharan Africa(Probe 1999).The world's largest number of out of school children, close to 59 million are found in India, 60 percent of whom are girls.(UN's HDR,2000) Thirty seven percent of the children are unable to reach class V(Haq and Haq 1998)

The directive Principles of Indian Constitution, in article 45, enshrines free and compulsory primary education for children up to the age of 14. But the reality is abysmally different. Although the number of primary schools has increased 2,82 times since 1951 and enrolments have improved, the responsibility of the Government for creating a satisfactory infrastructure has in practice not been matched by corresponding outlays which continue to remain woefully inadequate at around 3 percent of the GDP.

Disenchantment with education today runs high as educational facts and figures continue to reveal that the distribution of education follows the lines of not only class but also caste divides. Caste and class stratification of the Indian social fabric results in unequal educational opportunities. The dominant caste continue to wield their influence in education and the likelihood of the more marginalised groups accessing education becomes more difficult due to the social and cultural barriers they face as well as their compelling economic conditions.

Adverse sex ratio, high malnutrition., high maternal mortality rates, high drop out rates, poor school enrolment levels low skill levels, low value for work in India are all indicators of high preference for a male child due to the prevailing belief that girls are less of an asset and more of a liability. There is always a negative attitude towards girl's education. Seventy percent of the non-school –going girls state that apart from the fact that they came from families with low incomes, domestic work burden, sibling care and parental apathy towards their education keep them away from schools. Even women headed households prioritise their sons education over daughter's because son stay on in the family to look after the old parent, but daughter gets married and will go away.

In India it is very common to accept the stereotypical linkage between the per capita income and level of education/literacy. Low income status of our economy provides a convenient alibi only. There are many countries which have lower per capita income than India but significantly higher literacy rates. Policy oriented research over emphasise the supply side of the problem. Studies do not focus on the demand side and institutional factors in perpetuating the female educational disadvantage. The Problem is multi dimensional. While access is a necessary condition it is not a sufficient to ensure enrolment and retention.. The latter is contingent upon on the operation of whole host of factors: pedagogical factors, institutional factors and familial factors. There is no doubt that basic education and gendered nature of the problem continue to elude solutions not because of the intractability of the problem itself but more because of the fact that state refuses to take and implement certain hard decisions. The social hierarchy and economic hierarchy are interwoven in the livelihood of the majority Caste an important social unit, performs the most important function of division of labour and occupation. Employment of girl children in India is closely associated with its social attitude towards school education. The schooling of the girls is determined more intricately by factors such as caste, religion, family, occupation, etc. The subtle incorporation of Hindu notion of caste hierarchy and religious dogmas into the educational system has created a strong social belief that it is undesirable for lower caste people to acquire education No section of people advocate education as a force of liberation and equaliser. Gender and class continue to affect school attendance. Expenses involved in education as an explanation for sending children to work but not to school are more often used for girl children. Because returns from daughters education is considered to be zero by the parents.. Therefore the inaction of the state to abolish the practice of girl child labour has social acceptance.

5.9. EXPLOITATION OF GIRL CHILD LABOUR

Employment of girl children in India is closely associated with its social attitude towards school education. The schooling of the girls is determined more intricately by factors such as caste, religion, family type and size, occupation, kinship pattern and marriage etc. Thus girls are the worst victims of both class and caste hierarchy and gender discrimination.[16] Indian education system has remained elitist and urban-biased. The subtle incorporation of Hindu notion of caste hierarchy and religious dogmas into the educational system has created an educational dualism, which distinguishes between children with 'hands' and children with 'minds'. There is a strong social belief that it is undesirable for lower caste people to acquire education No section of people have advocated education as a force of liberation and equaliser. Caste an important social unit, performs the most important function of division of labour and occupation amounting to caste affiliation in rural India . Thus social hierarchy and economic hierarchy are interwoven in the livelihood of the majority.

The 'vested interests' tend to violate the constitutional provisions and legislations for protecting children. Everyone from middle class house-wife to the rich landlord, from parents to the employers in the informal sector needs a child labour and a domestic servant. Everybody behaves like an opportunist. There exists a tinge of aristocracy to be served. Everyone tries to pay less and get more work done through the children . The only person who suffers is the girl child who does not count. Socially concerned people salve their conscience by employing girl children ostensibly to save them from starvation and look upon it as a social service. Otherwise the child would have become a thief or street vagabond. All Bills and Acts give a carte blanche to employers and parents to exploit the girl children with the benign indulgence of the state. Given the ambiguities in definition and complexities of enumeration it is no wonder that estimates of child labour very so greatly in India. With this variation, It is particularly very difficult to assess whether child labour is increasing or declining. It makes any global comparisons, problematic. Therefore, school attendance can be accepted as a surrogate measure for child labour, because, child labour and child schooling are two dependent variables which are simultaneously determined by a set of exogenous variables. Analytical framework below exposed the reciprocal causation between child labour and child schoolingThe set of exogenous variables include caste structure, family size, land holding, productive asset, live stocks cropping pattern, rainfall, female labour input, school accessibility, parents (particularly father's) educational level etc. The exogenous variables for both participation of girl child labour and schooling attendance of the girl child are the same. Public policy can be directed towards the elimination of girl child labour and enhancement of the level of schooling of girls. For the purpose of the present study child labour may be defined as "any activity performed by a girl child in the productive process either in casual or regular basis with or without any remuneration attached to it" Thus girl child labour simply connotes a working girl child or employed girl child.

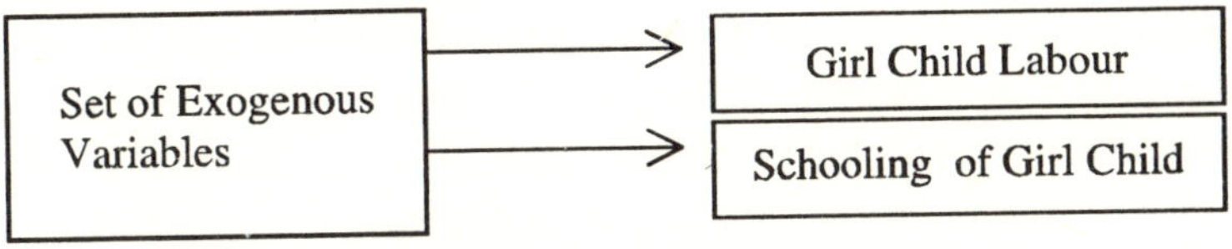

Fig. 5.1 : Girl Child Labour and their Schooling

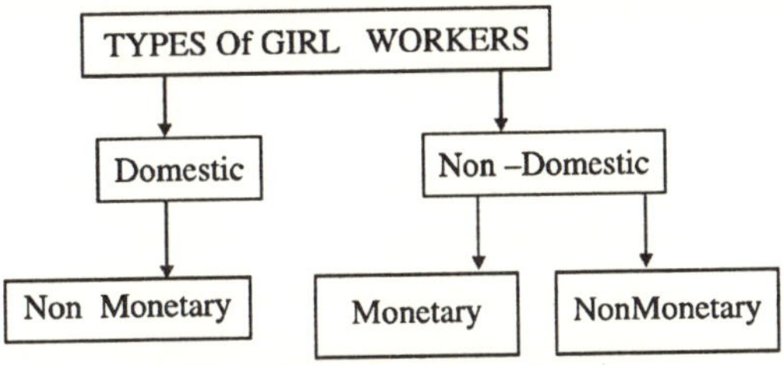

Fig. 5.2 : Types of Girl Workers

Girl children lend a helpful hand to their mother, once they are around. Their rearing does not involve any opportunity costs. Prospective husbands and prospective family-in-laws ,who will belong to a similar socio economic milieu will not expect the girl to have received much schooling. The bride should be a perfect housewife. Gender and class continue to affect school attendance. Attendance among girls is low in the villages. Expenses involved in education as an explanation for keeping children out of school are more often used for girls than for boys. The usually assumed underlying reason is that expenses should lead to returns. Returns from daughter education is assumed to be zero.

5.10. MAGNITUDE OF GIRL CHILD LABOUR IN INDIA

Girls engaged in cultivation constituted 56.64% in 1961. It decreased to 27.78% in 1971 and to 30.99% in 1981. Girls employed as agricultural labourer increased from 25.42% in 1961 to 57.34% in 1971 and to 55% in 19981. Boy workers in household industry decreased from 13.07% (urban) and 7.94% during 1961, 1971 and 1981 respectively.

Girl workers in the household industry (urban) has decreased from 31.50% to 17.96% in 1971 to 17.54% in 1981. Table 3.7 gives the estimated figures of labour participation of girl workers of India. It is useful to identify the industrial sectors in which child labour participation is rampant. In rural areas, 3.9% of child labour participation of boys is among cultivators families and 3.7% among agricultural labourer families. The corresponding rates for girl child work participation are 1.6% and 2.9%. This is not surprising since the dominant sector in the rural economy is agriculture. For similar reasons, in urban areas, the boy child labour participation rate is the highest in processing and manufacturing in the non-household sector. In order to adjust these structural differences, child labour as percent of workers aged 5 plus is calculated for each sector. It is found that in rural areas, This recent is the highest for both genders in livestock sector and next highest in the agricultural labour sector. In urban areas this percent do not show a large variation among the sectors as in rural areas. Hence one can conclude that child labour participation is rampant particularly in rural areas among families working in the livestock sector and as agricultural labourers. Families working in these sectors are also among the poorest in rural area. Therefore there is an empirical association between child worker participation and poverty.

In rural areas the percentage of child labour participation among the literates is 2.2 for girls (as against 13.4 for boys) and 6.4 for girls among illiterate children. Similarly in urban areas the percentage of girl labour participation is higher among illiterates i.e 2.5 for girls as against 0.5 for girls among the literates. Thus there is high degree of positive association between illiteracy and work participation among girl children . Therefore it is highly necessary to recognise the association between schooling

Table 5.1 : Girl Child Labour in Different Occupations if India

	Economic Activity	*% of population aged 5-14 year*				*% of main workers aged 5+ years*			
		Rural Girl		*Urban Girl*		*Rural Girll*		*Urban Girl*	
1	Cultivator	3.9	1.6	0.2	0.1	3.	7.4	2.0	3.6
2	Agl. Labr.	3.7	09	0.4	0.3	8.2	9.7	4.7	6.3
3	Livestock fishing etc	0.7	0.2	0.1	N	15.7	18.7	3.5	4.0
4	Mining-etc	N	N	N	N	2.1	8.2	0.5	3.4
5	H.H.I	0.2.	0.2	0.3	0.2	4.7	10.2	3.4	7.6
6	O.M.	0.2	0.1	1.1	0.3	3.2	10.7	2.2.	6.8
7	Construction	N	N	0.1	N	1.8	10.0	1.4	5.1
8	Trade & Commerce	0.1	N	0.7	N	1.9	3.2	1.6	1.5
9	Transport -storage etc	N	N	0.1	N	0.5	2.1	0.6	0.8
10	Other services	0.1	0.1	0.5	0.3	1.4	5.0	1.1	3.2
Total		9.2	5.3	3.6	1.3	4.9	8.9	1.8	4.6

Notes :- N denotes negligible, HHI=Household Industry ,O.M= Other Manufacturing

Source :- Report of Regstrar General, based on census of India, 1981.

Table 5.2 : Participation of Girl Children in the Work Force (000)

Category of child workers	*Population*		*Main workers*		*Child worker participation rate %*	
	Literate	*Illiterate*	*Literate*	*illiterate*	*Literate*	*Illiterate*
Rural Girls	18135	48536	392	3118	2.2	6.4
Urban Girls	11466	7476	57	190	0.5	2.5

Source :- Census Report ,1991. New Delhi.

and girl's work participation in framing policies for the reduction of girl workers and universal compulsory education .

5.11. INCIDENCE OF GIRLCHILD LABOUR IN ORISSA

Orissa has a bottom heavy population structure. The proportion of child population is very heavy for Orissa, because of its high fertility rate. It constituted 39.06% in 1961, 42.35% in 1971 and 39.64% in 1961,1981, and 1991 respectively .Urban child population accounted for 35.30%, 39.85 and 38.18% in 1961, 1971 and 1991 respectively. Child population in 1961 is the highest i.e. 43.15% in Kalahandi followed by 42.09% in Keonjhar. It was the lowest i.e. 37.10% in Cuttack The following table 5.3 shows the rural and urban distribution of girl child workers of Orissa. Percentage of Marginal girl workers is found to be the highest in Koraput followed by Ganjam and Sambalpur.

Table 5.3: Rural Urban Distribution Girl Child Workers

Districts	*Rural*		*Urban*	
	Marginal	*Main*	*Marginal*	*Main*
Sambalpur	10738	2535	181	461
Sundargarh	6461	459	47	349
Kenjhar	4051	381	28	140
Mayurbhanj	8605	1490	48	162
Baleswar	1602	417	46	208
Cuttack	1227	1038	60	388
Dhenkanal	4378	1557	27	108
Phulbani	5214	322	14	30
Bolangir	7853	490	106	123
Kalahandi	11153	451	49	106
Koraput	20971	605	125	288
Ganjam	12349	1167	221	299
Puri	1656	854	18	496
TOTAL	96258	11766	970	3158

Source: Census 1991,Govt of India Publications .New Delhi

5.12. SECTOR WISE DISTRIBUTION OF GIRL CHILD WORKERS

Here we analyse the incidence of child labour in different sectors of the Orissa. By looking into census reports of Government of India, it is found that child workers employed in the primary sector comprise 76.68% in 1961 and 88.15% in 1981. On the other hand child workers employed in the secondary sector comprise about 7.43% in 1961, 4,53% in 1971 and 5.67% in 1981 .Similarly child workers employed in the tertiary sector account for 15.89% in 1961. It declined to 9.01.% in 1971 and 6.18% in 1981. During 1981, primary sector of Orissa employs the highest i.e 96.49% of child workers of Phulbani district and the lowest i.e 74.31% in Cuttack. Secondary sector similarly gives employment to 11.24% 8.62% and 8.28% of child workers of Cuttack, Mayurbhanj and Sambalpur districts respectively. And the tertiary sector of Cuttack, Keonjhar and Mayurbhanj gives employment to 14.45% 10.19% and 8.87% of their total child workers. Employment of child workers in the tertiary sector and secondary sector of Orissa has declined over the decades. It is also true of the separate districts of Orissa. But in the primary sector employment of child workers has increased over last three decades. About 75.25% of girl workers account for 24.75% of the total child workers of the state of Orissa. Boy workers constitute the highest i.e 87.04% in district Balasore followed by that of Cuttack (85.89%) and Puri (85.77%). Girl workers account for the highest i.e 36.30% in Mayurbhanj district followed by Ganjam with 32.92% and Phulbani with 32.50% High proportion of boy workers are found in the rural areas of Bolangir, followed by Kalahandi and Puri. High proportion of girl workers are found in the rural areas of Mayurbhanj and Phulbani and Ganjam. High incidence of boy workers in urban areas are seen in Cuttack, Puri, Balasore and Sundargarh . These districts are industrially advanced districts of Orissa. High percentage of girl workers in urban areas are found in Keonjhar, Sundargarh, Balasore and Puri. It is observed (Table 4.10) that both boy workers and girl workers are predominantly engaged as agricultural labourer and cultivators. In 1981, 61.14% of girl workers were working as agricultural labourer as compared to 42.15% of boy workers in this occupation. Girl workers are found to be widely employed in household industry and other household industries in comparison to boy workers. Girls workers are also widely employed in other categories. But employers prefer boy workers in cultivation, mining and quarrying, construction trade and commerce, and transport.

Table 5.4 : Child Workers in Different Occupation of Orissa

Sl. No	*Occupation*	*1981*		*1991*		*2001*	
		Boy	*Girls*	*Boy*	*Girls*	*Boy*	*Girls*
1	Cultivators	48.72	46.41	34.48	10.71	37.85	18.80
2	Agrl. Labour	24.50	23.76	45.08	57.89	42.15	61.14
3	Livestock etc.	-	-	8.81	7.79	9.84	3.98
4	Mining etc.	4.70	2.27	0.10	0.96	0.16	0.69
5	Household Industry	9.96	10.93	1.96	7.26	2.01	5.46
6	Other Industries.	0.44	0.54	1.04	2.24	1.97	2.04
7	Construction	-	-	0.08	-	0.21	0.99
8	Trade/Comm.	0.73	9.42	1.41	1.33	2.09	1.07
9	Transport etc.	0.13	1.38	0.17	0.53	0.17	-
10	Other services	1069	13.94	6.82	10.82	3.49	5.72
	Total	100	100	100	100	100	100

Source :- Census of India, 1971, 1981 &1991.

5.13. THE REGRESSION MODEL

The inter district variations in the girl child labour ratio in Orissa is hypothesised to be due to the variation in level of poverty, level of literacy, population density, work participation rate, degree of urbanisation and dropout rates etc. In order to study the effects of these factors on rate of participation of child workers, the following two regression models have been used separately for urban girl workers and rural girl workers of Orissa.

1) Work Participation Rate of Rural Girl workers :

$$\text{Log } WPR_{GR} = G + gr_1 \log R_1 + gr_2 \log R_2 + gr_3 \log R_3 + gr_4 \log R_4 + gr_5 \text{ Log } R_5 + gr_6 \log R_8 + gr_7 \log R_{10} + gr_8 \log R_{11} + gr_9 \log R_{12} + gr_{10} \log R_{13} + \log U .$$

Table 5.5 : Regression Equation (Rural Girl Workers)

Sl. No.	*Independent Variables*	*Regression Coefficient*		*t-values*
1	Poverty ratio (PR) = R1	gr_1	-0.723	5.486 **
2	Rural poverty (RP)=R2	gr_2	-0.8742	0.7086**
3	Literacy Rate (LR) =R3	gr_3	-0.672	-0.5532*
4	Male literacy rate (ML) = R4	gr_4	-0.513	-0.4375
5	Female Literacy Ratio(FL) =R5	gr_5	-0.465	0.6165**
6	Degree of Urbanisation (UR) =R8	gr_6	-0.324	-0.4139
7	Male Work Participation (MW)=y10	gr_7	-0.137	0.0625
8	% of Girl(5-9)attending school at (GS)=R11	gr_8	-0.378	-0.7511*
9	Dropout(girl) rate at Primary stage (DP) =R12	gr_9	-0.306	0.1753
10	Dropout(girl)rate atMiddle School (DM)=R13	gr_{10}	-0.131	0.0129

R2 =0.796 B=9.432 * Significant at 5% level

F = 52.328 n=11 ** Significant at 1% level

2) Work Participation Rate of Urban Girl workers:

$$\text{Log } WPR_{GU} = G + gu_1 \log R_1 + gu_2 \log R_2 + gu_3 \log R_3 + gu_4 \log R_4 + gu_5 \log R_5 + gu_6 \log R_8 + gu_7 \log R_{10} + gu_8 \log R_{11} + gu_9 \log R_{12} + gu_{10} R_{13} \log U$$

Table 5.6 : Regression Equation (For Urban Girl Workers)

Sl. No	*Independent variables*	*Regression Coefficients*		*t-values*
1	Poverty ratio (PR) = R1	gu_1	0.8317	7.146**
2	Rural poverty (RP)=R2	gu_2	0.8915	1.827
3	Literacy Rate (LR) =R3	gu_3	-0.8676	-0.532*
4	Male literacy rate (ML) = R4	gu_4	-0.4351	0.956**
5	Female Literacy Ratio(FL) =R5	gu_5	-0.6345	0.391
6	Degree of Urbanisation (UR) =R8	gu_6	0.1342	-0.228
7	Male Work Participation (MW)=y10	gu_7	0.6993	0.084
8	% of Girl (5-9)attending school at (GS)=R11	gu_8	-0..5568	-0.836**
9	Dropout(girl) rate at Primary stage (DP) =R12	gu_9	0.6347	0.392
10	Dropout(girl)rate at Middle School (DM)=R13	gu_{10}	0.6134	1.752

G =8.671 $R^2 = 0.823$ *significant at 5% level

F= 37.15 n= 11 ** significant at 1% level

In the first regression equation (for rural girl workers) ten explanatory variables together explain about 79.6% of variations in the work participation rate of girl workers. Among the variables the poverty ratio, rural poverty ratio, literacy ratio and percentage of boys attending the school at the age of 5-9 years are found to be statistically significant. The regression coefficients(table 5.5) of gr_3, gr_4 ,gr_5,gr_7 and gr_8 are negative. All these negative coefficients imply that lower literacy rate, particularly lower literacy rate among male population, lower degree of urbanisation and lower rate of school attendance among the girls (of 5-9 age) all together tend to magnify the work participation among the girls. The corresponding t-values of gr_3 and gr_8 are statistically significant at 5% level. On the contrary the regression coefficients of gr_1, gr_2 and gr_6 are positive. The t-values of these coefficients are significant at 1% level. It implies that high ratio of poverty and rural poverty and high growth rate of population have positive influence on the work participation of girlchildren in Orissa. Similarly the regression coefficients of gr_1,gr_2, gr_9 and gr_{10} are positive .The t-values for gr_1 and gr_2 are statistically significant. But it suggests that higher rate of dropout both at primary schools and middle schools are responsible for high work participation of girl-children in Orissa.

In the second regression equation (for urban girl-workers) all the ten explanatory variable together explain about 82.13% of the total variation in the work participation rate of urban girl –workers. Among the independent variables, poverty ratio, rural poverty ratio in particular, literacy ratio, and female literacy ratio in particular and the percentage of girls attending the primary school at the age of 5-9 years are estimated to be statistically significant(Table 5.6). The regression coefficients of gu1 gu_2 , gu_9 and gu_{10} are positive and significant at 1% level of significance. It implies that high poverty ratio in Orissa and high incidence of rural poverty are the cause of high degree of girl child labour in Orissa. Similarly high dropout rate in primary schools causes high work participation for girl children. The regression coefficients of gu_5 and gu_7 are also positive. It means that high growth of population and high work participation of female are associated with high girl-child participation in the work force. But the regression coefficients of gu_3, gu_4, gu_5 and gu_8 are negative. The corresponding t-values of gu_4 and gu_8 are significant at 5% level. All these imply that lower literacy rate and lower female literacy in particular, of Orissa are the cause of higher work participation for girl-children. Similarly lower degree of urbanisation and lower percentage of girls attending schools at (5-9) age are the cause of higher incidence of girl child labour in the State. The findings of regression model fitted separately for rural girl workers and urban girl workers suggest that lower literacy, lower male and female literacy, lower degree of urbanisation and lower rate of school attendance on the one hand and high poverty ratio, higher rural poverty ratio, high growth rate of population and high dependency ratio on the other hand are the cause of high work participation of girl children in Orissa.

5.14. CONCLUSION

The problem girl workers reflects the character of society and polity. The roots of the problems of girl child labour are hidden in the socio-economic environment. The educational and health facilities for the majority of Indian population is woefully inadequate. There is urban bias and rural neglect. Economic distress of the people in the lower income group is responsible for the perpetuation of this malady. Social structure of India is characterised by both caste and class hierarchy. Children of the lower strata have no other option open than to enter into various activities of the informal sector. Practice of employing girl child is the byproduct of under development. There is high fertility and high dependency ratio and high population density in India. Infant mortality rate is very high in India. Literacy rate among male and female in India is very low. Degree of urbanisation is very low. SC and ST population in the state constitute about 16.2% and 22.2% of its total population. Literacy and work participation rate among SC/ST population is very lower. Educational and health facilities in the villages of India are deplorably very low. General work participation of both male, female is very low.

Problem of poverty coupled with rapid population growth has compounded the problem of girl child labour. Majority of girl workers exists in rural areas of India. Majority of parents consider the daughter as a part of socialisation process. But in reality girl workers are highly neglected and exploited. They are denied the liberty of human being and are treated as semi-bonded labourers. Problem of girl child labour in India is a very complex socio-economic malaise. Various social, economic demographic and educational forces mutually reinforce the incidence of girl-child labour. It is observed from correlation matrix that there is negative correlation between child work participation and literacy ratio. There is positive correlation between girl-child labour and school dropout rates both at primary and middle schools. High incidence of poverty and rural poverty have positive effect on high work participation of both girl and boy children .

In India there is very little critical analysis on girl child labour. Policy-oriented and action-oriented research on girl child labour is scarce and scattered. All studies and reports have only remained as a source of data, which endorses the passivity of the state. However many studies are done giving a vivid accounts of the work of children in particular place or factories. All research on child labour is increasingly concentrated on child labour intensive industries like, match , fire cracker, carpet, gem, brick industries etc. Much legislative attention, both national and international has been paid to the development and work of children. But there have been very few studies on the girl children working in various low-paid jobs in the informal sector and various domestic and non-domestic non-remunerative jobs in the villages and towns. The incidence of girl child labour in the informal sector has not been able to draw the attention of researchers to any noticeable extent. Very few studies exist on the economic role of girl children in the process of socio-economic transformation and economic development . Very few scholars have attempted to understand the causes, consequences and functions of child labour. Paucity of data and its non-reliability have been the major cause for refraining the researchers to carryout an indepth study on it. Some argue that it is unimportant because child labour is undesirable and must be stopped or regulated by law. So we do not need to understand its source. But the very failure to abolish child labour across the developing countries proves this view to be false. Therefore a critical probing into the problem is very much warranted . Better understanding of child labour and more particularly of girl child labour , its determinants and consequences and labour market and renewed emphasis on universalisation of primary schooling can lead us to reach the professed goal of eradicating child labour. Effective policy design requires an effective understanding of the roles of children within a broad social framework .

REFERENCES

1. Becker (1960) An economic Analysis of Fertility in G Becker (ed) Demographic and economic Change in Developed Countries, Princeton University Press. Princeton.
2. Burra Neera(1988) Exploitation of Children in Jaipur Gem Industry, Economic and Political Weekly, Vol.23(3) 10th January
3. Cain, MT (177) The economic activities of children in a Bangladesh Village, Population and Development Review, Vol.3(3)
4. Daniel, .C(1976) Child Worker has come to stay, Social Welfare, Vol. 22(8)
5. Das, Kumar (1990) Paradox of poverty and Planning in India, Economic Quarterly, Vol.25(4),Berlin
6. Fernades, W et al (1985) Child Labour in India, Indian Social Institute, New Delhi
7. George Ivy(1990) Child Labour and Child Work,Ashish Pub,New Delhi
8. Kanbargi, Ramesh(1991) Child labour in Indian sub-continent , Sage New Delhi
9. Nangia, PK(1987) Child Labour: cause –Effect Syndrome, Janak pub, New Delhi
10. Sarma, AM(1979) Child Labour in Indian Industries, Indian

Journal of Social Work, Vol.40(3) Singh S et al (1987) Child Labour in Agriculture, Print House, Lucknow

11. Singh, AN(1990) Child Labour in India, Sipra Pub. Delhi

6

Technology and Women in India

Economic growth and technological advancement in India in the current decade is very impressive . Technology, market and development are considered gender-neutral. But there is pronounced urban bias and rural neglect in the development process of India. Gender concerns and discourses survive within the development bureaucracies dominated by men. It is easier for them to ring-fence gender issues as a problem of poverty and to argue against 'feminization of poverty' than to admit the gender disadvantage which crosses the boundaries of class and ethnicity. Since the beginning of planned development, women have been viewed as a deprived section requiring welfare measures. Most studies and reports on women have only remained as a source of data, which rather endorses the passivity of the state. This chapter is based on a primary survey of 900 households of two villages of Orissa . It studies the impact of technology on various social parameters of village economy. It examines the link between technology and occupational pattern of women, the level of female education, and identifies the factors that influence women employment. It assesses employment potentials and opportunities for women in both farm and non-farm activities in the villages.It attempts to reveal the real scenario of the rural sector, and argues that rescuing gender from poverty trap means we need poverty-independent gender analyses and policies. Education and technology should ensure liberation and freedom of thought for all human beings. It should break gradually the shackles of tradition that binds women in the man-made gaol. The gender issue should be delinked both from myopic economics and insensitive politics.

6.1. DEVELOMENTALISM AND RURAL SECTOR

There is a global economic movement of economic integration through technology. The impact of this globalization process has become all pervasive and inexorable. All sectors of developing countries seem to be vibrating with economic buoyancy. It has generated an impervious atmosphere of over optimism of instant economic growth. There is expansion of trade, investment, market, and increase in GNP, productivity, per capita income, profit, efficiency, salary etc. Life styles of metro people in India have become more attractive , comfortable and fashionable than ever before. There is worldwide process of overproduction but unemployment and dramatic contraction of purchasing power of people.[1] The global economic system is thus characterized by two contradictory forces: the consolidation of cheap labor economy on the one hand and the search for new consumer markets on the other. Unfortunately the former undermines the latter in the long run. It generates social apartheid and undermines the rights of women. It is an insidious and inscrutable process, which is conducive to globalization of markets, which ultimately undermines human livelihood and destroys civil society in the south [2].

After India's independence and a long period of planning and development exercise, spanning over more than 56 years of in India, it is saddening to observe that the incidence of poverty and livelihood insecurity have remained as grave as ever. There is pronounced urban bias and rural neglect in the development process. The economic development has created an urbanization process, which is dysfunctional, and an industrialization pattern, which is regionally concentrated. The development planners have remained broadly myopic and complacent with trickledown effect for the rural sector. The result of the development exercises have been the persistence of a huge low productive primary sector, slender industrial sector and a bloated tertiary sector. All the benefits of the welfare measures have gravitated willy nilly towards the elite class and such other groups with political visibility.[3] The rural sector of India has remained closed to the subsistence level and sensitive to the vagaries of nature - flood, cyclone and drought etc.

With the euphoria of 'high-tech civilization', the concern for rural development, rural poverty, hunger and inequality virtually are dismissed as an obsession of egalitarian romantics. This insolent attitude and insouciance have generated dangerous consequences. It has spreaded an excitement of over optimism of instant change and pragmatism of high-tech-efficiency. It appears to be very logical and attractive. But its socio-economic impact and implications are not uniform across social groups, genders, regions, sectors, and generations. Its statistical mirage underestimates the ground reality and depicts a misleading picture. When one aims at gender equity, neither the earlier panacea of central planning nor the virtues of free marketism appears to carry much conviction for the common man of backward regions of India. The problem of economic vulnerability, livelihood insecurity and malnutrition among village people is becoming more pronounced .

6.2. WOMEN AND ECONOMIC DEVELOPMENT

The millennium development Goals (MDG) aims at eradicating poverty and promote gender equality and empower women by 2015. There is need to improve the policies and implement them with greater impetus. But poor women in India remain in traditional fields of employment. When traditional jobs become unavailable due to number of factors, women are forced to seek employment in other areas, which may have no relationship with their original experience and expertise. Women have a marginal role in family decision making, they are primarily responsible for keeping the hearth going. They are occasionally consulted on marriage negotiations but not on any financial matters in the villages. Women's economic contribution has been invisibilised in the industrial process of economic development. [4] This trend is not linear or unidirectional.

Women are also displaced and lost their share in the industrial workforce due to upgradation of technology, and reduction of labour intensity of production through automation and adoption of high-tech . Employers in the private sector ,in the process of modernization , eschew the responsibility for workers well being in the name of eliminating market distortions . Moreover, in the current globalized economy, women's social subordination coincides with the absence of economic alternatives. Employment of women in industries has been accompanied with deregulation of labour protection. Women fail to defend or promote their interest both as women and as workers. Even male-led labour unions either ignore or consider women's demand as divisive and irrelevant to the interest of the 'real working class'. The women-heads in the families face serious challenges in village economy due to low literacy levels, low asset holdings, lower productivity of land, lesser access to avenues of income- earning and governmental help and the declining kinship supports. The differential social evaluation of the sex roles, the male-orientation in running households coupled with rural poverty and household poverty enmesh in narrowing choices open to women heads of households. The capital intensive technology has rather trivialised the gender issue. The whole host of economic and social structures and processes that reinforce patriarchy, devalue and commodify the women. The confluence of modernization does not improve the fate of women.

6.3. TECHNOLOGY AND WOMEN OF INDIA

Modern technology is supported and directed by powerful institutions and interests. Men gravitate to science and technology . We must question, whether technology is male dominated because it demands some essentially masculine traits, or 'simply' because technology is where the power is?. Technology is socially constructed, or co-produced, alongside gender.[5] Technology itself gets gendered in the eyes of would be technologists. The continued male dominance in science and engineering is due in large measure to the enduring symbolic association of masculinity and technology by which cultural images and representations of technology converge with prevailing images of masculinity and power . The use of technology is always discriminatory.Technical prowess is what defines them as engineers *and* what gives them a sense of power. The symbolic gendering of technology extends beyond the artifactual, but it has material consequences. Within the masculinity-technology association, one can discern a series of highly gendered dichotomies . Most obvious of these is the distinction between being people-focussed and machine-focussed. It corresponds to the division between feminine expressiveness and masculine instrumentalism. Most women routinely interact with people *and* technologies. For example computer is implicitly rather than explicitly gendered. 'Hard' technology is inert and powerful, while 'Soft' technology is smaller scale. So the world of technology is made to feel remote and overwhelmingly powerful because of the hard-soft dualism. The hard-soft dichotomy also extend to styles of thought in technology [6]. On the masculine side of those dualisms we have an objectivist rationality associated with emotional detachment. On the feminine side we have a more subjective rationality associated with emotional connectedness. Males have dominated the ' internet culture' since its inception . The Internet culture can be discomforting and alien to females.[7]

India has achieved higher technological advancement during last decade. The Green Revolution, which focuses on increasing yields of rice and wheat, entails a shift in inputs from human to technical. Women's participation, knowledge and inputs are marginalized, and their role has shifted from being "primary producers to subsidiary workers." Technological progress in agriculture has had a negative impact on women. Women work longer hours and their work is more arduous than men's, yet their work is unrecognized. Men report that "women, like children, eat and do nothing."

There is tremendous effects of information technology on women's employment and the nature of women's work in all third world countries including India .[8] But in areas of technology, till today women represent about 10 % of researchers and about 5% of manager. The impact of information technology on society has not been uniformly beneficial, and the technological divide is being increasingly felt, especially in the developing countries. Serious obstacles still continue in achieving gender equality. The gender implications of digital divide is very serious in India. Access to and use of the Internet has important economic, educational, and social benefits, and those who are excluded from Internet participation will also be excluded from several benefits. [9] Lack of training does not allow them to escape from their sex-typed slots. The women from poorer families face challenges as they adjust to new technologies. Their jobs do not reintegrate them, leveling the hierarchies and adding responsibilities. [10] It is still believed by the elite class of Orissa that science improves their role and make them better mother, better wives ,enriching their domestic lives. They do not think beyond that. Women still face subtle resistance to their participation in science and technology, no matter how talented she is, from all corners, particularly from the husband, how so ever educated he may be. Women are expressly excluded from many activities .Because marriage has remained indispensable goal for the women, particularly in Orissa. All her achievements culminate in a good marriage and proving her motherhood. Not being married is a great social stigma both for the family and the girls. Not becoming mother is considered greater ominous. Therefore getting higher education for girls is an accident. Ninety percent of marriages are caste-based, arranged by the parents. Therefore parents feel it as a burden or duty. Girls continue their studies till the parent get a good boy for them. Education reduces the set of choice for the parents. So it is perceived as a problem for many girls. It is increasingly difficult to marry and get a partner . A good girl student experiences very encouraging motivation from the teachers, but cold attitude from the parents and relatives. Besides this, the amount of dowry-offer proportionally increases with the girls schooling for the parents. Even today many educated people(including the potential husbands) think that educated women would engage in deviant social and political behavior .[11] It is perceived that she would refuse to do household work and disobey their husband ,if their education is too higher than the husband. They would become musculinized and expect to be included in men's activities. Advocates of women's education argue that education will help women to fulfill their God-given duties toward their husband and family . Therefore women suffer greater subordination and deprivation both at home and in society. Oppression of women in Orissa can be described as hypocritical at its worst and schizophrenic at its best.

Women should be given various (both farm and non-farm) training to escape from their sex-typed slots. The aim with jobs should be to reintegrate them wherever possible, leveling the hierarchies, adding responsibilities to lower grade jobs and building in more interaction with the technologies in the case of routine operations and jobs. It should provide pathways for lower skilled women workers to learn and progress. The aim of training should be to encourage women of any age or occupation to consider on-the-job or off-the-job training for more technical work. Other wise they are more susceptible to displacement and deskilling by emerging push-botton technology. Technology should liberate women potential instead of hooking them up, or tying them in side the virtual prisons . Community-based women's organisations should be instrumental in the process of enabling women to cross the so-called digital divide .Technology should be powerful tools for women to overcome discrimination, achieve full equality and higher well-being.

6.4. RURAL POVERTY AND WOMEN IN ORISSA

India consists of 28 states and six union territories of which 17 are major states with a population of one billion. Orissa is the poorest state of the country. It is the state which depict the paradoxical situation of economic growth and coexistence of poverty and livelihood insecurity of people. Livelihood Security refers to the poverty line defining inadequate income, consumption, nutritional level, health status, life expectancy, and asset holding of the people. Livelihood consists of both generation of income as well as the ownership of productive assets that reduces the vulnerability of marginalized communities. [12] It involves the capabilities, assets of both material and non-material resource required for a means of living. A majority of the village population is still dependent upon the agricultural sector for their income .The income derived from farming is too little to improve their economic status. The rural poor are unable to save and do not have access to credit in order to invest in creating assets. The livelihood strategies of poor people in the villages are in reality different from those of rich people. The reduction in poverty in India is a myth. One fine morning the poverty level of India reduced from 36 % to 26% without any commensurate results. The definition adopted by the government at present has conceptual problem and therefore poverty is consequently underestimated. [13] The government uses that statistics to camouflage the real state of affairs.

Orissa is the poorest state of the India having 48% of its population below the line of poverty. The deprivation Index estimated for all states depicts the Indian scenario and place of Orissa in the national map. Orissa has the highest IMR, MMR and high rate of illiteracy .It has the maximum concentration of tribal population. Incidence of poverty is the severest on Women and children of Orissa. The standard prescription for growth have not ended poverty or hunger anywhere in the state. Poverty reduction is the bench mark against which success of development institutions must be measured.

6.1. HUMAN DEPRIVATION INDEX OF INDIA

Sl. No	Major States	Poverty line	Illiteracy 2001	IMR 2001	DI	Rank in DI	Rank in WEI
1	AndhraPradesh	15.77	38.89	66	40.21	9	20
2	ArunachalPradesh	33.47	45.26	44	40.89	7	13
3	Assam	36.09	35.72	78	49.93	5	19
4	Bihar	42.60	52.47	67	54.02	3	25
5	Gujrat	14.07	33.57	64	37.21	12	10
6	Haryana	8.74	31.41	69	36.38	16	12
7	HimachalPradesh	7.63	24.09	64	31.90	18	6
8	Jummu&Kashmir	3.48	45.54	45	31.34	19	21
9	Karnataka	20.04	32.96	58	36.99	13	16
10	Kerala	12.72	9.08	16	12.59	30	4
11	MadhyaPradesh	37.43	35.92	97	56.77	2	23
12	Maharastra	25.02	28.73	49	34.24	17	17
13	Orissa	47.15	36.39	98	60.50	1	22
14	Punjab	6.16	30.05	54	30.06	20	5
15	Rajasthan	15.28	38.97	83	45.74	6	24
16	Sikkim	36.55	30.32	52	39.61	10	8
17	Tamilnadu	21.12	26.58	53	23.54	23	11
18	Tripura	34.44	29.36	49	36.59	15	15
19	UttarPradesh	31.15	42.64	85	52.92	4	26
20	WestBengal	27.02	30.78	53	36.92	14	18
21	Delhi	8.23	18.18	51	25.80	22	2
	India	26.10	34.80	71	43.96		

Source : 1. National Human Development report 2001. India

2. Based on NHDR 2001 literacy rate

3. Economic and political report 2003, May. 10.

Note. DI=Deprivation Index, WEI=Women Empowerment Index

Poverty, hunger and starvation deaths persist in KBK districts of Orissa despite large sums are spent in various Govt programs. The ongoing poverty alleviation programes of the govt do not attack the poverty at its roots. Rather they tend to polarize the society by concentrating income in the hands of few and narrowing the social and economic opportunities for the poor[14] .Land degradation, water scarcity and growing vulnerability to economic stress are real threats to food security. Hunger is considered as the result of underdevelopment. Therefore there is need for appropriate mix of resources, food, water, land, credit, training, market and technology in order to create enabling condition for the poor people. Policy makers of India attempt to fight against 'Feminisation of poverty'.It does not mean that poverty is a gendered experience but that the poor are mostly women. The poorer the family the more likely it is to be headed by a woman. But poverty can not serve as the proxy for subordination of women. Therefore anti poverty policies can not be expected to necessarily improve the position of women.

6.5. LIVELIHOOD SECURITY FOR VILLAGE WOMEN IN ORISSA

The concept of livelihood is defined as a means of living or supporting life and meeting individual and community needs . It involves the capabilities, assets of both material and non-material resources required for a living. It refers to poverty line defining adequate income, consumption, nutritional level, health status, life expectancy, and asset holding of the people. Livelihood consists of both generation of income as well as the ownership of productive assets that reduces the vulnerability of marginalized communities. A majority of the village population is still dependent upon the agricultural sector for their income .The income derived from farming is too little to improve their economic status. The rural poor often are unable to save and do not have access to credit in order to invest in creating assets. As a result, there is over exploitation of natural resources such as water and forests in people's attempts to invest inputs into their agricultural production. The livelihood strategies of poor people in the villages are in reality different from those of rich people. Rich people always have the capacity to diversify their livelihood strategies because of the risks involved. The success of a livelihood strategy depends on both physical and human factors. In state like Orissa, which is economically not developed, the sustenance and management of a good standard of living and maintenance of secured livelihood is really difficult. The poor villagers are subjected to the prey of vagaries of nature and variance in monsoon, which lead towards very low level of production of crops and family income.

The livelihood becomes sustainable when it can cope with and recover from stresses and shocks and maintain or enhance its assets both now and in the future, while not undermining the resource base. Sustainable Livelihood System promotes equity between and among generations, races, gender, and ethnic groups; in the access to and distribution of wealth and resources; in the sharing of productive and reproductive roles; and the transfer of knowledge and skills. Sustainable livelihoods are based on the functional interrelationships in which every member of the system is needed and participates. Sustainable livelihood supports meaningful work that meets the social, economic, cultural and environmental needs of all the members of a community- human, non-human, present and future and safeguard cultural and biological diversity. It stimulates local investment in the community and help to retain capital within the economy.

A futuristic nightmare is visualized for women in the villages, where widespread unemployment leads to economic insecurity and cuts in government spending and employment mean, worsening health services, lesser access to education and deterioration in civic services. Since gender relations at the household level governing the sexual division of labour tend to remain rigidly in place, young women are forced to give up their education or prospects for gainful employment in order to help their mothers in household maintenance. Thus economic reforms, by ignoring the crucial cultural and structural aspects of gender, interact with the existing gender asymmetries affecting women of Orissa in negative ways.[16] Some of these factors especially those that concern gender ideology are indeed very difficult to measure quantitatively.

6.6. TECHNOLOGY AND WOMEN'S OCCUPATION IN VILLAGES : FIELD SURVEY

Livelihood options and occupational pattern of the people are directly and indirectly related with market mechanism. Sometimes market works friendly to the poor people and also sometimes expanded market access creates problems of livelihoods for them. Many social and cultural factors which influence women employment opportunities are persisting in the villages. Poverty and gender are not entirely separate social phenomena. The term "feminization of poverty" does not mean that poverty is a gendered experience. Previous studies used to focus on vulnerability context, livelihood assets, policies, livelihood strategies and outcomes. They never perceive the gender dimension of the issue. Women belonging to landowning rich class, being mostly dependent housewives, run the risk of higher livelihood insecurity with worst fallback position. Our survey focuses on both endogenous and exogenous processes that influence the livelihoods of rural women. It identifies the crucial variables that influence the livelihood pattern among both land-owning and labour-selling class of women in the villages of Orissa. It analyses various farm and off-farm activities, which contribute to the family earnings, pursued by village women. It explains various livelihood needs, potentials and opportunities for village women.

During our field survey we examine the links between technology and gender within the villages of Orissa. It analyses the occupational pattern of women, the level of female education, and identifies the factors that influence women employment. It assesses employment potentials and opportunities for women in both farm and non-farm activities in the villages. Orissa belongs to the coastal belt of eastern India. It has 30 districts. This study is based on the census study of two villages of two districts of Orissa .Two villages of Orissa have been selected purposively. The economy of both the villages centers around agriculture where as the first village has higher share of non farm activities. The first village is nearer to the town, second village is a remote one. It analyzes the occupational pattern of women, their decision making power and contribution towards to the family income. It analyses how women are contributing to their family income through various farm and non farm works. Mostly women are engaged in handicrafts, appliqué works and other small scale cottage industries.

6.7. CHARACTERISTICS OF THE STUDY VILLAGES

The study focuses on the scope ,potentials and opportunities of income generation among women in both the villages. It analyses, how women are utilizing these opportunities for getting employment and improving their earnings in the village economy. We observe the following difference between the two villages.

1. The average family size is lower in the occupationally diversified village, Nuasasana.
2. The dependency ratio of is higher in the agricultural village, Madhusudan pur
3. The percentage of housewives is higher in the pure agricultural village.

Villages	*Districts*	*Total House Holds (No)*	*Population below Poverty line(%)*	*Irrigated land(%)*	*Dependent on agriculture (%)*	*Distance from nearest town(Km)*	*Dependency ratio (%)*	*Male Literacy (%)*	*Female literacy (%)*
Nuasasan	Puri	430	53	80	75	20	76	52	30
Madhusudan pur	Jajpur	470	66	20	80	50	80	40	18
Orissa	30 districts		48	30	76	..	62	50	32

4. The work participation rate among women is higher in the occupationally diversified village
5. Higher literacy among the people motivates the people to diversify their livelihood in the first village.
6. Lack of or lesser irrigation facility fail to motivate the people to purse non –farm activities.
7. The higher percentage of marginal farmers encourages non-farm activities
8. The higher the percentage of wasteland, higher is the motivation for off-farm Activities among people.
9. The land-man ratio is lower in first village where people have high propensity to carry out non farm activities. The lesser the LAP higher is the propensity to carry out non-farm activities.
13. The occupational concentration is higher in second village and occupational diversification is high in the first village .
15. The dependency ratio is higher among higher caste and rich households due to many social constraints.

6.7.1. Employment of Women outside the Village

There is high degree of seasonal unemployment and disguised unemployment in both the villages. The agricultural productivity is lower in Madhusudanpur than Nuasasan. Among the hired agricultural labour of Madhusudanpur 56% are men and 33% are women. On the contrary among the hired agricultural labour of Nuasasan 55% are men and 53% are women. Therefore the work participation rate among women in Nuasasan is higher than that of Madhusudanpur. But there is male-female wage differential in the farm sector of both the villages. It is observed that 21 % of the house holds of Nuasasan are getting employment in service sector out side the village. While 11 % of the households of Madhusudanpur are doing services outside the village. But 9 % of households of Madhusaudanpur and 16 % of households of Nuasasan are engaged in wage labour works out side the village. Mostly women are found in the category of wage labour, working inside or nearby village. Women belonging to higher caste or rich class do not work outside the village at all.

The off farm activities of Nuasasan are mostly done by the women, while the off farm activities of Madhusudanpur are done by both, since they are family or caste-based occupations like carpentry, pottery , basket making etc. The orchard plantations and beetle vines supplement the livelihood system of the village economy. About 30% of farming households of both the villages have marketable surplus. The marketable surplus is generated from both non-cash crops like paddy and cash crops like vegetables, potato, pulses, fruit crops, groundnut and sugarcane. But lower agricultural productivity in Madhusudanpur reduces the marketable surplus of the farmers of this village.

6.7.2. Village Credit System

1. The credit system differs between two villages. In Nuasasan, 83% of households, who borrow from commercial banks, use the credit for buying products and raw materials, which they need in their non farm enterprises. But it is different in the second village, where people get the cash credit from the cooperative banks. They do not borrow for buying raw materials from the outside market.

2. The Cooperatives encourage many non-farm activities and provide training opportunities for women workers engaged in appliqué, chalk manufacturing, agarbati, candle making etc. About 31% of households of Nuasasan and 12% of households of Madhusudanpur get training from the cooperatives

3. In the entire sample, about 29%, 13% and 8% of the households have borrowed for health problems, appliqué works and purchasing livestock respectively. Other purpose of making loan includes investing in various types of non farm activities like candle, agarbati and chalk making. Loans for unproductive purposes amount to 24% of the total credit.

4. The investment in off farm activities is mostly self-financed in Madhusudanpur while it is mostly loan-financed in Nuasasan .This difference has strong association with the nature of non farm activities. Family based on non-farm activities depends more on self-finance, while skill-based non-farm activities depends more on loan-finance.

6.7.3. Income and Expenditure pattern

5. The occupational diversified village has higher average income than the agricultural village. It is due to two reasons; (a) The agricultural productivity is lower and (b) the average earnings from farm activities are lower than that of the farm activities.

6. But when we observe the expenditure pattern of villages separately we notice the difference that C is the modal expenditure class of Nuasasan while D is the modal expenditure class of Madhusudanpur . There is substantial difference in the average annual expenditure of two villages. It is due to the difference in the level of average earnings of the people.

7. When we examine the saving potential, we find that D is the modal group of both Madhusudanpur and Nuasasan. The average savings amount of household of Madhusudanpur is less than the average saving of the entire sample.

6.7.4. Women in farm and non farm activities

8. The non farm activities of Madhusudanpur are mostly family-based and self employed occupations, While in Nuasasan the off farm activities are mostly contractual and based on skill, knowledge and external supports.
9. The non farm women workers of Madhusudanpur obtain raw materials from the same locality, while the off farm women workers of Nuasasan procure raw material from out side the village. The network of intermediaries exist for supplying the raw materials to the non farm women workers of the first village.
10. The off farm activity in Madhusudanpur are mostly seasonal while in Nuasasan the non farm activities have no seasonality. It has connection with the nature of activity. When the occupation is family-based, then there are seasonal variations in production and demand. When the occupation is skill-based then there is no seasonal effect on production or demand.
11. The market for the products of family based non farm occupations is local, while the markets for the products of skilled based occupations are outside the village. The network of intermediaries exist for supplying the product to the marketing destinations.
12. Rise in household income and higher production are the main motivational factors for women to pursue off farm activities. There is inter-village difference in the impact of motivational factors.
13. Lack of or lesser irrigation facility has indirectly motivated the male to purse non –farm activities. Lack of irrigation is the cause of low land productivity. Therefore it constitutes a push – factor for the villagers to undertake off-farm jobs.
14. The higher percentage of marginal farmers and

landless peasants encourages more non-farmers activities. Nuasasan having higher percentage of marginal and landless farmers has more off farm activities.

15. Average earnings from non farm activities of households are higher than that of second village. But average earnings from farm activities are higher in Maddhusudan pur than Nuasasan.

6.7.5. Socio-Economic Status of Women

16. The percentage of housewives is higher in the pure agricultural village i.e Madusudan pur .And the proportion of women engaged in non farm activities is more in Nuasasan . The socio cultural factors are more restrictive in Madhusudanpur where women of are demotivated to earn from any economic activity.

17. The work participation rate among women is significantly higher in Nuasasan than in Madhusudanpur. It has brought occupational diversification in the first village. But the women of second village are mostly housekeepers. It is both the cause and effect of occupational concentration in second village. But there is no inter village difference in male work participation rate. It is almost the same in both the villages.

18. Higher literacy among the people motivates the people to face the challenge and diversify their livelihood base in the village economy. Higher female literacy encourages the women to seek alternative sources of income . Therefore Nuasasan having higher literacy has more non-farm activities.

19. The gender divisions of labour are socially rigid in both the villages. Women in all families of both villages are found to do the full responsibility of many jobs like cooking, cleaning, washing, child care, waste

disposal and gathering fuel, carrying fodder and water.

6.7.6. Participation of Women

20. None of the non farm women workers is very satisfied. In terms of fair price the non farm workers in both villages are marginally satisfied. It indicates the exploitation involved in the contractual arrangements with these women workers. The non producers expropriate the profit margin of the women workers.

21. The participation of women in decisions making pertaining to farming, village meetings, selling of crops, and purchase of animals, orchard plantation and purchase of durables in of sample households is very low.

22. Lower educational status and village tradition and caste system are the main constraining factors for availing employment opportunities of women in both the villages. Reduction in the rigidity of social and caste system leads to increase in women's' freedom to undertake some economic activity in order to supplement the household income.

Agricultural operations are mostly done by men. Off farm activities are mostly done by women. The seasonal and disguised unemployment is very high in both the villages. The male-female wage differential is higher in the farm sector of both the villages. There is no inter village difference in male work participation rate. But the work participation rate among female is directly connected with agricultural productivity

The higher caste households used to lease out their land to landless farmers or marginal farmers. People have high propensity to carry out non farm activities due to: a) low agricultural productivity b) lower land-man ratio or land availability per household (LPH) c) higher percentage of upland d) higher percentage of wasteland. The dependency ratio is higher among higher caste and rich households . Due to many social constraints and traditional values, the women belonging to higher caste and richer class are compelled to remain as housewives. Awareness and poverty among people encourage them to supplement their farm income and diversify their livelihood base.

The orchard plantation, fishery, appliqué, candle making and basket-making constitute a sustainable source of supplementary livelihood of the village people. The structures of landed property vary but the structure of non productive household assets does not vary according to the village category. The occupational diversified village has higher average income than the agricultural village due to: a) irrigation facility b) higher size of land holding, c) high income from non farm activities. Correspondingly, level of expenditure and saving are higher in the occupational diversified village. But the contractual arrangements in the non farm activities involve exploitation of the women workers. The borrowing for non productive purposes among village people is high.

Higher occupational concentration in a village does not encourage the women to be economically productive. The gender divisions of labour are socially rigid in the villages. Higher literacy among the people motivates the people to face the challenge and diversify their livelihood base in the village economy. Lower educational status and village tradition and caste system are the main constraining factors for village women in availing employment opportunities out side the village and carrying out non farm activities. Thus it is inferred that livelihood security of women in the village economy is determined by the following five factors: a) Economic factors, b) Social Factors, c) Demographic factors, d) Institutional Factors.

6.8. STATUS OF WOMEN IN VILLAGES

Although gender empowerment has been a buzzword in development circles, the concept has been used in so many different ways by different agents that it remains ambiguous. [17] Conceptualizing power and gender adequately entails understanding its multi dimensional nature, the complex ways in which women experience subordination and the ways in which they negotiate or manage this state of affairs. The gender-gap in indices such as life expectancy, literacy and earning has in fact increased from sixties to eighties in entire south Asia . The UNDP developed Gender Development Index (GDI) as a tool to capture gender inequality. It notes the inequalities between men and women on the same variables that make up the Human Development Index related to the over all achievements in that society. It considers only three variables: health, education and income. It fails to take into account important dimensions such as the quality of community life access to basic amenities and human rights. Important dimensions relevant for women such as safety and security, household allocation of resources, unpaid labour, mobility constraints and on sexual and reproductive freedom by patriarchal ideology do not find any place. Raising income of women may not indicate improved status for women. The GEM(Gender Empowerment Measure) is again based on three variables. It is built on a very narrow conception of empowerment. It does not include legal and human rights nor does it reflect the ways in which cultural constructions of gender identity are made. Thus it is clear from the above discussion that if one attempts to assess the impact of economic reforms differential on men and women, the conventional parameters used to measure gender disparity is not enough. It is therefore necessary to consider research methodologies that go beyond the quantitative in order to do justice to the complexity of these phenomena.

The situation in Orissa is counter logical. Paradoxically it is observed that in Orissa, there is a trade off between women's material well being and their autonomy. When the family becomes richer, the women lose her earning power and social autonomy. Therefore poverty and gender development can not be approached synergistically with the same policy instruments. When rising household income has a perverse effect on women's well being then policies which promote women's work participation rate even if successful, may not increase women's well being. Thus money is neither necessary nor sufficient for transforming the existing gender relations in Orissa.

In villages of Orissa, the child marriage practice still prevails in some communities. 'Drop out' rates and 'push out' rates in village schools for girls has been increasing. Practice of girl child labour has been endured as the "harsh reality". Case of selling of girl child has increased. Rape cases have been increasing. It is sheer hypocrisy that the so called modern civilisation with its pretensions to high thinking considers that to be born as a girl is a crime and burden . Unfortunately, education among women has not produced a reformative effect on the social outlook, nor encouraged any change conducive to social upliftment. Discrimination against women does not end by merely bestowing of judicial rights or by making women literate. The social problem can not be solved by legal bell or economic independence. Most urban women are literate today but they are also victims of domestic violence and social discrimination.

6.9. SOCIAL DYNAMICS AND FEMALE EDUCATION

While science and technology are advancing economic and social problems of backward states are worsening. In Orissa, discrimination and violence against women takes a dismaying variety of occurrences. All are violations of the most fundamental human rights. The pitiable condition of womanhood in Orissa trapped in the web of socio cultural factors such as superstitious and blind faith perpetuated by male dominance. Her struggle for survival continues from the womb to the grave without respite. The struggle for survival continues throughout the woman's life beginning with the female foetus. Although there is anti-abortion Act, private practitioners continue to conduct abortions with a sex bias. Though the technology has supported to help women to have safer births, it has resulted in female fetus being aborted and the practice is spreading in alarming manner. In fact prenatal Diagnostic Centres have become sex determination clinics. The legislation to curb the misuse of amniocentesis for sex selection and abortion of female fetuses calls for further punishing the women because they are under pressure to bear a male child. Son preference dangerously affects the women .Its consequences can be anything from foetal or female infanticide to neglect of the girl child over her brother in terms of such essential needs as nutrition, basic health care and education.

Orissa is a mosaic of many social riddles and contradictions. One such paradox is the gender inequality. There is a snark syndrome ,where there is no credible empirical base for the prejudices against women [18] .Educators and policymakers have internalized repeated social assertions . Even they do justify and implement such policies such as reservation of seats, women day celebration, welfare measure for widows, etc. The land which worships the woman most , has the highest violence against women . She is not only robbed of her dignity by the men outside, but also become a victim of cruelty by her saviours, within the four walls of her own house. However, her trauma does not end here, it may even go to the extent of forcing her to commit suicide or she may be burnt to death for various reasons. In the age of cyber culture and nanotechnology the horrendous phenomena as dowry in Orissa has also been increasing. [19] Girls are treated as commodity in the market . It transcends the rural urban dichotomy. Its incidence cuts across all caste and class boundaries. The cases of bride burning has been increasing. Many such case twisted as suicides. Some ideal parents who prefer not to take dowry for their well-qualified sons, are in fact considered 'strange' by the society and doubts about 'the respectability of the groom's family' are usually raised. Even on the final day, the marriage is cancelled on the suspicion that the boy may be impotent or having some ulterior motives. He may not find a girl to marry.The most common type of violence against women in Orissa is "domestic violence" . Although the family is a source of love, sympathy and support, it is also the great source of inequality, exploitation and violence. Domestic violence in Orissa is a horror they have to cope with in silence. The woman in

Orissa is a slave to the so-called institutionalized cultural shackles. Her mobility is restricted, her self-expression is monitored and her thoughts influenced by others in her milieu. She becomes the victim of suspicion by her brothers, parents, husband and in- laws. Domestic violence is one of the greatest obstacles to gender equality and right to life and liberty. Wife beating is generally accepted as a cultural phenomenon. Most men take it upon themselves to beat their wives to 'improve them.' Women too accept it as a part of life. The police, the doctor and the teacher all view it as a societal norm. The legal system is also hopeless in Orissa. There are pertinent rules and laws . But there are so many factors that prevent women of Orissa to seek justice through legal exercise such as :(a) Her apprehensions relating to ultimate consequences ,(b) Unreliable and expensive legal system, (c) Lack of support from her parental family and (d) Cultural and religious forces. Thus it is imperative that women themselves must be morally strong and empowered. Educational system should make them mentally strong.

6.10. INSTITUTIONALIZATION OF NEO-PATRIARCHY

The patriarchy is very strong among high caste households of Orissa. The women can not take the full advantage of their increasing access to education in order to enhance their autonomy. The most important factor affecting women autonomy is social prestige associated with higher caste Hindu families. In spite of being an essential economic contributor ,there are social constraints ,which work against the women to improve her status and position within the household . Female labour who work and earn do not automatically enjoy same rights and liberties .It is again dependent on caste hierarchy. A variety of cultural and socio psychological factors determine her autonomy . Even today man continues to exercises his subtler control on the family production and reproduction system. It is gradually institutionalized at several spheres: work, culture, customs, religion and education. Therefore liberation of women will not be easy or complete without the destruction of 'neo-patriarchy'. The social and economic structures that locks production and reproduction together , perpetrate male dominance and female submission. Thus liberation of women in the villages does not automatically follow from their economic citizenship. It can only be achieved if all structures in which women are integrated are transformed simultaneously. A modification of any one of them can be offset by a reinforcement of another, so that a mere permutation of the form of inequality is ultimately achieved.

6.11. CONCLUDING REMARKS

Although gender empowerment has been a buzzword in development circles, the concept is being used in so many different ways that it remains ambiguous. All studies and reports on women status have only remained as a source of data, which rather endorses the passivity of the state. We should reject the touristic observations of women in metro society , dispel misconceptions and portray the real scenario of Orissa. Effective policy design requires an accurate understanding of the gender issues within a broad social framework. We need poverty-independent gender analyses and policies in order to rescue gender from poverty trap. Women's income earning activity should not be temporary, exploitative and reversible. Education and technology should ensure liberation and freedom for all human beings. It should break gradually the shackles of tradition that binds women in the man-made gaol. Technological development can beboth a threat and an ally to women in their various roles. Therefore we should integrate gender into technology and development . More nuanced discussion of the complex interrelationships between gender and technology is needed. Training program for successful technology transfer is necessary to derive the benefits of existing market-driven technological promotion. The new technology should be used as a vehicle for gender equality in the backward societies like Orissa.

The gender issue should be delinked both from

myopic economics and insensitive politics. There is no substitute for a gender analysis , which transcend class divisions and material definitions of deprivation. Therefore 'adding women' is not necessary, but an insight and rethinking development concepts and practices as a whole through a gender lens is necessary. We have to initiate debate on state non action on gender issues. Despite several rules and acts in place, all rights of women are being violated and they have been suffering in silence. A vigorous multi-pronged and multi-professional effort is needed to establish the woman as a human being in her own right. With the hosanna of modernization it is imperative to dispel myths, superstitions and misconceptions about woman and her duties and adopt a rational attitude towards the woman as a human being.

Despite jamboree of techno culture we need a meaningful social transformation, which gives the equal independent human status to women .Economic citizenship is not sufficient for transforming existing asymmetric gender relations. In all backward states like Orissa , girls are educationally very successful but socially women are not. The wife may be happy but the women is not. The real progress should occur when the women become the producers of their own welfare and bounty, not the recipients of charity. The chance for a social transformation should begin and end with the womenkind in the ground, because, nothing grows from the top. Effective policy design requires accurate understanding of the gender issues within a broad social framework. Women development is a social process to be evolved from the society but not a technological product to be achieved by a triggered policy .

NOTES

1. Michel C (1997) , *Globalization of Poverty* , Madhyam Books, New Delhi
2. Kabra, K(2000) Indian Economy 98-2000, *Alternative Economic Survey*, Rainbow Pub.Delhi
3. Das Kumar(1997) Asian Profile of Underdevelopment and Poverty, *Asian Profile*,Canada, Feb.Vol.25 (1)
4. Boserup, Ester(1990) "Economic Change and the role of women" in *Persistent Inequalities: Women and World development,* (ed) Eren Tinker, Chapter-2, Oxford University press, New York
5. Faulkner, Wendy. (2000). The power *and* the pleasure? A research agenda for "making gender stick" to engineers. *Science, Technology, & Human Values, 25(1),* 88-120.
6. Edwards, Paul N. (1996). *The closed world: Computers and the politics of discourse in cold war America,* Cambridge, Mass: MIT Press.:167-72
7. Kiesler, S., etal 1985). Pool halls, chips, and war games: Women in the culture of computing. Psychology of Women Quarterly, 9, 451-462.. Turkle, S. (1984). The second self: Computers and the human spirit. New York: Simon & Schuster.
8. Swasti, Mitter (1997).*Women Encounter Technology(ed)* Routledge ,UK
9. Jannet (1998) *Women and Girls Last: Females and the Internet* ,IRISS '98 International Conference: 25-27 March 1998, Bristol, UK
10. Gattiker (1994). *Women and Technology (ed)* Walter de Gruyter
11. Geisman,Donna(2000). *Women, Science and Technology*, Routledge, London

12. Dorward, Andrew et al(2003) Markets, Institutions and Technology: Missing Links to Livelihood Analysis, *Development Policy Review*,Vol.21(3) pp.313-332
13. Meheta Jaya et al (2000) Poverty Statistics: Bermicide's Feast , *Economics and Political Weekly,* July 1st
14. Curie , Bob (2000), *The Politics of Hunger in India,* Macmillan India, Chennai
15. Katherine Jellison (1993) Top of Form Entitled to Power: Farm Women and Technology, UNC Press
16. Dewan , Ritu (1996) ,Gender: conceptual overview, *Economic and Political* Weekly April,19
17. Karlekar ,Malavika (1995), Search for Women Voices, *Economic& Political Weekly* 29th April
18. Byrne, Eileen M1993, Women and Science: The Snark Syndrome ,Falmer Press, Taylor and Francis Inc., Bristol)
19. The word dowry has been replaced by another more socially acceptable word ie presentation
20. Agrawal, Bina(1997) Bargaining and Gender Relations within and beyond theHousehold, *Feminist Economics* ,Vol.3(1) pp. 454-487

REFERENCES

1. Agarwal, Bina (1986).'Women, Poverty and Agricultural Growth in India', *The Journal of Peasant Studies,* Vol.13, No.4, July.
2. Agarwal, Bina (1994). *A Field of One's Own: Gender and Land Right in South Asia,* Cambridge University Press, Cambridge.
3. Bardhan, Kalpana (1979). 'Work as a Medium of Earning and Social Differentiation : Rural Women of West Bengal', Paper presented at *ADC-ICRISAT Conference Hyderabad*, India.
4. Chambers, Robert and Gordon R Conway,.(1992). *Sustainable Rural Livelihoods: Practical Concepts for the 21st Century.* IDS

Discussion Paper No.296. Brighton

5. Chattopadhaya, Molly and David Seddon (2002). Life histories and Long term Change: Rural Households and Gender Relations in a West Bengal village, *Economic and Political Weekly, Vol.* 37(49), Dec 7

6. Curie , Bob (2000). *The Politics of Hunger in India, Macmillan India*, Chennai

7. Das, Kumar(1993), *Rural Development in India,* Discovery Pub.House, New Delhi

8. Desai, Sonalde. (1994). *Gender Inequalities and Demographic Behavior: India.* New York: The Population Council, Inc.

9. Dorward, Andrew et al(2003) Markets, Institutions and Technology: Missing Links to Livelihood Analysis, *Development Policy Review*,Vol.21(3) pp.313-332

10. Dreze, Jean and Chen Marty (1995), Recent research on widows in India, *Economic and Political Weekly,* Sept.30, PP.2435-50

11. Dube, Leela and Rajni Palriwala (1990). *Structure and Strategies: Women, Work and Family,* (eds.) Sage Publications, New Delhi.

12. Folbre, Nancy, B. Bergmann, B. Agarwal and M. Floro (eds.) (1991). *Women's Work in the World Economy,* Macmillan, London.

13. Jain, Devaki and Nirmala Banerjee (eds.) (1985). *Tyranny of the Household*, Vikas Publishing House, Shakti Book Series, Delhi.

14. Karlekar ,Malavika (1995), Search for Women Voices, *Economic and Political Weekly,* 29th April

15. Krishnaraj, Maithreyi and Karuna Chanana (eds.) (1989). *Gender and the Household Domain,* Sage Publications, New Delhi .

16. Lingam, Lakshmi (1994). 'Women-Headed Households: Coping with Caste, Class and Gender Hierarchies', *Economic and Political Weekly,* Vol. 29, No. 12, pp. 699-704.

17. Saskia Everts(1998) Gender and Technology : Empowering Women, Engendering Development, Zed Books .London Top of Form

18. Sen, Amartya K. (1990). 'Gender and Cooperative Conflict', in Irene Tinker (ed) *Persistent Inequalities*, Oxford University Press, New York.

19. Faulkner, Wendy (2000), *The Technology Question In Feminism,* Women's Studies International Forum, University of Edinburgh

20. Venkateswaran, Sandhya. (1995). *Environment, Development and the Gender Gap*. New Delhi: Sage Publications.

21. World Bank (1991). *Gender and Poverty in India,* A World Bank Country Study, The World Bank, Washington DC.

7

Politics, Poverty and Women

Today the impact of modernization of the economy or advancement of the society is different for Indian women. Growth of consumerism has created the euphoria of advancement for all. In urban shopping centers , metro women appear to enjoy the freedom of a hedonistic consumers. Educationally, girls are very successful but socially women lag behind as before. The cascading declivity in women's social position debilitates her to a pretty-petty commodity. This is the unfortunate gift of education and technology for the women. This chapter argues that we need poverty-independent gender analyses and policies for rescuing gender from poverty trap. Education and technology should ensure liberation and freedom of thought for all human beings.The gender issue should be delinked both from economics and politics.

A discursive framework was evolved in late colonial India which included both proponents and opponents of the developmental model. Technology was recognised as a necessary means to the desired end of industrialisation, which was in congruence with the perceived path of progress and modernity. In late 19th and early 20th century the widely accepted view was that Industry and technology solve all problems. The connections of technology with human development and ultimately with modernity was a theme stressed during 1930s and particularly in the course of raising a polemical debate against the Gandhian indigenist philosophy. Modernity is always endorsed by science and technology. The opponents of Gandhian anti –technology views were presenting a somewhat caricatured version of his argument, for which they were given plenty of opportunities by the mystical and elusive nature of Gandhian rhetorics itself. Technology was a prevalent language of legitimacy which nationalists could not but confront and appropriate in one way or another. Industrialisation connotes production, wealth, power and modernity. It was generally agreed that a necessary component of development, what ever the wider parameters of development might require, would be the technology to overcome the backwardness and stagnation. Science became increasingly very important from late 19th century in all bourgeois ideologies of domination. The Gramscian "passive revolution " can be invoked as the proper explanation of the bourgeois leadership of Indian nationalism. The colonial education created a team of traditional intellectuals, an articulate multi lingual elite, often highly educated and self consciously cosmopolitan in outlook, dominated a good deal of space of organised political activity, economic system and especially the political philosophy behind it. This applied to politics of all kinds from right to the left. The discourse on development in late 19th century splited into two - growing pessimism regarding social progress of the masses and a high degree of optimism regarding technological progress.

7.1. HUMAN CAPITAL AND WOMAN

Human capital theorists only take into account the impact of education upon workers skill and productivity, but overlooks the 'social reproduction' function of schooling. Any expenditure on education ,health and training which raises one's productivity and future earnings in the labour market can be treated as human capital investment . A highly educated and highly skilled work force is not necessarily a profitable workforce. In a capitalist system the profitable production requires that the workers should have appropriate attitude and personality traits in addition to technical skills etc. The human capital investment therefore should inculcate this kind of attitude and values which are consistent with the functioning of capitalist system. The function of schooling is to generate a disciplined, obedient and a well motivated work force which accepts the capitalist ideology. There are two basic methods of comparing the benefits and costs associated with a human capital investment: The NPV approach which uses the discounting formula to compare the present value of costs and benefits. If NPV is positive then it is rational to invest. The IRR approach, which adopts the rate of discount at which NPV of the investment is zero. If IRR exceeds the interest rate, then it is rational to invest .The demand curve for human capital and supply curve of investment funds are combined to explain why people invest in different amounts of human capital. Difference in capacity, discrimination and varying access to financial resources all help in explaining differences in education and earning among individuals. The money market tends to provide funds for human capital investment in less favourable terms than for investment in physical capital , thereby providing some justification for public subsidization of human capital investments.

Human capital theory implies an obvious means by which society can mitigate income inequalities by increasing educational opportunities for the lower-income class of the society. In other words education is a potential equalising force, which can be used to offset or ameliorate the distributional inequities inherent in the market system. In India during the last century ,however the educational system not only plays a positive role in generating income and class inequalities but also provides a justification and tolerance for such inequality. In fact the children of well-educated ,high-income parents are much more likely to complete their higher education than the children of less-educated and low-income parents. Further more the quality of education and educational institutions available to the children of high-income parents are superior to those of low-income parents. The existing dualistic educational system creates an 'academic regimentation'. The education received by the children in the Indian villages and mostly by the working class children prepares them for jobs similar to those held by their parents. The children of a managers, technocrats, bureaucrats, and professionals are taught self-reliance within a broad set of constraints, while the children of production-line workers are taught obedience and endurance .

7.2. POLITICAL PROFILE OF WOMEN IN INDIA

We find two contradictory process in India's electoral system. On the one hand we have powerful, articulate women leaders who are mainly elite and on the other hand we have women who are mere rubber stamps. However the elite women's political presence derives their positional status from their relations with male politicians-husbands, brothers, fathers, uncle, father-in-laws. Between 1962 and 1984 the total number of women who contested the lok sabha has increased from 65 to 157 and the number of women who were elected was increased from 33 to 42. In the recently held election of 2004, the number of women parliamentarians has gone down from 49 (13th lok Sabha election) to 45 in 14th Lok sabha election out of total number of 543 parliamentarians. Womne's representation in lok sabha is less than 10% of the total. It is seen form the table that 45 elected women had to represent 50 crores Indian women's interest in the 14th loksabha election.

Table 7.1 : Woman in Political Sytem of India

Year of Elec-tion	No of Conte-stants	No of seats avail-able	Male			Female		
			Cont-ested	Elected	% win-ning	Conte-sted	Elec-ted	% win-ning
1952	1874	489	-	-	-	-	-	-
1957	1518	494	1473	467	31.7	45	27	60.0
1962	1985	494	1915	459	24.0	70	353	50.0
1967	2369	520	2302	490	21.3	67	30	44.8
1971	2784	520	2698	499	18.5	86	21	24.4
1977	2439	542	2369	523	22.1	70	19	27.1
1980	4620	542	4478	514	11.5	142	28	19.7
1984	5574	542	5406	500	9.2	164	42	25.6
1989	6160	529	5962	502	8.5	198	27	13.6
1991	8699	521	8374	492	5.9	325	39	12.0
1996	13952	543	13353	504	3.8	599	39	6.7
1998	4750	543	4476	500	11.2	274	43	15.7
2002	NA	543	NA	494	Na	446	49	9.1
2004	NA	543	NA	498	NA	432	45	9.6

Data for 1952 not available

Source: statistical Profile of Women in India, Govt of India, 2006

7.2.1. New Social Movement

Implication of increased political participation of women in India means increased visibility in the political scenario. We have seen increasing number of meetings, camps, welfare programmes, weekly meetings, national conventions organized by women cadre of different political parties It can be understood in following manner:

a. Rise in the number of women in the electoral process

and their meaningful contribution in highlighting the women specific issues

b. Qualitative change in political goals and processes as a result of accommodation of women's perspectives and priorities.

Though the social movement have thrown up new band of educated, sincere and hardworking women as leaders, their participation in the electoral politics is quite limited. Credibility of new social movements has been commodified by the electoral market. Women social activists who are ready to give thumb impressions are promoted by the man stream politicians. Women who stick out their necks have to create their own safety nets-financial security, gainful employment, credit-worthiness and self sustaining life style. Women in public life need to have special skills to scrutinize budgetary provisions in favour of empowerment of women. English educated articulate and aggressive women are tolerated by main stream only if they remain silent about budget. Elected women representatives can be successful in promoting women's development agenda only when their trusted soldiers and family members share their vision and so not force them to make unprincipled compromises. Each MP gets 2crores as MPLAD and each MLA gets 1 crore for local area development. They use the fund according to their political and personal priorities. Female –headed households have been most successful in all social movements right from the pre-independence days. Elected-women representatives whose decisions are taken by others is not respected by her own constituency. It is therefore very important for her to be aware of legal provisions, developmental schemes, help lines for emergency situations, tax structure revenue and expenditure in her department and constituency. She has to know the women component plan-schemes and programmes targeted for women and marginalized sections of the society, special need of the constituency, labour relations and labour processes in her constituency. After 73rd and 74th amendment of Indian constituition , provision has to be made for devolution of power in favour of women. One third of all seats in the local self-govt bodies have to be reserved for women Rural India has already elected village panchayats with one third elected seats reserved for females ie India has one million elected representatives. They are taking active interest in using budgetary allocations for promotion of women's education, safe drinking water and sanitation. But neither the people representatives at the center nor at the state level wish to give up their powers over their constituencies and to share their power to local level. Similarly bureaucracy having their past inertia, does not cooperate and does not support the decentralization of power to the local self government.

With out popular mandate if woman is elected/ selected for top position , they will have to face non cooperation from the administration and the law and order machinery. Women in public life need a protective shield of popular support and tremendous good will so that they can execute the development agenda more meaningfully. They should empower themselves with first hand experience of the operational reality, otherwise they become puppets in the hands of different power blocks. Knowledge base is necessary for each and every women decision makers to survive in public life for longer time. They should seek protection of the benevolent patriarchs. The n only 21st century will unfold an era of partnership between men and women dedicated to the cause of liberation of human kind, which will ensure social justice, safe environment and w communal harmony and world peace in the are of terrorism.

7.3. ECONOMIC DEVELOPMENT PROCESS

The post liberalisation period has marked a distinct upturn of the growth trajectory. Although the stagnation of the economy seemed to have been over by mid seventies, the crisis of 1991 underlined the unsustainability and fragility of a rather good growth performance of the eighties. The recovery of the growth since mid seventies is almost entirely due to the private sector. It can be observed from the following table. It is observed that the annual average economic growth of GNP and NNP during the pre reforms period was about 5.8. But it has become very slow during first two years of economic reforms. The annual average growth rate of per capita NNP has fallen to the lowest level of 0.9 only.

Table 7.2 : Growth of National Income After Economic Reforms

Five Year Plans	*Average Annual growth rates(at 1993-94 prices)*		
	GNP	*NNP*	*PCNNP*
Sixth Plan (1980-85)	5.5	5.4	3.2
Seventh (1985-86)	5.8	5.8	3.6
Annual plans(90-92)	3.3.	3.0	0.9
Eighth Plan(1992-97)	6.8	6.7	4.6

Then during eighth plan growth rates have improved but not very impressive in comparison to the pre-reforms period. The agricultural sector has lagged behind. Its growth rate during 1992-96 is only 2.9. The service sector's growth is 7.5 during that period. The private corporate sector in India has responded favourably to economic reforms with large investments. The overall post reforms growth rate of output has been robust at an average of 6.8 per The growth rate in the industrial sector and service sector has become very impressive.

Table 7.3 : Sectoral Growth rates of the Indian Economy

Sector	*1950-95*	*50-64*	*65-75*	*76-91*	*92-96*
Agriculture	2.4	2.5	3.1	2.9	2.9
Industry	5.6	6.8	4.2	6.4	10.1
Service	4.9	4.8	3.8	5.8	7.5
GDP (FC)	4.0	3.9	3.6	4.9	6.8

Liberalisation regime has provoked widespread restructuring and consolidation of Indian Industry. The private sector is vigorously restructuring itself to correct past inefficiencies of pre reforms era and promote competitiveness. But research and development has suffered. Export orientation is also very limited (Basant 2000).Indian industry has relied more on technology imports and affiliations with MNCs and less on in house R&D activity. Increased dependence on imported technology and industrial consolidation, however have not yet resulted in any measurable productivity improvement. The neglect of R & D is a matter of grave concern for sustaining industrial growth and competitiveness as the access to technology is becoming increasingly crucial to industrial success in knowledge-based world economy.

7.4. JOBLESS GROWTH

The employment in the organised sector has grown. It is observed from the table that since the Govt is withdrawing itself from active participation in production activities the growth of employment in the organised sector has remained very slow. Employment in the public sector has increased from 190.57 laks to 194.18 lakhs during 91-98. On the contrary the employment in the private sector has risen from 76.7lakhs to 87.48 lakhs during 91-98.During 1998 the growth rate of employment in the public sector was —0.09 percent while it is 1.72 percent for the private sector. The private sector has contributed predominantly to the increase in the employment in the organised sector except in the year 1993 under the reforms regime. The growth rates of employment in the organised sectors reveals that the employment in the public sector has become negative while in the private sector it is not very impressive. In the entire country the employment has grown from 281.66 lakhs during 91-98. The rate of growth of employment is only 0.46 percent. The employment trend shows that the large scale industries with its heavy emphasis on capital-intensive high tech absorbs most of the investible capital of the country .

The work participation rate among male has remained 51.55% and among female it is only 22.25 %.The corresponding percentages for Orissa are 53.79 and 20.79 .The period of 1998 –2000 is the period of market fundamentalism. At the end of November 1999 there were more than 4.1 crore job seekers compared to nearly 3.92 crores at the end of 97-98.Clearly this does not represent the total unemployment The labour force in 1995-95 is estimated at 194.4 million rural men, 96.9 million rural women, 71.9 million urban men and 15.2 million urban women giving a total labour force of 378.6 million. With nearly 8 million new entrants every year labour force may be around 400 million at present. With 90 percent of farm holdings being small and marginal the poor peasantry can not be considered employed in the sense of having work and or asset capable of ensuring livelihood security. Thus the number of the virtually unemployed working poor is many times larger than that shown by statistics. The situation is really grave and complex. Therefore any analysis without incorporating this trend makes little sense.

There is obvious neglect of the problem of unemployment in the country. Public sector employment in March 1998 was lower at 19.42 million compared to 19.56

million in March 1997.Private organised sector employment depicted a small rise from 8.69 million to 8.75 million. Obviously overall employment scene with huge backlog and large annual increment of about 8 million to labour force remains very bleak. The trends in poverty and other social indicators bear witness to this phenomenon. It is also reflected in the growth rate of employment in the organised sector in 1998, which was negative (-)0.99 % for the public and 1.72 % for the private sector. Thus during the period when the GDP growth rate was estimated at 5 % employment growth rate was a negligible 0.46 percent. So during liberalisation regime employment growth has become lower than the rate during the eighties. T he rate of capital formation ie the rate at which capital stock is growing is much higher than the rate of growth of labour absorption in the economy. As a result the 'reserve army' of job seekers is ever increasing. Capital intensity is ever increasing and labour intensity is ever declining. The growth fundamentalists have embraced a perverted set of objectives: higher growth of output, investment, profits etc are the highest values in their commodity-centric world. It amounts to dethroning our society and polity in favour of an economy which disempowers the common masses, a large majority of whom subsist not as parts but on the edges of the market economy. There is a growing infatuation with knowledge based new economy. It tends to ignore the real economy pulsating with life and work of millions, which continuously intensifies the exclusion of common man. What is saddening is that the market fundamentalists fails to notice the ominous menace inherent in these process and facts. On the contrary they continue to posit its theoretical faith in the imported advice or dictates of the reforms. The external advocacy are found convenient vehicle by the urban-rich-elite class for promoting their narrow sectional interests. The power to implement SAP regarding disinvestment, power purchase agreements, sanctioning of mega projects, tax and incentive policies for industry and trade, huge defence deals etc open up enormous scope to follow the model of cronyism for the ruling party and bureaucracy. .So SAP inevitably leads to crony capitalism. True but insidious western cultural influences are inherent in western FDI,technology, foreign travel, freedom of media and internet. (The expenditure on foreign travel has gone up from Rs.703 crores in 90-91 to over ten times to rs.7326 crores in 98-99)All these things are conducive for the power game. Besides these other routes are also advocated. Constitutional reviews, electoral reforms, public funding of elections, media management, saffronisation of bureaucracy, intimidation of dissidents, attack on minorities, unleashing of cultural terrorism etc are parallel routes for realising the power goals. The consequences of the NEP would travel far and wide not only for specific industries ,groups, or regions but for the whole economy, polity and people at large. Its success can at best be treated as a pyrrhic victory, when means win and ends lose. Majority of the rural sector and the unskilled and illiterate section of the urban sector tend to lose their right to livelihood and economic citizenship. With inadequacy of public services carrying unaffordable user charges caused due to inefficient and corrupt bureaucratic mismanagement and inflationary situation the common man will be pushed into vicious circle of vulnerability. Optimism of the elite may go haywire. The growth of employment in the organised sector is very unimpressive. It is observed from the table-4 that since the Govt is withdrawing itself from active participation in production activities the growth of employment in the organised sector has remained very slow.

Table 7.4 : Employment in the organised sector (in lakhs)

Post reforms period	*Pub.Sector*	*Pvt.sector*	*Total*
1991	190.57	76.76	267.33
1992	192.10	78.46	270.56
1993	193.26	78.50	271.76
1994	194.45	79.30	273.75
1995	194.66	80.59	275.25
1996	194.29	85.12	279.41
1997	195.59	86.86	282.45
1998	194.18	87.48	281.66
1999	194.15	86.98	281.13
2000	193.14	86.46	279.60

Source: Economic Survey,Govt of India, various Volumes.

The private sector has contributed predominantly to the increase in the employment in the organised sector except in the year 1993 under the reforms regime. The growth rates of employment in the organised sector is observed from the following table. The role of public sector has reduced substantially with the drive towards downsizing over the last decade.

Table 7.5 : Contribution of Public and Private Sector

Sectors	*1991*	*1992*	*1993*	*1994*	*1995*	*1996*	*1997*
Public sector	1.52	0.80	0.60	0.62	0.11	-0.19	0.67
Private Sector	1.24	2.21	0.06	1.01	1.63	5.62	2.04
Total	1.44	1.21	0.44	0.73	0.55	1.51	1.09

7.5. CASUALISATION OF JOBS

India is a mosaic of paradoxes and contradictions. One such paradox is the gender inequality. The nation which has been preaching the messages of love, equality and compassion for centuries, ironically, has the deplorable socio economic status for women even today . The realities are worse than the scenario that is published in reports and newspapers. Some scholars dismiss the problem of gender-disparity as a 'non-issue' by invoking the economistic theoretical explanation of a 'dual economy'. Ironically they also contribute to either the notion of 'feminization of jobs' or 'feminization of poverty'. Almost all Indian studies on gender have tended to overstress the personal and under stress the societal consequences of gender asymmetries .

The votaries of structural adjustment programme argue that now there is a trend of continued "feminisation of employment" in all developing countries. It seems to be a myth. It does not reflect the sign of progress or prosperity. It does not imply the success of economic reforms or emergence of new technological breakthroughs either. But there are two major reasons which make us believe the feminisation of work: (I) The structural shift of employment from manufacturing to service sector activities in these countries and (2) the incidence of poverty(economic strain on the household inflicted by double squeeze) and question of survival.The contemplated industrial growth is tending to generate a process of jobless growth. Now while every country of the world is characterised by joblessness, women as class had to bear a much heavier burden of unemployment over the past two decades. It is observed that unemployment among women has increased in almost all countries even under reforms regime.On the contrary, the present economic reforms, particularly in India are likely to (1)Promote highly sophisticated technology (so called High -Tech) and (2) Create imperfections in the rural factor (particularly labour) market. These two factors tend to continuously displace the female workers from high productive activities to low productive activities. It is tending to accentuate the concentration of women in domestic works and non-market roles and activities.

An economy which sharply aims at export oriented production and multinational investment is hardly likely to generate jobs for the women and other vulnerable sections of the society. There is inherent male bias in the formulation of macro adjustment policies. It is creating a system which is ultimately as centralised and undemocratic as any that can be imposed by the meddlesome bureaucracy. The main thrust of globalisation measures is greater commodification of all aspects of everyday life and work. With the LPG policy the jobs in the formal sector are continuously reduced and jobs in the informal sector have been increasing. The LPG model is tending to generate a vicious TRAP involving jobs like Tailoring, tutoring, Receptionists, producing Achar and Papad and agarbati working in beauty Parlour. All these jobs are visible and no doubt make the females more active and smart. But most of these jobs , belong to the inside spheres and semi domestic sectors. The best job in the entire set is perhaps the receptionist, which is unfortunately based upon the candidate's beauty smartness but not on her intelligence,or skill or experience. Rest of the jobs are low paid and under paid categories. Most of these belong to the informal sector, which is unregistered, and unprotected, subject to all types of exploitation and intimidation.. It is unfortunate that greater availability and casualisation of these jobs makes us believe in the feminisation of jobs. Moreover these jobs are available to the upper and better off section of the women. Market forces undervalues everything which is not directly calculable. The globalisation of prices (and not income) and nationalisation of poverty are likely to spell further economic strain on women, in term of work burden and curtailment of family expenditures. Therefore feminisation of work is likely to result in feminisation of poverty and promote the process of neo housewifisation.

With the confluence of economic growth and high-tech industrialisation the caste-class-specific gender bias against the women is likely to remain more pronounced in all backward regions like Orissa, MP, Bihar. Because market is never friendly neither to the weak, unskilled, illiterate, ignorant, vulnerable people nor to backward resource- poor regions.

Economists see women's poverty as the consequence of underdevelopment rather than subordination. They myopically prescribe anti-poverty approach or efficiency approach. They collapse all forms of disadvantage and deprivation into poverty. That approach believes that women are victims of development. Thus Gender issue can never be approached with poverty reduction policies. Gender concern exists with in the development bureaucracies which deny the otherness of the poor and direct the attention to the gendered character of development agencies themselves. Rescuing gender from poverty trap implies that we need poverty-independent gender analyses and policies which recognize that poverty reduction policies are not necessarily appropriate to tackle gender issues because gender subordination is not caused by poverty. But in India, there is a trade off between women's material well being and their autonomy. This situation is not faced by the poorer section. This is one way of looking at the limited degree to which poverty and gender development can be approached synergistically with the same policy instruments. If rising household income has a perverse effect on women's well being then poverty reduction policies even if successful, does not increase women's well being. There is great variations in the degree and manner by which women gain from rising family incomes and poverty reductions. Much depends on the transactions and transfers with in the households. Thus Money is neither necessary nor sufficient condition for transforming gender relations in Indian society. So non financial leverage gained by women from her participative role in the development process is relevant to changing gender relations.

7.6. POVERTY AND WOMAN

India consists of 28 states and six union territories of which 17 are major states with a population of one billion. The process of globalisation and economic liberalisation ushered in during the early nineties have contributed to the acceleration of economic growth. But these policies appear to have resulted in a widening of the gap between the man and woman. . The gains of development are not evenly distributed across the states and among various sections of the society. Nearly one-third of the population continues to live with meagre resources and income barely enough to replenish daily individual nutritional requirements. After 60 years of independence the level of poverty has not declined significantly, but instead has increased in certain states and regions. One of the most important reasons for the sluggish progress with respect to human resource development is the low level of spending by both the centre and states on social sectors including health, family welfare and education. India barely spends eight percent of its GDP on health and education services and expenditure on family welfare is just one percent of the national income.It is lower than that of other developing countries with similar per capita income. At the all India level there are wide inter-state, inter-regional ,male-female and rural –urban disparities in terms of social development.

This table 7.6 depicts the Incidence of Poverty across the states of India. It also analyses the rural and urban poverty separately. There is no disaggregated dada on incidence of poverty among women. It is observed that in 1973 rural poverty was the highest in West Bengal and urban poverty was the highest in MP. During 1993 the rural poverty was the highest in Orissa followed by that of Bihar. But urban poverty is the highest (ie 48%) in MP. It is seen that Poverty in the rural sector is the highest in Orissa followed by that of Bihar. Rural poverty is the least in Punjab and less in Gujrat.

Table 7.6 : Poverty Profile In India

States	*1973*		*1977*		*1983*		*1987*		*1993*		*2000*	
	R	*U*	*R*	*U*	*R*	*U*	*R*	*U*	*R*	*U*	*R*	*U*
AP	46	51	38	43	27	37	21	44	16	38	11	27
Assam	52	38	62	34	42	23	22	29	17	08	11	10
Bihar	64	51	63	50	65	50	42	55	44	35	39	33
Gujrat	45	51	41	41	27	38	28	38	22	29	13	16
Haryana	34	40	27	34	19	20	18	21	27	18	08	10
K'tak	55	53	47	49	35	40	34	34	21	40	17	25
Kerala	59	61	49	59	39	48	30	44	27	26	10	20
MP	63	61	63	59	49	51	41	46	41	48	36	37
M'rastra	59	44	63	39	45	38	43	38	38	35	23	28
Orissa	69	58	73	52	68	49	59	45	50	41	48	43
Punjab	29	28	15	26	14	23	13	16	14	12	06	05
Rajstan	44	57	37	44	34	38	29	43	27	31	13	21
Tnadu	58	52	58	49	54	45	46	43	33	39	21	22
UP	57	60	48	54	46	49	41	42	42	35	32	31
WB	73	35	69	36	62	31	49	33	41	23	32	16
India	56	47	51	42	43	38	37	37	37	33	27	24

However in Table 5 it is observed that per capita calorie intake among rural population has declined over the decades while it has remained almost stagnant among the urban population. There is lack diaggregated data , yet we are certain that per capita caloie intake of women in villages and urban areas are always lower than the males and children.

Table 7.7 : Per Capita Calorie Intake Per Diem In India

Years	*Rural*	*Urban*
1961-62	2511	2063
1971-72	2168	2179
1972-73	2266	2107
1973-74	2328	2003
1983-84	2221	2089
1993-94	2153	2071

7.7. POVERTY IN ORISSA

Nature of Poverty in Orissa is inherently vicious. It is basically a rural phenomenon. Various problems of the rural people of Orissa are interrelated, which need to be solved simultaneously. For instance, poverty together with its attendant problems of malnutrition ill health, disease, poor housing, low productivity etc. are all interrelated. Fig.1 illustrates the relationship among cluster of problems: some relations are dependent and others are interdependent. The association between poverty and human resources is a two-way relation. Poverty tends to reduce one's access to better health, nutrition and better education, which itself tends to limit his ability to escape from the vicious circle of poverty. The interrelationships are mutually reinforcing. In the process the women in the family suffers the most due to poverty: high drudgery, ill health, high malnutrition, low calorie intake, low productivity etc.

Fig. 7. 1. Misery-go-round

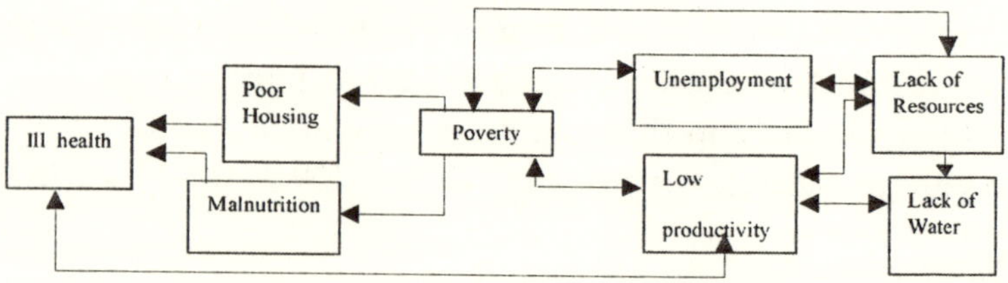

7.8. UNEMPLOYMENT AND WOMAN

In order to analyse the incidence of unemployment among women, let us first examine the nature of the nexus between economic growth and employment situation in pre and post reforms period. It is observed that

i) Relationship between economic growth and unemployment was negative and statistical significant during pre-economic reforms period

ii) Relationship between economic growth and unemployment was positive and statistical significant during post-economic reforms period

Let examine the real face of the rising trend of feminization of jobs.

Table 7.8 : Unemployment Rates(daily Status) In India

Year	*Rural*		*Urban*	
	Male	*Female*	*Male*	*Female*
1972-73	6.8	11.2		
1977-78	7.1	9.2		
1983-84	7.5	9.0		
1987-88	4.6	6.7	8.8	9.2
1993-94	5.6	5.6	6.7	10.5
1999-2000	7.2	7.0	7.3	9.4

Here in table 7.8 it is observed that unemployment among the female is always higher among female than among male population. In table 7 it is observed that per capita calorie intake among rural population has declined over the decades while it has remained almost stagnant among the urban population.

Unemployment rate in pre and post reforms period is presented in the following table.

The 61st round of NSS has provided us the information about the state of unemployment in 2004-5 and has also provided the comparative analysis with previous rounds. We observe the following points:

a. the unemployment rate of the usual principal status during 2004-5 has remained about the same in rural and urban areas for males as compared to 1999-2000.But it has increased by 2% for females. This implies that there was no improvement in the usual principal status employment.

b. The unemployment rate in terms of current daily status has increased by 2 % more for females in both rural and urban area. This indicates deterioration in the female employment. In terms of males, CDS rate has increased from 7.2% in 1999-2000 to 8 % in 2004-5 for rural areas. However there is a slight change in male CDS rate in urban areas from 7.3% to 7.5%. The upshot of this analysis is that the major problem of the Indian economy is under employment and not so much as open unemployment. High usual status of unemployment rates for females in urban areas up from 7.1% in 1999-2000 to 9.1% in 2004-5 is however a cause of great concern.

Table 7.9 : Unemployment Among Women in India

Round Year	*Male*			*Female*		
	Usual Status	*Current weekly Status*	*Current daily status*	*Usual Status*	*Current weekly Status*	*Current daily status*
Rural						
61st(2004-04	2.1	3.8	8.0	3.1	4.2	8.7
55th (1999-00	2.1	3.9	7.2	1.5	3.7	7.0
50th(1993-94)	2.0	3.1	5.6	1.3	2.9	5.6
43rd(1987-88)	2.8	4.2	4.6	3.5	4.4	6.7
38th(1983-84)	2.1	3.7	7.5	1.4	4.3	9.0
Urban						
61st(2004-04	4.4	5.2	7.5	9.1	9.0	11.6

55th (1999-00	4.8	5.6	7.3	7.1	7.3	9.4
50th(1993-94)	5.4	5.2	6.7	8.3	7.9	10.4
43rd(1987-88)	6.1	6.6	8.8	8.5	9.2	12.0
38th(1983-84)	5.9	6.7	9.2	6.9	7.5	11.0

Source: NSS Report No.515: Employment and Unemployment Situation in India (2004-05)

In the table 7.10 the unemployment rates for 2004-5 for rural and urban areas are illustrated. In both the rural and urban areas, the unemployment rates(CDS basis) was over 8% which was quite high. On the contrary the difference in CDS rates for males and females in rural areas indicates minor variations. In urban areas, male CDS rate was 7.5% whereas the female CDS rate was quite high at 11.6 %. The usual principal status rate for rural areas was very low at 2.5%, but it was quite significant in urban areas at 5.3%.

Table 7.10 : Unemployment Rates during 2004-2005

Types of Unemployment	*Rural*			*Urban*		
	Male	*Female*	*Total*	*Male*	*Female*	*Total*
Usual Principal Status	2.1	3.1	2.5	4.4	9.1	5.3
Current Weekly Status	3.8	4.2	3.9	5.2	9.0	6.0
Current Daily Status	8.0	8.7	8.2	7.5	11.6	8.3

Source: NSS Report No.515 (2004-05)

The entire Indian economy has experienced a peculiar trend of falling the real wage rate along with relatively less regular employment for most workers(Chandrasekhar and Ghosh 2006).The large part of the increase in self-employment and therefore in employment is a distress – driven phenomenon, led by the inability to find adequate gainful paid employment. This indicates that shift towards self-employment is part of the survival strategies of the working people. Though the labour productivity has tripled between 1981-2004 from 0.7 to 2.1%, the workers share in value added has declined from 0.3 to 0.15 during the same period. The benefits of this sharp increase in labour productivity are largely appropriated in the form of rent, interest and profits incomes by the propertied class. The women workers are more exploited in this perverse trend . Therefore high economic growth does not reduce poverty or unemployment, and therefore does not ensure higher social welfare or higher economic prosperity either.

7.9. ECONOMIC CITIZENSHIP OF WOMEN

Main stream Economics which endorse capital intensive technology has rather trivialised the gender issue. At the most it addresses the issue of unequal wages among men and women.. Economics as a discipline is predominantly male dominated. Therefore all planning and policies are geared to promote economic growth through technological advancement. Technology, market , development are considered gender-neutral. But in reality we experience that rate of unemployment is always severe among females. It is observed from the following table 7.11 that rate of unemployment has increased from 5.6% to 7% in 2000, though we see that girls are hijacking more jobs in the service sector and the work participation rate among women has been increasing. There is no significant increase in their economic citizenship.

Table 7.11 : Unemployment & Poverty In India

Years	*Rural Unemployment(%)*		*Poverty Ratio(%)*	
	Male	*Female*	*Rural*	*Urban*
1972-73	6.8	11.2	56	47
1977-78	7.1	9.2	51	42
1983-84	7.5	9	43	38
1987-88	4.6	6.7	37	37
1993-94	5.6	5.6	37	33
1999-2000	7.2	7	27	24

7.10. HUMAN DEVELOPMENT

Human development is the end and economic growth is the means. It defines the basic objectives of the development as enlarging the choices of people primarily by providing them with education, health and employment opportunities. Human development has three essential qualitative components: (a) equality of opportunities for all people in the society(b) sustainability of such opportunities from one generation to others and (c) empowerment of people so that they participate in and benefit from the development process. HDI attempts to measure the country's achievement in the enhancement of human capabilities. It is an equally weighted composite index of three components: index of life expectancy, index of educational attainment and index of adjusted per capita income. India ranks quite low in the comity of nations with a rank of 115 among 100 countries studied by UNDP. There is a good deal of variation in HDI values across the states.

Table 7.12 : Indicators of Human Development

Countries	*Human Dev. Index*	*Gender Dev. Index*	*Gender Empow-erment Index*	*Human Poverty Index(%)*	*HDI (1999)*
India	0.44(138)	0.41(118)	0.22(86)	36.70(47)	.571(115)
China	0.62 (108)	0.61(90)	0.48(28)	17.50(18)	.718(87)
Pakistan	0.44(139)	0.392(120)	0.189(92)	46.80(64)	.498(127)
Bangladesh	0.36(144)	0.33(128)	0.27(76)	48.30(67)	.470(132)
Sri Lanka	0.71(91)	0.69(70)	0.30(70)	20.70 (22)	.735(81)

It is observed from table 7.13 over the years and decades that India continues to have very low position in terms of HDI among the comity of nations. HDI Rank of US, UK,

Table 7.13 : Human Development Index : Comparison

Countries	*1975*	*1985*	*1995*	*1999*	*(rank)*	*2003*	*(rank)*	*2004*	*(rank)*
India	.406	.472	.544	.577	(115)	.602	(127)	.611	(126)
China	.522	.590	.679	.718	(87)	.755	(85)	.768	(81)
Thailand	.604	.676	.749	.762	(70)	.778	(73)	.784	(74)
Bangladesh	.332	.383	.443	.470	(132)	.520	(139)	.530	(137)
Sri Lanka	.614	.674	.717	.735	(81)	.751	(93)	.755	(93)
Pakistan	.343	.403	.476	.498	(127)	.527	(135)	.539	(134)
Japan	.851	.891	.920	.928	(9)	.943	(11)	949	(7)
UK	.839	.856	.914	.923	(14)	.939	(15)	940	(18)
US	.861	.896	.923	.934	(6)	.944	(10)	948	(8)
Canada	.867	.904	.930	.936	(2)	.949	(5)	.950	(6)
Norway	.856	.887	.924	.939	(1)	.963	(1)	.965	(1)

Japan is always much higher, India can never be compared with G-7 countries. Its postion is better than Bangladesh, Pakistan but worse than Srilanka and China.

Table 7.14 : Economic Development Vs Human Development

Country	*PC GDP**	*G- Index*	*L-Index*	*E-Index*	*H-Index*
India	3139	0.58	0.64	0.61	126 (0.611)
China	5896	0.68	0.76	0.84	81(0.768)
USA	39676	1.00	0.88	0.97	8(0.948)
UK	30821	0.96	0.89	0.97	18(0.940)
Japan	29251	0.95	0.95	0.94	7(0.949)
Norway	38454	0.99	0.91	0.99	1(0.965)

* Per capita GDP in terms of PPP US $, 2004

G-Index= GDP index, L-Index= Life expectancy Index,

E-Index= Educational Index,

H-Index= Human Development Index

The above table 7.14 illustrates that though India is growing very fast in economic growth its performance is very dismal in terms of human development. Among these six countries, India has the lowest per capita GDP, lowest GDP index, lowest life expectancy index and lowest educational index. HDI rank if India is 126 among the comity of nations, while China has 81 st rank. Norway, Japan and USA have their ranks 1,7 and 8 respectively according to UNDP report of 2006.

The gender implications are erased from their analysis. With the immense sophistication in methodology that emphasizes exclusively on quantification, uncomfortable issues such as patriarchy has remained as non issue and invisible. Gender concern and discourses survive with in the development bureaucracies which are themselves dominated by men. It is easier for them to ring-fence gender issues as a problem of poverty and to argue against 'feminization of poverty' than to admit the realistic view of gender disadvantage which crosses the boundaries of class and ethnicity. In India since the beginning of planned economic development, women have been always viewed as a deprived section requiring welfare measures and charity.

Independence in India, like all other countries, has brought economic development and modernization. Decolonization, with accelerated industrialization and spread of female education has increased urban wage employment of unmarried educated women. But the traditional role of unskilled and uneducated women in villages of India continue to becomes worse due to acceleration in the male migration from the villages .Rural-urban migration has multiplied the work burden for village women. In India there is hyper growth of tertiary sector in the last decade. Modernisation has brought mechanization in agricultural sector, automation in industrial sector and computerization in tertiary sector. It has brought radical changes in the traditional hierarchy for men but much less for women . The educated class of male refuse to do any manual work. Modernization of agriculture had reduced the work burden of male due to mechanization and tractorization. But women continue to perform their drudgery- ridden traditional hand operated tasks like collecting food, fuel and fodder unless their family income is sufficient to shift some work to another women from less well-off families

7.11. GENDER DEVELOPMENT INDEX

Human Development (HDI) is a measure of overall levels of human development in the society and does not measure the gender disparities that exist. About half of the population in developing countries comprise of women. It is a culturally stubborn problem. In India there is discrimination against women at the familial and societal levels. Any development process and programme in which women do not actively participate and fruits from which are not shared equitably is neither sustainable not desirable. Development if not engendered is indeed endangered. [2] The Gender-related Development index (GDI) is a measure of gender inequalities in a state ,in selected health and education related parameters. The discriminatory care given to the female infant immediately after birth is a direct reflection of the gender biases prevalent in the society

Data given in Table 7.15 reveal the gender inequality across the countries. In terms of Gender Development Index India's rank is 105 among 162 countries The second column indicates the difference between the ranks of HDI and GDI. It is negative for India, Bangladesh, Pakistan and Japan. It implies that there is gender inequality in these countries. In terms of gender Empowerment Measure(GEM) India has the 86th rank, while China has 28th position in the world. Physicians per thousands of population in India is only 48 while it is 413 in Norway and 279 in USA. Female Literacy

Rate in India is only 44, while it is 89% in Srilanka and 75 % in China. Adult literacy in India is only 52 % as compared to 93 percent in Thailand and 80 % in China.

Table 7.15 : GDI and GEM

Countries	*GDI*	*HDI-GDI*	*GEM*	*PPTP*
India	.553(105)	-1	.22(86)	48
China	.715(76)	3	.48(28)	16
Pakistan	.466(117)	-1	.189(92)	57
Bangladesh	.459(121)	-1	.309(62)	20
Sri Lanka	.732(70)	4	.409(56)	37
USA	.932(4)	2	.738(10)	279
UK	.920(12)	2	.671(16)	164
Japan	.921(11)	-2	.520(31)	193
Norway	.937(1)	0	.836(1)	413
Canada	.935(2)	0	.763(5)	229

Source : Human Development Report , UNDP ,different Years

GDI = Gender Development Index,

GEM = Gender Empowerment Index,

PPTP = Physicians per Thousands of Population during 1999

Table 7.16 GDI and HDI of Different Countries

Indices and Variables	*Thailand*	*China*	*India*	*Japan*	*USA*
Education Index	0.84	0.80	0.57	0.93	0.98
FLR (Female Literacy ratio)	93.9	76.3	45.4	99	99
GDI(rank)	0.760 (60)	0.724 (77)	0.560 (105)	0.927 (11)	0.937 (6)
HDI rank –GDI rank	1	3	-2	-2	0

Status of women in terms of gender development index(GDI) is very low in developing countries. Rank of India and China are 105 and 77 respectively. The difference between HDI and GDI is positive for Thailand and China but negative for India and Japan.(table 7.16) It implies that there is again incompatibility between human development and gender development. Higher human development does not necessarily imply better gender-neutral development. Because an educational system ,which is viable and economically efficient may not be socially just and desirable. The knowledge-based society never emerges from this kind of regressive educational system. Every body now used to believe that there is ' knowledge explosion' in the entire globe. This is a semi-myth. There is simply information-boom and explosion of awareness about facts and market functionings. In the search of marketability of new courses and seeking tangible returns from the degrees, the real pursuit of enhancing the quality of education in academic institutions is undermined; and the academic excellence, expertise, and scholarship are safely ignored. Thus academic institutions are not likely to become centre of excellence but centers of mediocrity only.

The following table 7.18 depicts the inter state imbalance in gender disparity index. It is based on the census data of major 15 states of India. Kerala is having the best position always. Tamil Nadu and Andhra have 2nd and 3rd position respectively. It is the lowest in Bihar followed by UP and Assam. Table 7.18 : Gender Disparity Index across Different States After globalization, the educational dualism is becoming more pronounced in developing countries. The success of higher education system (HES) thrives on social polarization and pillage of economic vitality and vulnerability of the civil society. As a result the renteer economy expands very high and parallel economy grows very fast. The Higher Education in developing countries may not be sustainable because its present success is not based upon quality but upon a powerful educational dualism. Ironically this dualistic pattern is very stable. But this stability and strength in the educational system is socially most undesirable and unacceptable in the long run. This educational dualism manifests in and perpetuates, inter alia, the persistence of:

- Difference in employability of male and female
- Wage/earning differential between male and female
- Casualisation/ contractualisation of jobs
- Gender disparity, subordination women
- Rural urban disparity, hierarchy in access
- High dropout rates in academic institutions
- Child labour and semi-bonded labour practice
- Prostitution, child trafficking

In developing countries, general household characteristics like income, caste, occupation and educational level of parents continue to determine access and educational achievements of students. The gender bias is more pronounced in higher education system of India . It is the daughter who is sent to government colleges and public universities. The son is admitted in the private institutions with huge spending. The son's education is considered to be an investment while that of the daughter is accepted as an unproductive expenditure. This is particularly true for girls and for children from poor and middle income families. The national picture always conceals wide regional differences in gender-inequality again.[15] The early socialization of girls by parents and teachers contribute to the development of 'superiority feeling' in boys and 'inferiority feeling' in girls. Machismo being all pervasive in educational, political ,economic and social subsystems is a maelstrom for Indian society. We can no longer look at gender disparities in isolation. The intermeshing of geographic location, social status, economic position, gender, occupation and displacement/ migration has resulted in new forms of disparities and disempowerment. The dualism involving low cost options does not do either ; they merely accentuate existing cleavages in the society. Therefore we need to have value-based education for building a society which automatically rejects any type of malfunctioning and maldevelopment.

7.12. CONCLUDING REMARKS

Political system in India is never gender neutral. Economic development is never gender-neutral. The nexus between political system and economic system goes against women. Poverty can not serve as the proxy for subordination of women. Therefore anti poverty policies can not be expected to necessarily improve the position of women. Money is neither necessary nor sufficient for transforming existing asymmetric gender relations. Thus Gender issue should never be approached with poverty reduction policies. Because this approach believes that women are victims of misdevelopment

Even today man continues to exercises his subtler-control on the family production and reproduction system. It is gradually institutionalized at several spheres: work, culture, customs, religion and education. Therefore liberation of women will not be easy or complete without the destruction of neo-patriarchy . The social and economic structures that locks production and reproduction together , perpetrate male dominance and female submission. The liberation of women can only be achieved if all structures in which women are integrated are transformed simultaneously. A modification of any one of them can be offset by a reinforcement of another, so that a mere permutation of the form of inequality is ultimately achieved. Thus a social transformation, which gives us real modernity is warranted. Modernity does not come from technology, economic development or consumerism. Real modernity implies social prosperity which treats both male female as equal and free human beings.

When one aims at true modernization neither the earlier panacea of central planning nor the virtues of ongoing globalization appears to carry much conviction for women section or social development of India. Although gender empowerment has been a buzzword in development circles, the concept has been used in so many different ways that it remains ambiguous. All studies and reports on women status have only remained as a source of data, which rather endorse the passivity of the state. Policy strategy should reject the touristic observations of the metro life , dispel misconceptions and attempt to reveal the real Indian scenario. Effective policy design requires an effective understanding of the gender issues within a broad social framework. We should have poverty-independent gender analyses and policies in order to rescue gender from poverty trap. Women's income earning activity should not be temporary, exploitative and reversible. Education and technology should ensure liberation and freedom of thought for all human beings. It should break gradually the shackles of tradition that binds women in the man-made gaol. The gender issue should be delinked both from myopic economics and insensitive politics. There is no substitute for a gender analysis , which transcend class divisions and material definitions of deprivation. Therefore 'adding women' is not necessary, but an insight and rethinking development concepts and practices as a whole through a gender lens is necessary. The debate on state non action on gender issues should be initiated.

REFERENCES

1. Chambers Robert (1993), *Challenging the Professions: Frontiers for Rural Development*, Intermediate Technology Publications, London
2. Das, Kumar (1997), Asian Profile of Underdevelopment , *Asian*

Profile, Canada, Vol.25(1),Feb

3. Das, Kumar (1998), Sustainable Growth and Equity in the context of Free Marketism, in
4. Abdur Rab (ed) *Management of Development*, University of Dhaka, Bangladesh
5. Das, Kumar (2002) Economic Development and Human Capital Formation in India, Paper presented in *World Economic History Congress* held at Buenos Aires, Argentina, 22-26, July
6. Ramachandran, Vimala (2002), *Hierarchies of Access: Gender and Social Equity in Primary Education,* (ed) European Commission, February
7. Agrawal, Bina(1997) Bargaining and Gender Relations within and beyond the_Household, *Feminist Economics* ,Vol.3(1) pp. 454-487
8. Cohen, Phillip N (2004) The gender Division of Labour: Keeping house and occupational segregation in the united states, *Gender and Society,* April
9. Cotter, D A et al(2001) Women's Work and working women: the demand for female labour, *Gender and Society*,Vol.15(3) PP.429-52
10. Das, Kumar (1997) Asian Profile of Underdevelopment and Poverty, *Asian Profile*, Canada, Feb. Vol. 25(1),1997
11. Geeta V, (2002)God made you different and Nature made us different, *Gender Theorizing Feminism*, Stree Publications, Madras
12. Maher, V (1990) Work Consumption and authority with in the Household, in *Of Marriage and the Market* (ed) Kate Young et al, Routledge London
13. Sullivan, (2004) Changing Gender Practices within the Household: a theoretical perspective, *Gender and Society*, April
14. Sen, A K (1990) Gender and Cooperative conflicts in Persistent Inequalities: Women and World Development (ed) Irene Tinker Oxford University Press, New York

8

Women and Health Care System

India has experienced substantial improvement in the health status of people due to significant modernization of the health care system. But the disaggregated scenario is quite dismal. This chapter examines the disease burden by focusing on short-duration diseases and major morbidity among Indians. It highlights pertinent issues confronting the Health Care System in India. It analyses the gender bias and urban bias existing in health care system of India and brings out the policy implications in the context of ongoing free market policy.

Social prosperity is embedded in human development. It is the end and economic growth is a means. The modern concept of Human development depends on health status of people. It is an inseparable dimension of development process of any nation. Therefore it is warranted to examine the health status of people and analyse the emerging health care system of India under globalised regime. The impact of globalisation has become all pervasive in India. All sectors of Indian economy seem to be vibrating with economic buoyancy. The new economic reforms has generated an atmosphere of over optimism of instant economic growth. There is expansion of trade, investment, market, and increase in GNP, productivity, per capita income, profit, efficiency, salary etc. Life styles of metro people have become more attractive , comfortable and fashionable than ever before. The new reform process pursues economic growth to the best of its ability until it is distracted by other issues like health and environment. It adopts the rhetoric of all these issues pretty easily. It puts over emphasis on economic efficiency and modern urban sector at the cost of the larger society . After 60 years of independence India ranks 127 in terms of Human Development Index (HDI). Its disease burden and morbidity rate has remained at very high level. Infant mortality rate and mothers mortality rate are very high in India. Female foeticide is also very high as indicated by ever declining demographic ratios: sex ratio and child(0-6) sex ratios.

8.1. HEALTH CARE SYSTEM

Health of the people is the natural wealth of the nation The axiom "Health is wealth" is relevant in all ages. It is the health of people on which survival of the people and wealth of the nation depends. Health is the most germane issue of India's development process India has worked continuously to improve its health care system in the last several decades, and considerable progress has been made in expanding the public health system and reducing the burden of disease. Other notable achievements include the establishment of an extensive network of Government health care facilities both in the rural and the urban areas and determined efforts to upgrade the skills of health care workers, particularly in rural areas. In just over five decades, life expectancy in India has doubled, and the infant mortality rate halved. However, during the same period India's birth rate has declined by only 25%. Nevertheless, its performance requires much improvement in comparison with other emerging economies, including most comparable nations in the region. Deficiencies persist with respect to access, affordability, efficiency, quality and effectiveness, despite the high level of overall private and public expenditure on health. Through out the history, life of most Indians has been a constant struggle for survival in an insanitary environment against poverty, malnutrition and disease. India face the cruelty of '*double burden*' of old problem of" ill health"(resulting from malnutrition, undernutrition, communicable diseases) and of new problem of ill-health (Price of development, resulting from environmental degradation and industrialization, mining etc).The lack of proper preventive, promotive and curative facilities in the rural areas constitute a more pronounced facet of dualism .

After globalization significant changes have occurred in different sphere of life of Indian people. But after 60 years of independence there is a 'benign neglect' of the majority. Government's high priority on 'rural health' are not effectively translated into the budgetary priorities. It is only a very small percentage(less than 3 percent) of the budget is spent on health of people in rural sector where more than 80 percent of the population live. The basic health infrastructure in rural areas has remained as weak as before. Despite concerted efforts, India continues to record high levels of infant-and-mother-mortality and morbidity ,especially among infants, children ,the elderly and women specially of backward regions of the country.

Health care system in India is highly elitist and strongly urban biased. It is not only inefficient but also regressive in character. All priorities of promoting rural health care has not yet been translated into budgetary priorities. The modern hospital only deal with the tip of the ice berg. The medical profession in India has neither the capacity or training to deliver health to the common man in the villages. In Indian democracy all activities and programs are carried out in the name of rural people and especially of the under privileged. But pitiably almost all benefits of development gravitate to the elite class or urban class. It reveals the extent of the hiatus between preaching and practice and this applies perfectly well to the field of health both in its public as well as private sector.

In India the concept of primary health care(PHC) was a response to the growing recognition that development policies of the fifties and sixties has largely failed to improve the conditions of majority of the population in the world. Disease control programs driven by renewed confidence in the technological achievements of medicine failed to eliminate many endemic diseases The diseases which cause morbidity and mortality continue to exact an unacceptable toll. The central message of the PHC strategy was a call for equity and social justice. After one year of PHC and alternative approach known as Selective primary health care, SPHC was widely disseminated. It argues that more effective method of decreasing mortality depends on the selection and prioritization of limited number of diseases. In spite of many sociological and epidemiological criticisms this SPHC model was accepted by the World Bank, USAID and other donors Later it was extended to include three Fs : female literacy, family planning and food supplements. So PHC model has been now supplanted by selective strategies. SPHC adopts a technocentric managerial approach in delivering medical care .In India SPHC adopts a powerful measure in its armory known as DALY (disability adjusted life year)which captures disability and life lost to disease rather than mortality alone. DALY projects and justifies the scientific base of SPHC. DALY model is being extensively used in various consultation process. They are oriented toward the expert's view which often entailed with cost benefit analysis and other verifiable indicators for the funding agencies. They try to over professionalize rather than deprofessionalize health. The SPHC goes away from equity consideration and detracts from the need for a long term social, economic and political change.

After privatization of health sector, the out-of –pocket expenditure(OPE) of common people has increased significantly. The OPE as percentage of consumption expenditure is 5.8% for urban and 6.1% for rural sector . Public health expenditure is only 0.8 % of GDP and Per capita public health expenditure is only Rs 163.

% of public HE to THE = 26.46%

% of private HE to THE = 73.54

%Per capita average public HE = Rs. 163

Per capita average private HE = Rs. 473

Per capita average total HE = Rs. 617

Public HE as % pf GDP = 0.8

Private HE as % of GDP = 2.2

%of OPE in urban consumption exp = 5.82

%of OPE in rural consumption exp. = 6.15

HE = Health expenditure , THE = Total Health Expenditure

8.2. DISEASE BURDEN OF INDIA

The disease burden of India is as high as dependency burden in India. There are eight clearly identifiable diseases, namely epilepsy, hypertension, diabetes mellitus, heart diseases, mental illness, tuberculosis ,leprosy and cancer. Short duration morbidity is very high in Madhya Pradesh, West Bengal, Tamil Nadu, Punjab, Haryana, Orissa and Andhra Pradesh and low in Gujrat, Maharastra and Kerala, UP and Rajstan. Female morbidity is very high in comparison to male morbidity in Tamil Nadu followed by Punjab, Haryana and Orissa. The incidence of diarrhoea was 31 ,cold and cough 72 and fevers 25 per thousands populations. At the state level the incidence of diarrhoea is very high in MP, Orissa, WB and very low in Kerala, Gujrat,

Maharastra and Punjab. Incidence of cold and cough are high in WB and Tamil Nadu but low in Gujrat and Maharastra. It is very high among less developed villages and low among women. Prevalence of fever is uniform across all ages. Gender disparity is very high among 15-34 years age group in comparison with other age groups. It is probably related to pregnancy and child birth related problems.

Point prevalence Rate(PPR) for all ages and all types of major morbidity worked out to be 4578 per lakh population. It was very high in AP,Kerala, TN, Haryana and Punjab. It is considerably higher among adults and the older population. It was only 966 per lakh population among 0-4 year age group followed by 1138 among 5-14 age group. PPR increases sharply with the age. It is about 23 times higher among the elderly(above 60) in comparison to 0-4 age group .Thus it is higher among the states which have higher life expectancy such as Kerala, TN, Haryana and Punjab. The prevalence of major morbidity among the poor could be low because the severely affected would already have dead. Incidence of leprosy among ST population is three times higher than the national averages. The highest morbidity has been recorded for hypertension(ie 589 per lakh) followed by Tuberculosis(ie 423 per lakh). (Table-1). However the prevalence of tuberculosis, leprosy and cancer falls as household income increases. The prevalence of hypertension and heart diseases has been reported to be high for the salaried and professional class in urban areas. The prevalence of tuberculosis is high among the SCs and STs and might be related to their low level of living and consequent malnutrition. It is very much positively related to the incidence of poverty. The gender disparity in TB is only 0.59, which may be due to under reporting or non treatment of women.

Table 8. 1 : Major Morbidity in India

States	*Epil-epsy*	*Hyper-ten-sion*	*Dia-betes*	*Heart dis-ease*	*Men-tal disease*	*TB*	*Lep-rosy*	*Cancer*	*Major Morb-idity*
Gujrat	103	381	215	188	160	276	30	7	2551
Kerala	81	1443	980	914	283	504	-	39	7319
M'stra	147	241	130	151	84	282	65	62	3487
Orissa	369	863	116	245	99	206	31	74	5011
Punjab	103	1475	196	166	268	230	-	28	6692
Rajstan	60	64	55	84	79	303	-	37	3150
T'nadu	205	1191	377	949	80	583	83	15	6775
INDIA	120	589	221	385	132	423	57	43	4578
Gender D	0.71	1.31	0.65	0.86	0.75	0.59	1.64	0.95	1.00

It is observed that different types of physical disabilities such as bitot spot, night blindness and impairment related to visual, auditory, vocal, and loco motor system are prevalent among the children up to 12 years of age. The incidence of these physical disabilities is 2042 per lakh among 0-4 years age group and 2896 per lakh among 5-12 years age group. The prevalence of physical disabilities among the younger is over 70% than the older age group.(Table-2) .This suggests that the most physical disabilities are genetic, biological and even birth defects . There are very wide variations across the states . Physical disability are higher among the boys. Under reporting in case of girls may be due to cultural factors. There has been high incidence of bitot spots in MP and Rajstan and Tamil Nadu. It is a manifestation of extreme malnutrition due to calorie and protein deficiencies. For rural India as a whole the prevalence of bitot spot is 1135 and 2090 per lakh population in 0-4 and 5-12 years age groups respectively. Children from families of wage earners and minorities have a higher incidence of disabilities.

Table 8.2 : Forms of Disabilities in India

Type of Disability	*0-4 year(millions)*	*5-12 Yr (millions)*
Physical Disability	3.6	5.1
Visual Impairment	0.9	2.3
Hearing impairment	0.3	1.5
Speech Impediment	0.6	0.8
Bitot Spot	2.3	4.2
Locomotor Disability	0.4	1.0
Total	8.1	14.9

Average annual household expenditure on short duration morbidity and major sickness worked out to be Rs.121 and Rs. 49 per person respectively. The cost per sick person of major sickness was Rs. 1071 for rural India. The high cost treatment is due to both extended duration of major morbidity and high cost of medication. On the other hand cost of treatment for infants and the very old is relatively low with high levels of gender disparity. The proportion of expenditure on doctors fee and medicine alone account for about 76 % of the total cost in case of short duration morbidity and about 65% of the cost incase long duration major morbidity. Thus the household expenditure on treatment of sickness has become very substantial. Short-term morbidity and major morbidity are disproportionately higher among the vulnerable section groups in India . Therefore the burden of both short duration and major morbidity falls on the weaker section of the population, including the wage laborers, minorities, and low income groups. A large private sector for health care is therefore growing very rapidly. Cuts in public expenditure as a result of structural adjustment and privatization of health care adversely affect the relatively poor and vulnerable.

8.3. FEMALE INFANTICIDE

The sex composition of any region has significant demographic and social implications. The sex ratio in USA is 1029, Japan is 1041, Brazil 1025 and China is 944. But the pattern of sex ratios in India as they emerge in 2001 census have sent shock waves throughout the country. The dramatic fall in sex ratios in India, especially in states like Punjab, Haryana and Orissa in the last decade has alarmed demographers and sociologists. It is the same in both the poorest state and the richest state of India.

Table 8.3 : Declining Child Sex Ratio(0-6) In India

Year	*Child Sex Ratio in Punjab*	*Sex Ratio in Orissa*	*Sex Ratio in India*
1961	894	1001	941
1971	899	988	930
1981	908	981	934
1991	875	971	927
2001	793	972	933

Similar situation prevailed during the paramountcy of Bristish East India company and the crown. The earliest census of India, 1891 shows the glaring gaps in sex ratios. Social scientist agree that female infanticide has historically been responsible for such alarming scarcity of females in India. The British claimed to have discovered this heinous practice and made concrete efforts to curb such practice. They identified the high caste khatris, bedis, rajputs as primarily responsible for infanticide in colonial India. The imperial reports regarded caste pride, hypergamy and the exorbitant expenditure on marriage.dowry as primarily responsible for these infanticidal deaths. But contemporary scholars examined the effects of british methods of governance and development which produced the milieu in which sons became even more preferred and dowry gradually increased. It then increased due to the caste system, cultural and religious factors. It is an established custom that a female has to marry. It is a indispensable. The unmarried girl is looked in an eye of hatredness. And the girl has to marry a boy of her caste or tribe which is at least equal rank with her own. To marry in a inferior caste is considered a degradation and the option to remain unmarried is actual dishonour. These two difficult options are risky for many parents, who choose to escape the responsibility and destroy her before birth. It is prevailing now even more among the educated class and rich people. It has no direct connection with poverty. The sex ratio decline among children in the 0-6 age group turns out ot be sharper in the urban areas than in rural . The traditional north-south divide stands significantly modified and the northernisation of sex ratios is rapidly taking the urban route. The sharp decline in the urban female –male ratios among children can not be explained away by three popular escape hatches of yesteryears ie. migration, undercount or biologically ordained high sex ration at birth. The continuous decline clearly points to one factor, sex selective abortions or female foeticide that has gained currency during 1980s and more sharply in the 1990s, which the slogan of women empowerment and gender equality has become more louder. This is the stark reality of gender discrimination. It is the sharpest indicator of a gender-biased society. The problem of female foeticide and impending gender bias needs a fresh look .

8.4. URBAN BIAS IN PRIVATISATION

The health care system under privatization process has the following characteristics.

1. Majority of the population of India do not have the basic health facilities and services. About 70 percent of the population do not have sanitary facilities and about 40 percent of the population do not have the

access to safe drinking water. In the vast country like India only 50 percent of the population get the minimum health care facilities. Even today dysentry, diarrhoea, tuberculosis , malaria and filaria continue to cause an enormous number of deaths in the rural areas.

2. In terms of allocation of resources rural areas are always neglected. The most contrasting observation is that only 17 % of the hospital beds are available for the rural population which constitutes more than 75 % of the populations. Allocation of resources are always biased in favour of richer states, which affects the backward states and poor people adversely. Further , the govt expenditure on preventive and curative services tends to favour the urban and richer groups. Health care delivery system has been biased against the unorganized sector and particularly the urban poor.

3. The public health expenditure is heavily skewed .Therefore in many of the richer states average expenditure is almost twice as all India average. With stagnating public health expenditure, sky rocketing prices of drugs and rising cost of other health services and increasing unregulated privatisation of health care sector raises serious concerns .

4. The investment pattern in the health sector in India largely determines the quantity and quality of health care available to the population. Total health expenditure of India is classified into three types:

   a. Public expenditure by the govt(center and State)

   b. Private sector expenditure including the companies and NGOs

   c. Direct expenditure of the households(Out of pocket expenditure)

The first two are important in determining the health care system of India. But after globalization, the role of public sector is shrinking ,therefore out-of –pocket expenditures(OPE) on health has substantially increased . As a result the proportion of OPE is approximately 97% of total private expenditure (WHO,2003). Many rural families are plunged into poverty due to the sudden rise in the out-of–pocket expenditures(OPE) on health. It has impoverishing effect on poor families.

6. Developed countries have better health insurance system, leading to lower OPE. But in India, financing through public health expenditure is a better mechanism in comparison to insurance system as later deals with the curative care, while the former has the potential of addressing the comprehensive health care (both preventive and curative). The nascent health insurance sector in India accounts for a meager portion of the overall market. Only the very rich, govt employees and some formal sector workers enjoy health insurance. The entire rural sector depend on public health care system.

7. The OPE as a share of family income is determined by 3 important factors: i). availability of public health system (ii) health seeking behaviour iii) affordability of private health services.(table 8.5) OPE is directly related to last two factor while inversely related to the first one. Per capita Health expenditure of both rural and urban areas are shown below. It is seen that the poorest 20% spend only 3% while richest 20 % spend about 7% of total consumption expenditure.

Table 8.4 : Out of Pocket Expenditure in India

Quantile	*Share of OPE in total consumption Expenditure*		
	Rural	*Urban*	*Total*
Poorest 20%	3.06	3.50	3.22
Middle class	4.69	4.61	4.66
Richest 20%	8.44	5.61	7.10

8. The present techno-centric managerial approach of the health sector, has remained top- down and expert-oriented. It is highly insensitive, over professionalized and strongly urban biased. The modern hospital only deal with the tip of the ice berg. Under privatization regime the government PHC service is virtually non-existent in the villages. All the vertical programs introduced one after another during last 60 years have perennially suffered not only from lack of sufficient fund but also from ignoring ground reality.

8.5. GENDER BIAS IN HEALTH CARE

Govt. expenditure on health service in India has remained very low. It is worse in backward states like Oissa and Bihar, MP and UP. As a result the standard of health services is very poor. The communicable diseases have not been arrested effectively. Malnutritional diseases are increasing and above all health care facilities are not accessible to the teeming millions due to high burden of out of pocket expenditure. Poor financing of the health services lies at the root of these problems. The state and central govt of India are facing resource constraints. The govt of Orissa has a heavy debt burden- the highest among all the states of India. Further loans are being incurred to meet the revenue expenses and this is an unsustainable situation. It is therefore very unlikely for the state govt to allocate more resources to the health sector. Perspective health plans have been formulated at the national and state levels. But implementation of these plans with state funding will be very difficult

Physical access to health center has remained very low in all the backward districts of the country. Even if health facilities are available, people on the remote areas seem to be either ignorant of or rather non chalant about the beneficial impact of these measures. The malnutrition and anemia are rampant among women. The rate of malaria endemicity in India is more among women. The morbidity and mortality from malaria is also very high among women. Diarrhoeal diseases are also common among women. Women health remains neglected in each family. It is due to poverty and more due to gender discriminatory attitudes and approaches. Women in the remote villages suffer more from polio, chicken pox, malaria, tetanus, tuberculosis, measles, whooping cough, typhoid and diphtheria etc. Lack of public health care and sanitation affect the female very acutely. More over in India, women face a higher risk of poverty than men, due to lack of access to economic resources(credit, land, inheritance, education etc)O and lower remuneration for different economic activities. Within households, poverty places a particularly heavier burden on women because of the time and energy demands of managing the family consumption and welfare in the context of scarcity. Poverty and health have clear inter relationships through impacts on nutrition, exposure to risks of unhealthy housing and unsafe water and sanitation, higher workloads, and generally on vulnerability to illness. Poverty is also a major contributor to sexual and reproductive ill-health.

Patterns of health and illness in women and men show marked differences. Men and women experience different health risks that stem from their biological differences as well as their different social economic and cultural roles . Most obviously women as a group tend to have longer life expectancy than men in the same socio-economic circumstances. Yet despite their greater longevity women in most communities report more illness and distress than men. The precise details of this excess in female morbidity and the factors behind it vary in different social contexts. Women's advantage in relation to life expectancy is partly biological in origin. Economic development and social changes that remove some of the major risks to women's health such as introduction of birth control technologies improvements in living standards and the introduction maternity services also led to a significant improvement in life expectancy. Thus a range of social factors combined to enhance women's inherent biological advantage. For men, the emergence of the male breadwinner in industrial economies requiredmen to take on life threatening jobs in much greater number than women. As a result, male deaths from occupational causes have historically been higher than those among females and that. At the same time men's increase access to resources and their growing freedom from religious and other constraints led many to take up potentially dangerous substances and these new habits came to be defined as inherently 'masculine'. These factors contributed to reduce life expectancy among men. The net effect if socio-economic conditions favour longer life expectancy among female. However, in African countries men outlive women, possibly because of the harsh living conditions and the marginalization of women. In India and Pakistan the two sexes have almost equal life expectancy. In these societies there is an excess of female deaths both in childhood and in childbearing years and most can be attributed to the material and cultural discrimination against girls and women . Therefore, these are societies in which the biological advantage of the women is entirely cancelled out by their social disadvantage.

The female preponderance in morbidity is difficult to interpret, but three contributing factors are suggested: (a) Women's greater longevity is itself a cause of their higher rates of morbidity. (b) Women are more likely than men to suffer health problems connected with their reproductive system. Their capacity to conceive and bear children as well as the desire to control fertility brings them to the health care system more often than men. (c) Studies from many parts of the world show that women are more likely than men to report symptoms of mental distress . Therefore, being a male or being female has a major effect on an individual's health and wellbeing. The combination of their biological sex and gendered nature of their cultural economic and social lives put individuals at risk of developing some health problems while protecting them from others. The course of a disease may be different in women and men because of differential response to illness between men and women; differential societal response, to male and female sickness; and difference in accessing health care. Varying biological factors between the sexes influence susceptibility and immunity to diseases. Gender roles and relations influence the degree of exposure to infection and access to disease prevention and control resources shared by both sexes, they may have different manifestations or natural histories or differ in the severity of their consequences in women and men: For example TB is the single leading cause of deaths among women of reproductive age, accounting for 9% of the deaths worldwide; compared with HIV 3% and heart disease 3% (11,12).progression from infection to disease is as much as 130% high in women and case fatality rates are 27-41% higher among girls and young women

Thus there is the relevance of a gender perspective in health. The gender perspective facilitates a more contextualized understanding of differences between women and men in relation to: the rate of and vulnerability to infection, differences in access to and use of available health care resources, differences in the effect of the social meanings, especially stigmatization, of infectious diseases, the effects of disease on women as primary health care providers in their homes, and key dimensions of structural differences based on factors such as age and social status. Stigma associated with any disease (say TB, leprosy) seems to have a greater impact on women than on men and often places them in an economically or socially precarious position. Because the health and welfare of children is closely liked to that of their mothers.

The health care delivery system in India is not only inefficient but also discriminatory in character. It discriminates between rich and poor, educated and uneducated, and between male and female. The male-dominated society and the health care system of India remain callous and insensitive to the specialness of the health problem of women. The medical profession has not yet realized it. None is more blind than who does not see. The blind can not see, but we do not see. In the words of Sarveswar Sexena, the famous poet, " if there is a corpse rotting in your house, can you sing hymn in the next room?. It is only when the struggle for gender equity and women empowerment in health and health care joins the struggle for freedom from imperialism and expropriation, than we can move towards a truly health society.

8.6. ROLE OF LOCAL COMMUNITY

Health is a fairly elusive and esoteric concept for the majority. It has a broad spectrum of determinants. Modern health facilities has a strong urban bias. It is only hospital based and disease oriented. But the frontier of health care extends far beyond the narrow limits of medical care. 'Health for all' and "Education for all" means extension of these services, to the remote villages. It entails the removal of various obstacles to these services. Such as elimination of ignorance, malnutrition, unhygienic housing, contaminated water supply etc. All these aspects warrant concerted efforts in all directions. The nature of the problem is community -specific and region-specific. Hence a bottom up approach is the imperative need., which can ensure effective peoples empowerment.

There is a plethora of schemes for promoting health services. But they do not build PHC outside their campaign. In fact resources that could otherwise be spent in developing appropriate community level health care are spent on expensive campaigns. Any health provision which is technocentric in character triggered from the outside is destined to falter. Recent effort to socially marketize the insecticide treated mosquito nets as a magic bullet are likely to be counter productive. This will merely divert huge funds. Monumental failure of Malaria eradication is the best example. Many such programs have failed. They are bound to fail because they rest upon the medical and technical approach. Their target oriented social marketing approach is planned and implemented by experts with a view to maximize efficiency. It takes no account of equity or social, political and economic realities in which people live. Policy makers are unable and unwillling to learn lessons from the past. We must understand that any health programme which is to build a sustainable long term health for its people, has to involve the community . To ensure a more all-encompassing approach, women's voices and experiences need to be better incorporated into the ongoing planning process for better health status of the community and economic development.

More efficient management of health service through high technology medicines is only one aspect of the problem. It is equally important to mobilise communities and individuals to take a more active role in promoting health. The health care is a complex phenomenon, involving four aspects :

- vulnerability aspect
- morbidity aspect
- preventive aspect and
- curative aspect

An effective health care delivery system should take all these four aspects into consideration. The purposes of health care services should include saving lives, preventing, relieving and curing diseases and disability and ameliorating the consequences of diseases when it can not be cured. Rural health Care system of India does not involve the common man or the village community. And with the global euphoria of and movement towards free market policy ,with the development of the private health sector, 'efficiency' is being over emphasized at the cost of 'equity' or common. It negates the women health problems and neglects the gender perspective in health care. Therefore HFA(Health for All)slogan ,which has become the powerful leverage of the officialdom before and after privatization process is likely to be a myth for the majority. Because the commercialization process and commodification of health products/services neglects the gender issues, social priorities and cultural values.

There is the need for better allocation and more efficient use of resources. More funds should be directed towards primary health care. The share of non salary component of expenditure on drugs and maintenance of health infrastructure should be augmented and timely disbursement of funds to different sub sectors can kick start the improvement in the health sector. There is need for awareness building in the community and change of mindset of people. The Chinese concept of bare-foot doctors extending the basic facilities like immunization , pre and post natal check-ups , treatment for diarrhea., malaria along with making the people aware of basic health care ad sanitary measure would not only improve access to health service s but also generate demand for information. Inclusion of information n on health status ,nutritional status, sanitary condition, food value of indigenous food materials, medicinal properties of different plants and herbs in the school curricula may improve awareness among women and make people more health conscious.

8.7. LOOKING AHEAD

Human health is the most fundamental requirement of any society/ economy. It is the inherent source of production and capital. Rural economic development squarely lies on the improvement in community health and spread of education. But both continue to be neglected entities for the rural people .Both are usually subjugated to other needs of the rural poor, conceived as more important i.e. efficiency, income, wealth, and security.

The problem does not lie so much in inadequacy of health services but in the approach and in our inability to make them reach the common people through over professionalized and over bureaucratized health system both in the public as well as private sector. The doctor and nurses wherever present are only concerned with curative services which mainly favored the local elites. The enjoyment of the highest attainable standard of health (if not living) should be one of the fundamental rights of every human being without distinction of region, race, caste, religion, political belief, economic or social status. Thus deprofessionalization of the health sector is required. The HFA strategy should meaningfully lead us to a state of complete physical, mental and social wellbeing where health should become the fundamental human right.

The present approach has a focus on efficiency but not on equity or quality. It emphasizes on market but not on social reality, the disease but not health. Therefore HFA reflects only neo liberal ,right wing prescriptions at the expense of the poor. It is mere a return to economic trickle down and disease control.. It gives a message of benign neglect for those who can not afford to be part of the market. Therefore HFA is a myth for the poor people and backward regions.

Given the synergistic relationship between education, health, nutrition, energy, adequate allocation of public investment needs to be made on the social overheads and efficient measures should be adopted to magnify its trickle-down effect on rural people. The crux of the matter is that the new approach requires human development goals to be an integral part of the economic development . It should be more and more inclusive process. Combination of conscientization of the rural people and sensitization of the bureaucracy at all levels can ensure human prosperity

The present top-down techno-managerial approach to 'delivering' healthcare in India is known for its lack of sensitivity to cultural and social factors of the local people and for its lack of accountability to the people, whom it is intended to serve. It is necessary to explode the myth that health care has to be delivered to the people by very highly trained people and professional experts. It is necessary to liberate the people from the clutches of experts and professionals. Unless the people are involved in the planning process, it is impossible to evolve meaningful, rational and cost-effective health care system that can provide adequate amount' of "appropriate" health care to the people.

Thus effective disease control (say TB or leprosy) cannot be achieved so long as the disease is considered in isolation from the social process that maintain it, create the condition facilitating its spread and act as barriers to care or cure . Insights into the economic and social burdens incurred with a diagnosis of disease are essential to understand why many patients especially the most disadvantaged are unable to seek health care and unable to comply with treatment regimens . Socio- economic and cultural factors play important roles in determining overall gender differences in rates of infection and progression to disease; and access to case detection and successful treatment of TB. Therefore, disease control and research programs need to be gender sensitive and take the necessary measures in all their efforts.

There is the need for health program to operationalize and institutionalize a gender perspective in reproductive health services in rural India .It can result in a significant reduction in unmet need for contraception, increased client satisfaction, an improved communication between stakeholders. The gendered approach should include categories related to institutional policies and practices, provider practices, personnel knowledge of reproductive health, client comfort, use of gendered language, information, education, communication and training, client satisfaction, and monitoring and evaluation. We should incorporate a gender perspectives in the private and public hospitals . A regular evaluation and monitoring of the gender-neutrality of health care system is necessary. We should create effective systems of accountability to improve the delivery of core public services. This can be achieved in a variety of ways: internal reform of public sector agencies; providing citizens with regular, relevant and reliable information; strengthening local governments and decentralizing responsibilities; and expanding the role of state.

Our policy goal should ensure that men and women

are given equal opportunities to realise their potential for health . A crucial strategy to achieve this goal is the gender mainstreaming of national health policies. This entails integrating attention to sex and gender differences in all stages of health policy development: conceptualisation and agenda setting; policy design; decision-making; policy implementation and monitoring. The gender mainstreaming of national health policies is a crucial strategy in achieving equal opportunities and reducing inequalities in health between men and women. The sex ratio should be reveresed by social transformation. Applying a gender perspective would necessitate that all health statistics be engendered and a comprehensive women's health profile be made. In order to ensure equality between the sexes, particularly in the area of health following barriers should be removed and following steps must be taken:

- Provision of sufficient funding/investment to promote gender mainstreaming
- Need for comprehensive collection of gender disaggregated data, in order to make the situations of both men and women clear.
- More attention should be paid to the monitoring of gender equality within national health policy
- .Specific targets should be developed, and time scales for their achievement and indicators of progress should be set.
- Creating a woman-friendly health service, increasing representation of women in the health services
- Encouraging gender-specific data collection and gender-disaggregated research on many aspects of women's health

REFERENCES

1. Banerjee, D (1989),Health and Family Planning Services in India, New Delhi : Lok Prakashan
2. Barros P P (1998) The black Box of Health Care Expenditure growth determinants, Health Economics, Vol 7, pp.533-544
3. Blomquist, A.G. and RAL Carter (1997) Is Health Care Really a Luxury? Journal Of Health Economics, Vol16, pp.207-230
4. Dasgupta, P (1993) , An Enquiry into Well being and Destitution, Oxford: Clarendon Press
5. Das, Kumar B (1990) Rural development Through decentralization, New Delhi: Discovery Pub. House
6. Doyal L. Sex, Gender and health preliminary conceptual framework. In:Diwan V, Thorson A, Winkwist A. (Ed): Gender and Tuberculosis. Nordic School of Public Health, Gotebor; 1998: 29-40.
7. Kothari ,V and I Gulati (1997),DALYs as a guide for health Policy, Economic Political Weekly,Vol.32(41) : 2612-17
8. Macintyre S, Hunt K. Sweeting H. Gender Differences in Health: are things really as simple as they seem? Social Science Medicine 1996, 42(4): 617-624.
9. McCoskey ,SK and TM Selden (1998) Health Care Expenditures and GDP, Panel Data unit root test results, Journal of Health Economics, Vol.17 pp.369-376
10. Parikh, K.S.(1999), India Development Report, New Delhi: Oxford Univ. Press
11. Pritchett, L and L H Summers (1996) Wealthier is Healthier, Journal of Human Resources, Vol.31, PP.841-868
12. Reddy, K.N. and V Selvaraju (1994) Health Care Expenditures buy Govt of India, Seven Hill Publication ,New Delhi
13. Shariff, A(1999), India: Human Development Report, National Council of Applied Economic Research, New Delhi
14. Tulsidhar, V B (1989) Public Expenditure, Medical Care and Infant Mortality: A comparative study of States in India, State Finance Unit Research Paper-2, National Institute of Public Finance and Policy, New Delhi
15. UNDP (2007), Human Development Report, New York: Oxford University Press.
16. World Health organization. Gender and Health: Technical paper. World Health Organization 1998bhttp:,'/www.who.int/ reproductiv-health/pulication /WHD_98 16_gender_and_health.

9
Water, Woman and Sanitation

Water is essential to the well-being of humankind, vital for economic development, and a basic requirement for the healthy functioning of all the world's ecosystems. Access to water and sanitation is necessary for health, education, economic development and the environment. Clean water, together with hygienic sanitation, is necessary to sustain human life and to ensure good health and human dignity. Yet more than 1 billion people do not have access to a safe water source . And over twice that number are denied access to adequate sanitation continues to shock and appal. Millions of lives are at risk from preventable diseases and t he futures of millions of the world's children are blighted by the multiple deprivations of poverty, lack of education and ill health that often accompany poor water and sanitation. Access to a sufficient quantity of safe water is fundamental to the health and dignity of all. Water and sanitation are not just the subjects of one of the targets of the Millennium Development Goals; they have a part to play in the realisation of all the Millennium Development Goals.

The International Year of Sanitation, which has just begun, calls for all nations to recognise that access to hygienic sanitation is equally important to ensure health and dignity. The international community has committed to meeting the Millennium Development Goal of halving, by 2015, the proportion of people without sustainable access to safe drinking water and basic sanitation. This is a great challenge. A human rights approach to water and sanitation, with its emphasis on accountability, access to information, non-discrimination, attention to vulnerable groups and participation is a crucial aspect of achieving this goal. It requires a focus on the most marginalised sectors of society, including over one billion people living in informal settlements the world over.

Nationally and internationally, the allocation of resources to water and sanitation is insufficient . The lack of access is exacerbated by a challenging social and environment context: accelerating urbanisation, increasing pollution and depletion of water resources and climate change. It is estimated that at any one time nearly half the population of developing countries is suffering from health problems linked to inadequate water and sanitation. Approximately 4 billion cases of diarrhoea each year cause 2.2 million deaths, mostly among children under five – about 15 percent of all deaths of children under the age of five in developing countries. Lack of access to water and sanitation undermines economic and social development, due to the costs of disease, the unequal burden on women and children and the high costs of accessing water (in terms of time and money) that reduce people's ability to secure other essential goods. In addition, without sufficient water, the ecosystem, for example the proper growth of trees and other flora necessary to prevent soil erosion, cannot be supported. The current water and sanitation crisis is caused by issues related to poverty, inequality and unequal power relationships. Water and sanitation policies and programmes all too often exclude marginalised groups and areas such as informal settlements and arid areas. In addition, institutional changes, such as shifts in land ownership, decentralisation and delegation of responsibilities for public services are in some circumstances reducing the reducing the accessibility of water and sanitation.

9.1. MDG AND WATER-SANITATION

The United Nations General Assembly Millennium Declaration resolved to halve the proportion of people who are unable to reach or to afford safe drinking water by 2015. The Johannesburg Plan of Implementation of the World Summit on Sustainable Development (WSSD), 2002, reiterated this commitment, and added a similar target in relation to the proportion of people who do not have adequate access to basic sanitation. The Millennium Development Goals are a set of goals and indicators that operationalise the commitments in the Millennium Declaration and the sanitation target set at the WSSD. Millennium Development Goal 7 on 'Ensuring Environmental Sustainability' is to *"halve, by 2015, the proportion of people without sustainable access to safe drinking water and basic sanitation"*.

There are also clear links between the other MDGs and access to water and sanitation, such as the importance of clean water for the eradication of extreme poverty and hunger, and adequate sanitation to achieve universal primary education and the reduction of child mortality. The MDG targets are understood by the United Nations to apply globally and within each country. While some countries are on track to meet the target for water and sanitation, many, particularly in Sub-Saharan Africa, are not. Even if the MDG target is met, there will still be millions of people without access to safe and adequate water and sanitation services. It will be necessary to set a further target date for reaching the rest of the population currently without access to these essential services.

9.2. WATER-SANITATION AND HEALTH

Nearly half the population of developing countries is suffering from diseases linked to inadequate water and sanitation. Drinking contaminated water transmits waterborne diseases such as cholera, typhoid, diarrhoea, viral hepatitis A, dysentery and dracunculiasis (guinea worm disease). Insufficient water for washing and personal hygiene leads to water-washed diseases, such as trachoma, and a lack of sanitation facilities can exacerbate water-based diseases such as schistosomiasis. Stagnant or still bodies of water can serve as a habitat for insects, such as the mosquitoes responsible for malaria, dengue fever and yellow fever. The effects are widespread:

- Approximately 4 billion cases of diarrhoea each year cause 2.2 million deaths, mostly among children under five – about 15 percent of all child deaths under the age of five in developing countries.
- Intestinal worms infect about ten percent of the population of developing countries. Intestinal parasitic infections can lead to malnutrition, anaemia and retarded growth. They can be controlled through better sanitation, hygiene and water supply.
- Six million people are blind from trachoma. Five hundred million people are at risk from this waterborne disease.
- Two hundred million people are infected with schistosomiasis, with 20 million suffering severe consequences.
- At any one time, close to half of all people in developing countries are suffering from health problems caused by poor water and sanitation. It has

been calculated that 443 million school days are lost each year to water-related illness.

- Over 1.2 million people die of malaria each year, the majority of whom are children. Poor management of water and wastewater drainage is a contributing factor to the incidence of malaria in many countries.

In addition, inadequate sanitation has a negative impact on the bladder and bowels, which are placed under undue pressure through insufficient access to sanitation facilities. The presence of a flushing toilet in the house can cut the risk of infant death by more than 30 percent. Carrying heavy vessels of water long distances also damages children's growing bones and causes back pain. The financial cost of treating such diseases goes far beyond the cost of ensuring access to water and sanitation services for all. While the diseases described above are not always life threatening, they can have negative life-long consequences, reducing a person's ability to learn effectively at school, continuing poverty into adulthood.21 The lack of adequate water and sanitation services also compound other illnesses or diseases - such as measles and pneumonia- and contributes to maternal mortality during childbirth. Poor water and sanitation services are a significant factor in high infant mortality rates.

9.3. SANITATION COVERAGE

Improved water sources' refers to sources that are likely to be safe, such as household connections, boreholes or public standpipes. Sources such as rivers or ponds or vendor-provided water are assumed unsafe. A household is only determined to have access to an improved water source if the source is within 100 metres of the home. 'Improved sanitation facilities' refers to facilities that are likely to ensure privacy and hygienic use, such as a connection to a public sewer or a simple pit latrine. Sources such as public or shared latrines are assumed unsafe. The definition of 'improved water supply' does not address certain aspects of the right to water and sanitation, for example, whether the cost of the water is affordable, whether the supply is continuous, how long it takes to collect water (including waiting time) and whether there are security concerns in collecting water. Therefore, the number of people with access to water short of the requirements in general is certainly much higher than the number of people with access to 'improved water supply.'

Table 9.1: Water and Sanitation Coverage, 2004

Region	*% without access to improved water*			*% without access to improved water*		
South Asia	6	19	15	27	63	62
Developing Countries	8	30	20	27	67	50
Developed countries	0	5	1	0	2	1
World	5	27	17	20	61	41

9.4. SANITATION IN INDIA

In India, many people in rural areas collect water of dubious quality from unprotected wells or surface water sources, often at a great distance from their homes, deterring them from collecting sufficient quantities. Toilets are often seen as unnecessary or unaffordable. In urban areas of India low-income groups - particularly those living in informal settlements - often lack access to adequate water supply and sanitation. Piped water supplies and sewers seldom cover informal areas, which means that people living there access water from a variety of generally inadequate water supply options, such as wells built close to latrines or small-scale water providers, such as door-to-door water vendors, whose water supplies may not be of good quality. Sanitation in most states is severely neglected by both governments and households. The number of toilets per inhabitant is generally inadequate, with no guarantee that they are hygienic to use. Because of the lack of sanitation at a household level (or, in many cases, at any level), many people use plastic bags, streets or other unhygienic places for defecation. The lack of access to water and sanitation has a severe effect on human health, particularly women health, exacerbates poverty and undermines economic development. Water shortages and unreliable access to water reduces crop production and livestock health and can undermine the viability of businesses run by poor women and men, including home-based activities.

Affordability of water and sanitation services is crucial to accessibility, but is all too often ignored, both in project implementation and in data collection on access to water and sanitation. Unless water and sanitation services are affordable to all, access to an adequate quantity of safe water and to safe toilets is threatened. In addition, human rights standards stipulate that the direct and indirect costs of securing water and sanitation should not reduce any person's capacity to acquire other essential goods and services, including food, housing, health services and education. This implies that 'ability to pay' will need to be considered in addition to 'willingness to pay' in designing water and sanitation tariffs.

9.5. INDIA'S RAPID URBANISATION

Urbanisation process in India is continuing at a significant rate, dramatically increasing the populations of urban informal settlements. Lack of access to water and sanitation services will increasingly become an urban problem, exacerbated by the insecure tenure of those living in informal settlements and the lack of planning for urban growth. This is often a symptom of the fact that informal settlements are frequently not politically accepted and the people who live there are not seen as a crucial part of the urban economy.

- Increasing levels of human and animal waste, agricultural run-off and industrial waste are polluting water sources in cities of India. There is frequently little control over wastewater, with insufficient legislation, regulation and monitoring to ensure that wastes are properly treated.
- Levels of drought are being exacerbated by alterations in weather patterns due to climate change and by desertification due to poor farming practices. Climate change is causing increasingly extreme weather patterns, which will have an impact on water availability and accessibility. Large section of India's population are in the most vulnerable position, not just because they lack the necessary resources to deal with emergencies effectively, but also because people are more likely to be living in vulnerable areas in sub-standard housing. Often governments lack the necessary resources and human capacity to tap new sources of water.

Majority of the population of India do not have the basic facilities and services. About 70 percent of the population do not have sanitary facilities and about 40 percent of the population do not have the access to safe drinking water. In the vast country like India only 50 percent of the population get the minimum health care facilities. Majority of the rural population do not have the access to these services. The following Table 18 depicts the comparative position of India with those of three other developed countries. All these advanced countries provide 100 % access to health care facilities.

The present techno-centric managerial approach of the health sector, has remained top- down and expert-oriented. It is highly insensitive, over professionalized and

Table 9.2 : Access of Population (in %)

Country	*Health Care*	*Safe Water*	*Sanitation*
India	50	63	29
U S A	100	90	98
U K	100	100	96
JAPAN	100	95	95

strongly urban biased. The modern hospital only deal with the tip of the ice berg. The medical profession in India has neither the capacity or training to deliver health to the common man in the villages. In India SPHC(Selected Primary Health Care) adopts a techno-centric managerial approach in delivering medical care but it does not encourage participation of the community in defining their health needs It adopts a powerful measure in its armory known as DALY (disability adjusted life year)which captures disability and life lost due to disease rather than mortality alone. It appears to offer an exciting opportunity for appropriate planning ,implementation and evaluation of health care. The government PHC service is virtually non-existent in the villages. All the vertical programs introduced one after another during last 50 years have perennially suffered not only from lack of sufficient fund but also from ignoring the need to involve people in a meaningful way.

9.6. WATER-SANITATION AND POVERTY

In many countries with an abundance of water and financial resources, communities living in poverty are denied sufficient water for drinking and other basic needs. Poor people are less able to cope with the negative health consequences of poor water and sanitation due to other factors such as malnutrition and poor educational standards. Lack of water also undermines people's ability to grow food and engage in income-generating activity.

This lack of safe water and sanitation also has an impact on society as a whole in terms of health costs and loss of human potential and resources. There is a strong overlap between poverty and the lack of access to safe water and sanitation, with a lack of access to water contributing to levels of poverty, as well as poverty being a factor in why people do not have access to water.The same is true regarding access to sanitation and levels of poverty. The continuing unequal access to water exacerbates existing poverty in the following manner:

a. It has high costs in terms of reducing ability to purchase other essential goods. Often it is those who can least afford it that pay higher prices for drinking water. On average, those on low incomes spend a significantly greater proportion of their income on water than do the wealthy, thereby affecting their ability to provide for other basic needs such as food, shelter, clothing, housing, health and education. The absolute price they pay to water can be ten times or more the price per litre supplied through the pipes.

b. It increase the Burden of disease in the poor households. Disease caused by lack of safe water and sanitation leads to illness and death. It also burdens those with low, or no, income with high health care costs and loss of ability to work to secure one's livelihood. Disease also causes children to miss school and adults to miss work. Safe water is also essential for home-based care of the sick or those who are HIV positive.

c. It involves unequal burden on women and children. The lack of adequate access to water in the context of poverty affects women and children in particular. Women and girl children have the traditional role of collecting water, often from great distances, affecting their health, their access to education and ability to earn a livelihood.They are in greatest physical contact in the domestic environment with contaminated water and human waste, exposing them to a host of biological pathogens and chemical hazards, including when disposing of their own family's waste.

Constant carrying of heavy weights of up to 20 kilograms (the weight of 20 litres of water) can lead to back and joint problems as well as sprains and fractures from falls. In some countries, spending five hours per day collecting water to meet the family's needs is not unusual. Girls shoulder the burden of water-hauling in Asia and Africa. In Africa, forty billion working hours, or 25 percent of household time, are spent each year carrying water. As the collection of water often has to take priority over other activities, it prevents women and girls from engaging in other productive activities, adult or basic education or other domestic responsibilities, rest and recreation. Lack of adequate sanitation causes women in particular significant physical and social distress, and can lead to long-term damage to the bowels. Growing evidence suggests that inadequate water supply and sanitation facilities in schools lead to decreased attendance and drop-outs.28 Better access to water increases school attendance by 15 percent in Tanzania, while 12 percent more girls stay in those Bangladeshi schools that offer the privacy of basic sanitation facilities.

d. It retards productivity in the entire economy.Developing countries lose a significant percentage of GDP due to lack of productivity and other related costs from lack of access to adequate water and sanitation. The main burden rests with those living below the poverty line. The international community has recognised the importance of alleviating these problems, reflected in the Millennium Development Goals.

Water resource management is crucial for poverty, food, fodder and ecological security. It is more crucial for gender equality. Agriculture accounts for 70-80% of the total water consumption in the country. Infact livelihood security is critically linked with water security, which means: People and communities have reliable and adequate access to water for different needs, present as well as future and able to take the advantage of different opportunities that water resource present and are protected from water related hazards. Water security is indispensable for livelihood security. It addresses inter and intra regional as well as inter household inequalities in the process of growth, development and ecological balance. In the context of scarcity, allocation of water should be governed by optimality rather than productivity (as optimality combines both economic and social benefits)

9.7. ENVIRONMENTAL SUSTAINABILITY

In recent years some of the gains made in the provision of safe water are being threatened by over-extraction, competition and environmental pollution. In many regions throughout the developing world, sources of water traditionally available in abundance for domestic use is now disappearing. As technological advances were being made in the drinking water sector, parallel advances were being made in the irrigation sector. These advances, together with the increasing demand to produce more food and cash crops from the same land has led to massive programmes of intensive irrigation in many countries. While the technology has allowed drinking water to be pumped from the ground through a borewell and handpump at the rate of thousands of liters per day, the same technology has provided the means to pump hundreds of thousands of litres per day from irrigation borewells (or from surface water sources, whose depletion ultimately affects the groundwater aquifers). Parallel to the over-exploitation of water is an alarming increase in the pollution of water from industry and agriculture, and from other sources. As a result, some handpumps which once provided clean water are now abandoned because of quality problems and people are forced to return to ponds and streams (which are also likely to be more polluted than they were 10 or 20 years ago) for their drinking water needs.

Water should be treated as a environmental, social and cultural good, and not primarily as an economic good. But the present practice of people is different. They use it as if is a free gift of nature. They think to have free riding on the free good. Water should be priced so that all persons, including the poor, can afford an adequate supply of safe water. It also indicates that "The manner of the realisation of the right to water must be sustainable, so as to ensure that the right to water can be realised for present and future generations." Charging for the use of water above the essential amount is one means of ensuring water services are also environmentally sustainable. This would suggest that it is necessary to price water in such a manner to discourage wasteful consumption. From an economic perspective, water services need to be paid for, either from user payments or from public funding. From a human rights perspective, public funds need to be directed towards extension of service for the poor and for ensuring that such service is affordable.

9.8. CHANGING CONTEXTS

A number of issues common to all countries explain current levels of lack of access to water and sanitation: In many situations it excludes particular groups

- Poor people are excluded from decision-making, and their needs are seldom prioritised.
- Resources are used to provide high quality services to a few or to fund prestigious large-scale projects,

such as dam construction or river diversion, rather than low-cost alternatives, such as rainwater harvesting or sand dams. The latter would be more likely to reach the majority of people without access to water and sanitation services, who live in rural areas.

- Unpopular minorities are excluded from access to water and sanitation for political reasons
- Deprived urban areas, remote rural areas, semi-arid and arid areas are frequently neglected or intentionally excluded from government programmes for infrastructure development and maintenance. This results in insufficient infrastructure and facilities for water and sanitation.
- There is a lack of culturally sensitive and pro-poor policies for the allocation of water resources between the different sectors of water use, and also within the different sectors (agriculture, education, health, water resources.)

9.9. PUBLIC AUTHORITY

Governments can act to ensure affordability of water and sanitation services by:

1. Setting standards for water and sanitation pricing according to ability to pay in order to ensure that payment for water, including indirect costs, does not reduce a person's ability to buy other essential goods and services.
2. Designing, monitoring and controlling charges by water and sanitation utilities and small-scale service providers to households, schools, health institutions and workplaces.
3. Prioritising available public investment towards the construction and maintenance of water and

sanitation infrastructure and facilities and subsiding these costs for low-income users.

4. Reducing costs of securing access by ensuring that a broad range of levels of services and facilities areavailable and ensuring the potential for progressive upgrading.

5. Establishing flexible payment terms, such as phased connection charges, removal of requirements for deposits, grace periods and contributions in kind, based on participation of users, in particular low-income users and vulnerable and marginalised groups.

6. Providing subsidies for water and sanitation services that target the lowest income, vulnerable and marginalised persons.

7. Increasing public financing for subsidy programmes for the poor through measures such as: cross-subsidies between higher and lower income groups, reducing high-cost interventions, eliminating subsidies that primarily benefit upper and middle income groups, ring-fencing of water and sanitation revenues, improving efficiency, increasing national budgetary allocations and better targeted and increased international assistance.

8. Reviewing laws, regulations and taxes that may raise costs beyond affordable levels, for example taxation of equipment required for service provision, in particular small-scale provision.

9. Integrating ability to pay considerations into disconnection policies and ensuring that where disconnections are carried out, they do not lead to denial of the minimum essential amount of water.

A. Non-domestic Use

Water is required for a range of different purposes,

besides personal and domestic uses For instance, water is necessary to produce food (right to adequate food) and ensure environmental hygiene (right to health). Water is essential for securing livelihoods (right to gain a living by work) and enjoying certain cultural practices (right to take part in cultural life). Nevertheless, priority in the allocation of water must be given to the right to water for personal and domestic uses. Priority should also be given to the water resources required to prevent starvation and disease, as well as water required to meet the core obligations of each of the Covenant rights.

While personal and domestic uses of water are primary, it is also essential for other uses, such as agriculture, industry (whether small- or large-scale), and to protect the environment. Water is also essential for food security and income-generating activities. Water shortages and unreliable access to water can reduce crop production and livestock health32 and can undermine the viability of businesses run by poor women and men, including home-based activities. Ecosystems also require water to remain viable. Without sufficient water, the ecosystem, for example the proper growth of trees and other flora necessary to prevent soil erosion, cannot be supported. Water availability, allocation and sustainability involves trade-offs between these uses.

b. Lack of Awareness

Many actors in the water and sanitation sector are unfamiliar with international law and human rights standards. We should make wider campaign and contribute to the learning required for both the development and human rights communities to effectively deal with the right to water and sanitation. WE should clarify the implications of the right to water and sanitation.

Misconceptions	*Clarifications*
It entitles people for free water	Water and sanitation needs to be affordable for all
It allows for unlimited use of water	It ensures every one for sufficient water for domestic use ,to be realized in a sustainable manner for present and future generations
It entitles everyone to a household connection	Water and sanitation need to be within or immediate vicinity of the household
If all people do not have access to water and sanitation, then country violates the rights	State should take steps to progressively realize the right
It entitles to get water from other countries	People can not claim that. However water courses can be shared equitably

There can sometimes be unrealistic aspirations about what recognition of the right can achieve. Recognition of the right to water and sanitation can help shape policy development and legitimise claims for access, but it does not automatically lead to implementation. Significant efforts are required to implement and advocate for the right.

c. High Cost and Affordability

A common barrier to accessing a sufficient quantity of safe water and sanitation is the cost involved, in terms of both money and time, leading many to seek cheaper, if less safe, alternatives. The cost of obtaining water and sanitation often reduces the ability of individuals and communities to pay for other essential goods including food, housing, education and health.

In the rural areas of many countries, as the water table changes due to erosion or overuse, and ground and surface water becomes increasingly polluted, traditional sources no longer provide safe water. Deeper wells, involving expensive equipment and a specialised workforce are required to improve and maintain water supplies. In urban areas, large numbers of residents, (primarily those in informal settlements) are excluded from the piped network, forcing them to turn to alternative supplies of water delivered by small-scale providers that can be unreliable and unsafe – in some cases originating from shallow wells or surface water, which is likely to be polluted. This water generally costs more per litre than water provided by municipal water companies. This has led to inequitable access to resources, with the poor paying significantly more per litre for an inadequate service than their richer counterparts in serviced areas. Those who do not rely on small-scale providers rely either on wells or on surface waters that are likely to be contaminated, or they are forced to travel long distances to secure supplies from alternative piped sources. The affordability of sanitation is equally a challenge, primarily the high cost of connecting to a sewerage system or of constructing and maintaining a latrine.

d. Lack of Gender Disaggregated Data

Due to a lack of adequate statistics, the number of people without access to water is often underestimated. As many of the informal settlements in urban areas are unrecognised by the local or national governments, the exact number of residents living in these settlements is often unknown, as is the status of water provision. Tenants may also be missing from the statistics where landlords do not declare them. Water can also be prohibitively expensive, so that even where water is available, people do not have access to a sufficient quantity for health and hygiene practices. As a result, there is considerable inequality in distribution of water and sanitation services in urban areas, with smaller urban centres particularly badly affected. Statistics for access to water and sanitation services in urban areas therefore tend to be uneven –more urban-focused, which uses different criteria to measure access to water and sanitation in urban areas. Further to this, while people may use safe sources of water for some of their purposes, such as for drinking, this source may be prohibitively expensive to use for all domestic uses, forcing people to use unsafe sources for washing or cooking. This is not reflected in the statistics of access to water supply.

9.10. MAIN STAKEHOLDERS

Different stakeholders can act to implement the right to water and sanitation. National, regional and local governments (both the executive/administrative branch of government and legislative branches/municipal councils) are the key actors in setting up the conditions to ensure the right to water and sanitation services. Achieving this objective involves actions by governments at national, regional and local levels, in the roles of policy making, resource allocation, and service provision regulation.

The main actors involved in the realisation of the right to water and sanitation are:

1. International organisations.
2. Industrial and agricultural water users.
3. Policy makers - allocators of resources and regulators – including national and local legislative and administrative authorities, catchment management bodies and officials who are responsible not only for water and sanitation provision but also for related services, such as social, health, development, information gathering and statistics, and budget issues.
4. Services providers- Agencies providing water and sanitation– ranging from public, private or cooperative large-scale network providers to small-

scale water or sanitation providers composed of private, civil society or community efforts.

5. Public institutions- that promote, monitor and enforce human rights and those which are responsible for monitoring and regulating delivery of water and sanitation services – including human rights institutions, ombudsmen, judicial courts and regulators.
6. Civil society organizations- such as non-governmental organisations, academic institutions, the media and professional bodies.
7. Right holders - all individuals: man, woman or child, whatever their residential status.

A. Role of the Government

Governments, in most cases local authorities or public companies, operate the vast majority of water and sanitation utility services although some services are managed by public water companies . Basic sanitation and hygiene promotion is considered a responsibility of public health services, although some responsibilities are borne by water and education agencies. In addition to complying with relevant legislation and policies, water, sanitation and health service providers have the following roles:

i). In the case of utilities, extending water and sewerage services to schools, health centres and other public centres where these are needed (with separate facilities for males and females) and to households, including those occupied by marginalised and vulnerable groups.

ii). Improving affordability of water and sanitation services through increased efficiency and flexibility of services.

iii). Carrying out sanitation and hygiene promotion and training and providing financial assistance to small-scale providers and households that rely on small-scale facilities.

iv). Ensuring environmentally sound disposal of waste.

B. Role of the Community

The communities and Individuals can play the following roles:

i. Identifying the needs and priorities and monitoring service provision,

ii. proposing appropriate water and sanitation policies to government

iii. participating in consideration of such policies.

iv. obtaining information about their rights and disseminating it to others

v. advocating for implementation of their rights

vi. contributing to the operational and financial sustainability of such facilities and services

vii. taking the responsibility for constructing household toilets.

viii. avoiding contamination of water resources, spreading knowledge of good hygiene practices.

ix. assisting vulnerable and marginalised section of community to have such access

9.11. NON-DISCRIMINATION

In India section and sectors tend to gain more due to their higher political visibility. Many of those who develop, influence and implement law and policy consider certain groups to be less valued members of society. Consequently, members of these groups lack access to basic entitlements. It is therefore necessary that water and sanitation policies prevent and remedy discriminatory political decisions and practices. Human rights principles highlight the need to actively design water and sanitation policy that prioritises and addresses the needs of vulnerable and marginalised groups, rather than treating all persons as facing identical challenges in accessing safe water and improved sanitation. It is important for policy-makers and implementers to dedicate time and resources to reviewing whether vulnerable and marginalised groups are being included, and that their needs are being taken into account. The following list encompasses both vulnerable and marginalised groups which include:

- Women.
- Children.
- Inhabitants of rural and urban deprived areas.
- Indigenous peoples.
- Nomadic and traveller communities.
- Refugees, asylum seekers, internally displaced persons and returnees.
- Older persons, persons with disabilities and people with serious or chronic illnesses.
- Victims of natural disasters and persons living in disaster-prone areas.
- People living in water scarce-regions (arid and semi-arid areas and some small islands).
- Persons under custody.

Vulnerable groups are those, such as children and the disabled, who require special attention due to their developmental or physical limitations. Marginalised groups, such as women and ethnic minorities, require special attention due to their historical and cultural discrimination, as well as from their general under-representation in political decision-making, which has led to the neglect of their needs in policy making. Everybody, including the most vulnerable and marginalised, is entitled to have access to water and sanitation without discrimination. The principle of non-discrimination is a fundamental human right in itself and is included in all international human rights treaties. It prohibits any distinction, exclusion, restriction or preference, which is based on any ground – such as race, colour, sex, language, religion, political or other opinion, national or social origin, property, birth or other status - that differentiates without any legitimate reason.

9.12. ENSURING AFFORDABILITY

The governments can act to ensure affordability.

i). Setting standards for water and sanitation pricing according to the ability to pay,

ii). Designing and monitoring chargesof water and sanitation utilities

iii). Prioritising public investment towards the construction and maintenance of water and sanitation infrastructure

iv). Reducing costs of securing access by ensuring that a broad range of levels of services and facilities are available.

v). Establishing flexible payment terms, grace periods and contributions in kind, based on participation of users, particularly marginalised groups.

vi). Providing subsidies for water and sanitation services that targeted towards the vulnerable and marginalised people.

vii). Increasing public financing for subsidy programmes for the poor through measures such as:

- increasing national budgetary allocations
- better targeting
- cross-subsidies between higher and lower income groups, reducing high-cost interventions

- eliminating subsidies that primarily benefit upper and middle income groups
- ring-fencing of water and sanitation revenues
- improving efficiency

The greatest role of the civil society is to raise and maintain public awareness of the challenge of securing the right to water and sanitation for all, which can otherwise can be easily forgotten, or reduced solely to policy considerations, and dealt with without adequate reference to human rights dimensions. They should expose of the contextual issues surrounding the water and sanitation crisis in India They should offer incisive examples from rural scenario that enrich the description of the human right to water and sanitation. Scepticism about the human right to water and sanitation – as with all economic, social and cultural rights – will usually focus on questions of resource allocation. Therefore, they should focus on affordability and financing of water sanitation.

9.13. PROTECTING WATER CATCHMENT AREAS

The destruction of forests, through methods such as slash-and-burn cultivation, can have serious, detrimental effects on the reliability of water resources. As a result it may be necessary to restrict certain forms of cultivation and logging in forest areas that form the catchment for water sources relied upon by local communities. Such measures require close co-operation between a wide range of government bodies, including those responsible for land use, agriculture, water resources management and environmental protection. Such restrictions may undermine the livelihoods and food security of the affected people, and therefore the right to an adequate standard of living, housing and food. In addition, there are situations where communities may need to be re-located from a catchment area in order to maintain its protected status. Relocations can undermine the human rights to housing and the right to an adequate standard of living, and, where no public services are available to evictees, the right to water and sanitation, health and education. Thus *national measures designed to realize the right to water should not interfere with the enjoyment of other human rights.*"27 Thus, such circumstances call for the provision of alternative land for housing and agricultural purposes and for evictions. Forced evictions are becoming increasingly common as communities are displaced in order to facilitate economic development, and in some cases, environmental protection. Evictees are normally not provided with alternative land, or where land is provided, water and sanitation services are lacking. As a result forced evictions normally lead to deprivations of access to water and sanitation.

9.14. INTERNATIONAL COOPERATION:

The global crisis in access to water and sanitation is one of the central issues that the international community as a whole has pledged to address through the UN Millennium Declaration. Specifically, the Declaration undertook to halve, between 2000 and 2015, the proportion of people who are unable to reach or to afford safe drinking water. At the 2002 Johannesburg World Summit on Sustainable Development, all governments further committed to halving the proportion of people without access to basic sanitation by 2015. However, providing all those unserved with access to basic water and sanitation services poses considerable financial and technical challenges, particularly as the vast majority of people that lack access to these essential services live in developing countries, many of which, in particular the least developed countries, do not have sufficient financial resources and administrative capacity to provide for the right to water ad sanitation. International co-operation is often seen as relevant only in regard to development assistance.

However, the right to water and sanitation is dependant on a number of international dynamics that are beyond the control of any one government. These dynamics include international trade and investment, economic sanctions, pollution of shared resources such as the atmosphere and transboundary resources, the use of transboundary resources and international armed conflict. The full realisation of the right to water and sanitation globally is therefore not possible without international co-operation in these areas.

9.15. NATIONAL COORDINATION

It is very much necessary to ensure co-ordination between all relevant ministries and departments. When developing national and local plans of action for water and sanitation it is important to take into consideration the wide range of ministries and departments with responsibilities for water and sanitation. For example, sanitation falls within the responsibilities of agencies responsible for water, sanitation, health, local government, land use management, education, among others. As water is required for more than personal and domestic uses, its allocation involves agencies, those that are responsible for health, environment, finance, land, housing, energy, agriculture and industry, in addition to those involved in water and sanitation. Coordination between all relevant ministries and departments to ensure that there is no overlap of efforts or contradictory policies formed is very crucial.

9.16. COMMUNITY PARTICIPATION

The right to water and sanitation is an entitlement held by all people, and which has a legal foundation. It therefore provides a strong basis for holding all relevant actors accountable. There has to be acccess to information and participation. Each policy, programme or strategy concerning water and sanitation is to include, as an integral element, the right of all people to participate in decision-making processes that may affect their rights.Special efforts are made by governments to ensure the equitable representation in decision-making of marginalized groups, in particular women. Communities have the right to determine what type of water and sanitation services they require and how to manage those services.13 All people will have full and equal access to information concerning water, sanitation and the environment. Accountability: Persons or groups denied their right to water and sanitation have access to effective judicial or other appropriate remedies, for example courts, national ombudspersons or human right commissions

It should follow the principle of non-discrimination and inclusion of vulnerable and marginalised groups: This means that access to water and sanitation is ensured for everybody, including vulnerable or marginalised groups, and without discrimination. Non-discrimination implies that there is no distinction, exclusion, restriction or preference - based on any ground (e.g. race, colour, sex, age, language, religion, political or other opinion, national or social origin, property, birth, physical or mental disability, health status (including HIV/AIDS), sexual orientation and civil, political, social or other status) - which has the intention or effect of impairing the equal exercise of the right. Non-discrimination also includes proactive measures to ensure that the particular needs of vulnerable or marginalized groups, such as women, persons with illnesses, people living in informal settlements, and excluded minorities are met.

Human rights, and their underlying values of dignity, freedom and equality, emerged from a variety of sources, including religious convictions and concerns for social justice. They are rooted in historic global struggles, such as the struggles for freedom, democracy and independence. Treating human beings with dignity and equality – universally shared values – requires that all people have access to water and sanitation. International human rights treaties, negotiated by State officials representing all cultures and civilizations, provide an authoritative definition of human rights and a tool with which to implement them. The right to water and sanitation is founded in a number of international legal treaties and political declarations in the fields of human rights, environmental law and humanitarian law. It is also reflected in a number of national constitutions, legislation and cases.

9.17. CONCLUDING REMARKS

Integrated water management can only be possible if the community is empowered through decentralization and is free to make decisions on their natural resource management. The four main important resources are land, water, livestock and forest which form the village ecosystem. Without a balanced management of all of these four basic resources, the development process cannot be sustainable. The development programmes must be built around a sound land-water-forest-livestock oriented model with decision making at the micro-level. Rural water supply should not be treated as a mere service delivery process but as a step towards household water security. Water security requires household, community and national actions to protect and preserve water sources, to use water as a scarce resource and to ensure its equitable supply. Investment in the capacity building of the community in planning, development, implementation and maintenance of the water supply project is one of the first steps toward sustainable development. To analyze the complete socioeconomic impact of a water supply, sanitation and hygiene project, the full impact should be taken into consideration. They include less disease, better education for children (particularly girls), better nutrition for mothers and children, time energy saving for women and secure livelihoods. To achieve maximum impact through water and sanitation interventions in rural communities there is a need for multilevel and intersectoral actions.

The MDGs are not an end in themselves. Full coverage of safe water and sanitation and resulting poverty reduction is the end, but the goals are probably the best method we have to move us in that direction. The spirit of the MDGs is global and the MDGs target those countries that are in most need of help rather than simply aiming to achieve an arbitrary goal.It is necessary to have social and gender equity in the availability, access and control of all potential resources. Communities should be perceived as informed consumers, clients and managers, capable of making choices as to the type of services they have the capacity to provide rather than passive receivers. Communities must also acquire management and organisation skills with leadership capable of defining tasks and managing facilities. Public authorities responsible for water and sanitation must change from "benefactors" to "facilitators" who enable communities to make their own decisions. Self-help activities in the construction phase are often ambiguous.

The resources need to be organized to cultivate an empowering environment by promoting and supporting selfmotivation, building skills, communicating knowledge and aligning social service systems. The only way the goal of sustainable development can be achieved especially in fragile eco-regions is through deepening democratic values and participation at the grassroots level. Institutional decentralization along with empowerment will ensure the survival base of the rural economy and will promote growth.

We should make appropriate policy design and corresponding efforts to improve access to water and sanitation. The governments, policy makers and practitioners should implement the human right to water and sanitation. National and local governments should adopt practical, affordable and sustainable strategies, policies and solutions to address the problems they are facing in realising the right to water and sanitation. The public authorities in India should distinguish between the challenges facing urban and rural areas, and propose policy approaches for each that address their different circumstances. We should bring a gender perspective to the task ahead - ensuring that the human right to water and sanitation is realised for all.

REFERENCES

1. Agarwal, Anil and Narain, Sunita. *Dying Wisdom: The rise fall and potential of India's traditional water harvesting systems. A Citizen's report*. New Delhi: CSE, 1997.
2. Bhattacharya, S., and Dave, P.N. *Project Nutrition, Health Education and Environmental Sanitation: an impact study*. Delhi: National Council of Educational Research, 1991
3. Biswas, Asit K. *United Nations Water Conference: Summary and Main Documents*. Oxford: Pergamon Press for the United Nations, 1978. Agency: United Nations
4. Bijlani, H. U. and Rao, P. S. N. *Water supply and sanitation in India* . New Delhi: Oxford& IBH Pub. Co., 1990
5. Black, M. *Thirsty cities: water, sanitation and the urban poor*. London: WaterAid, 1995. Agency: Water Aid
6. Davis, J., Garvey, G. and Wood, M. *Developing and managing community water supplies* Oxford: Oxfam, 1993. Agency: OXFAM
7. Gleick, P., 'The Human Right to Water', Water Policy, Vol. 1 No. 5 (1999).
8. Mitra, Swati. *Communication materials data bank for rural community-based water and sanitation initiatives*. New Delhi, World Bank, 1994.
9. Munasinghe, Mohan. *Water supply and environmental management: developing world applications* . Boulder: Westview Press, 1992
10. Nigam, Ashok and Heyward, Richard. *Improving Cost-*

Effectiveness of Rural Water Supply and Sanitation Programmes. New York: UNICEF, 1993. Agency: UNICEF

11. Narayan, Deepa. *The contribution of people's participation, occasional paper series ; no. 1).* Washington, DC, USA, World Bank, 1995. Agency: World Bank

12. Okun, Daniel Alexander. *Capacity Building for Water Resources Management.* New York:UNDP, 1991. Agency: UNDP

13. Postel, Sandra. *The Last Oasis: Facing water scarcity.* London: Earthscan, 1992

14. Serageldin, Ismail. *Toward sustainable management of water resources* . Washington, D.C.: World Bank, 1995. Agency: World Bank

15. Subramanian, A et al (eds . *UserOrganizations for Sustainable Water Services. World Bank Technical Paper No. 354* . Washington: World Bank, 1997. Agency: World Bank

16. UNDP. *The New Delhi Statement from the GlobalConsultation on Safe Water and Sanitation for the 1990s, Sept. 1990, New Delhi.* New York: UNDP, 1990.

17. UNICEF. *Planning for Health and Sanitation Programmes: A Workshop Summary (April 21-22, 1993).* New York: UNICEF, 1993.

18. World Bank. *Water Resources Management: A World Bank Policy Paper.* Washington: World Bank, 1993. Agency: World Bank

19. WHO. *Community Water Supply and Sanitation in South-East Asia Region: International Drinking Water Supply and Sanitation Decade Assessment· and Perspective for the 1990s.* New Delhi: World Health Organization, 1993

20. Wakeman, Wendy. *Gender Issues Sourcebook for Water and Sanitation Projects.*

21. Washington: World Bank, 1995. Agency: World Bank/ Collaborative Council.

10

Natural Disasters and Women

The public authority are myopic in regards to the economic effects of natural calamities. They suffer from inaccurate understanding about natural calamities and their consequences and remedies. With hasty understanding they respond very randomly to post disaster crisis. Each natural disaster contributes to social distortions and environmental imbalance. An integrated development of disaster affected areas has the real danger of floundering on tile rock of departmentalism. Hence this chapter argues that in order to overcome these problems it is imperative to devise an engendered approach with in a sound organisational framework.

Natural calamities[1] occur in all countries of the world. Natural disasters refers to the catastrophic situation in which day to day pattern of life on the earth are suddenly disrupted and people are plunged into helplessness and sufferings. Globally, approximately 2 billion people were affected by natural or technological disasters between 1990–1999, with almost 600 000 fatalities. More than 86% of people killed by disasters during this period succumbed to natural events. Windstorms claimed the largest proportion of lives (35%) while floods accounted for the largest proportion of people affected (75%).. Since the mid-1990s there has been an increase in the recorded number of all types of disasters and the number of recorded fatalities resulting from disasters, especially in developing areas and despite disaster preparedness programmes. People in low-income countries are 4 times more likely to die from extreme natural events than those in high-income countries. During the 1990s, more than two-thirds of the deaths from disasters occurred in Asia, which was also the continent most frequently hit by disasters· The frequency and intensity of all disasters in the third world countries is very high. The gravity of the problem associated with each type of disaster and with each region significantly differs. But the public authority suffers from inaccurate understanding about natural calamities and their consequences and remedies, be it Bhuj-Koch quake, Latuer's quake, Orissa's super cyclone, Andhra's super flood or Kalahandi's drought or Bhopal gas tragedy. Two third of world's population live in developing countries and ninety five percent of disaster related deaths occur in these countries. Among all continents 87 percent of deaths have occurred due to disasters in Asia alone. Earthquake, Typhoon, cyclones, hurricanes and Tornadoes together account for 70 percent of all disaster related deaths in India. The annual average number of people killed and affected by various kinds of natural disasters is always increasing. The Asian scenario is worsening continually[2]. It is revealed from the following table 10.1.

Table 10.1 : No of People died and Affected

	Annual Average Number of People killed (1972-96)		
	World	*Asia*	*India(1987-96)*
Killed	136,790	46,353	5,063
Affected	143512,164	126092,412	56563,631

Every natural calamity, though varying in its cause,

frequency, predictability, impact, duration and controllability rolls back the economic growth. Sometimes people's actions responses to natural disasters tend to be careless, spontaneous, unplanned and uncoordinated, which leads to further man made crises. Generally the coping capacity to these calamities is more in advanced countries than in the underdeveloped countries. A large portion of world's natural disasters is experienced in poor regions, which are badly equipped to deal with such events. This results in substantial loss of life, social upheaval in the first instance and destruction and disruption of vital production and communication in the second instance[33] Awasthi et al (1982) p.2.

It is estimated that the material value of losses in these countries exceeds the annual increase in GNP, thus retarding the development or even resulting in negative economic growth, despite substantial aid currently being given by advanced industrialised nations to developing countries for disaster relief.

Within Asia 24 per cent of deaths due to disaster occurred in India. Roughly 60 per cent of all disasters in India emanate from floods and high winds. This is yet another indicator that India urgently needs to pay attention to mitigating the effects of disasters. The total expenditure on relief and reconstruction in Gujarat after the earthquake has been to the turn of Rs.11,500 crore. About 54 per cent of the subcontinents land mass is vulnerable to earthquakes while about four crore hectares is vulnerable to periodic floods. India's key vulnerabilities are: (1) coastal states, particularly the east coast and Gujarat are vulnerable to cyclones; (ii) four crore hectare land mass is vulnerable to drought; (iii) fifty-five per cent of total area is in the seismic zone III-V, and so is vulnerable to earthquakes, (iv) sub-Himalayan/Western Ghat is vulnerable to landslides.

Table 10.2 : Damage due to Natural Disasters in India

Year	*People affected (in lakhs)*	*Houses and buildings, partially or totally damaged*	*Amount of property damage/ loss (Rs. In crore)*
1985	595.6	2,449,878	40.06
1986	550.0	2.049,277	30.74
1987	483.4	2,919,380	20.57
1988	101.5	242,533	40.63
1989	30.1	782,340	20.41
1990	31.7	1,019,930	10.71
1991	342.7	1,190,109	10.90
1992	190.9	570,969	20.05
1993	462.4	1,529,916	50.80
1994	235.3	1,051,223	10.83
1995	543.5	2,008,355	40.73
1996	549.9	2,376,693	50.43
1997	443.8	1,103,549	n.a
1998	521.7	1,563,405	0.72
1999	501.7	3,104,064	1,020.97
2000	594.34	2,736,355	800.00
2001	788.19	846,878	12,000.00

Source: Annual Reports, NDM Division, Ministry of Agriculture, cited from Disaster Management - The Development Perspective; Vol.I,Ch.7, The Tenth Five Year Plan Document (2002-2007) GoI.

The table 10.2 quantifies the damage to infrastructure, property and the lives, spanning 16 years from 1985 to 2001. The figures definitely reflect an upward graph, asserting the urgency and the severity of the ever-increasing disasters in their scale as well as nature.

All this highlights how we are constantly facing the increase in the number of disasters more than in the past, in addition to the dangers that we are already coping with. Having said this, humanitarian aid (in terms of government, international non-governmental organizations (INGOS), non-governmental organizations (NGOS) etc.) which earlier became active only at the stage of post-disaster has now started to proactively plan to mitigate the effects of looming disasters. This is a multifaceted task, yet it is being planned by different departments and organizations and approaches. Development programmes are now consciously trying to link disasters with supporting concerns of development. Disaster management in itself has begun to introspect on its approaches, thus giving way to the "disaster risk reduction" approach, which involves planning right from preparing the groups at the village level to prepositions of stocks at the state and district level. While this effectively strengthens the efforts canalized towards mitigating the effects of disaster, we still need to streamline managing disasters. The statistical data given in the table highlights the urgency and the magnitude with which disaster preparedness has to be undertaken, to ensure the lives of women and men

10.1. NATURE'S CRUELTY

In India, eight states: Orissa, West Bengal, Andhra, Tamilnadu, Karnatak, Maharastra and Gujrat are more cyclones prone, flood prone and quake prone states. It is irony to observe that disaster prone areas have been high-density centers of population. So all these disasters have tended to be more destructive by affecting ever-larger concentration of population. The aftermath effects of these disasters should be viewed not only in humanitarian and broad social terms but also in terms of economic terms since it is indeed a formidable obstacle to economic development of the region. One should be concerned with the effects on the population they afflict. We should examine the demographic and environmental consequences of such crises in terms, for example, of their effect on morbidity, mortality, fertility, migration as well as their impact on social, economic and political structures.

India has such diversity that one can form contrary opinion about its hydrological conditions and ecological characteristics. When drought occurs in KBK districts regularly a feeling that nature has been too niggardly in the matter of water endowment comes to many of us. As news of flood havoc in almost every year in the coastal districts, with the excessive rainfall pours in, we begin feeling a sense of tyranny of our water bounty. In between these fluctuating moods, one gets really baffled. Unfortunately India has suffered from simultaneous occurrence of drought, flood and earthquake with in one year. One tends to believe in Malthusian theory of population. Although human-made technological disasters reportedly claim fewer lives than natural disasters (13.5% during 1990-99), they have profound implications for public health. For example, about 5 million people, including 500 000 children, are estimated to have been affected by the Chernobyl nuclear disaster in 1986. Nearly a decade and a half later, there continues to be a large case load of health problems linked to the Chernobyl disaster. Many of the survivors of the 1984 Bhopal industrial disaster have suffered respiratory damage or are affected by repeated infections because of compromised immune or metabolic systems.

10.2. SUPER CYCLONE IN ORISSA

Cyclone is the most menancing natural calamity, which haunts the Indian peninsula and repeats every few years. In the state of Orissa, which belongs to the eastern part of India, constitutes the coastal belt of Bay of Bengal. It is the poorest and most backward region of the country. In this region it is observed that from prehistoric time flood plains, adjoining the banks of rivers and cyclone prone areas have been high-density centers of rural population. So all types of natural calamities such as flood, cyclone and droughts are annual recurring phenomena in this state.

So all these disasters have tended to be more destructive by affecting ever larger concentration of population Orissa has such diversity that one can form contrary opinion about its hydrological conditions and ecological characteristics. When drought occurs in KBK districts regularly a feeling that nature has been too niggardly in the matter of water endowment comes to many of us. As news of flood havoc in almost every year in the coastal districts, with the excessive rainfall pours in, we begin feeling a sense of tyranny of our water bounty. In between these fluctuating moods, one gets baffled by seemingly paradoxical phenomenon of simultaneous occurrence of drought and flood in the same calendar year.

10.2. IMPACT OF SUPER CYCLONE

The super cyclone had exposed the people and the landscape to the impact of three natural hazards: storm surge, high speed wind and heavy torrential rain. The combination of these three resulted three types impacts ie. Physical destruction, saline inundation and flooding respectively. Consequently the cyclone caused damages in different ways, affecting villages /towns either in single or multiple ways. Such was the fury of nature that two district head quarters in worst affected areas ie. Jagatsinghpur and Kendrapara could not be reached for 4 days. Massive fallen trees, uprooted electric poles and wires blocked the roads. All channels of communication had failed. The state remained cut off with the outside world during the cyclone. All major coastal towns of Orissa had been badly affected. Vast tracts of coastal areas and parts of Cuttack and Bhubaneswar remained submerged by tidal water and rainwater respectively. Thirty five villages along the seas coast in Erasama block (Jagatsinghpur district) have been washed away. In addition ,the rivers like Baitarani, Budha balanga, Subarnarekha, Salandi and Kharasrotta were in spate due to incessant rain. As a result the flash of flood cut off almost all roads to Jagatsinghpur, Kendrapara , Jajpur and Bhadrak districts had hampered rescue and relief operations in these districts. About 400 villages were not accessible even 4 weeks after the cyclone. Part of Puri district bore the burnt of the onslaught of the cyclone with reported storm surge of over 7 meters. In some areas saline water had penetrated to 15 to 25 km inland and had swept away many coastal villages. In port town of Paradeep ,where the water column of 8 to 10 meter entered the town for about I km water spread inside. The inland districts of Cuttack and Khurda were also affected by the storm and flood. Other districts affected by heavy rainfall were Jajpur, Mayurbhanj, Nayagarh ,Dhenkanal and Keonjhar.

Table 10.3 : Super Cyclonic Storm (Oct. 29-30, 1999)

Population affected	15681072
Villages affected	14586
Districts affected	12
Human lives lost	9893
Livestock perished	444531
Houses Damaged	1661683
Crop area damaged(ha)	1843047

Water logging due to flooding and saline inundation caused serious damages. About 90 to 100% of the crop in the affected districts was cyclone hit at the most vulnerable time of paddy. The loss of stored food, seeds and crops were overwhelming as the harvest was about to take place within 3 weeks. As a result the food security of many households was severely endangered on long term basis. There was wide spread contamination of drinking water sources due to large scale inundation. Most of the hand pumps were damaged. Numerous wells, tanks, ponds and canals got severely polluted. In 10 cities water supply system were completely broken down. Over 84000 tube wells in rural areas had been submerged and rendered defunct. Thousands of open dugwells were contaminated. The municipality sewerage system has also extensively damaged It has affected more than 15 million people in the 12 districts.

The rural population(13.7 million) was much worse hit than the urban (1.9 million) It had taken a toll of 9893 human lives [3] and left 7507 persons injured. As per the estimates , about 7000 lives lost due to tidal surge and about 2000 lives due to cyclonic flood . And 8119 lives were reported lost from Jagatsinghpur district alone. A total of 3.7 million children were affected and 1500 have been orphaned. Practically all kutcha houses ,which comprises about 95% of rural dwellings, either completely or partially destroyed. More than 2 million households were affected. About 1.8 million houses were damaged, 25956 have been washed away and 747863 fully collapsed [4].

The scene of devastation and cries of victims of the super cyclone is not easily believable, unless one sees in own eye. No description will be adequate to depict the real story. The people after cyclone hopelessly lie tired, looking to the sky and counting the number of helicopters flying over their village every day. Some Villages had become completely inaccessible. It was even difficult after 20 days of the cyclone to reach some villages even by bicycle because of flood. Heavy rain from the rivers and tidal water from the sea washed away many houses. People used to move from one house to another with the help of floating buoy made of bannana trees. There was no land or space as a result village people used to climb trees to make toilet. There was no radio or television or news papers. There was common kitchen cooking one meal a day (Bhat and dalma, or khechri).There was no fuel to cook that bare rice or boil the contaminated water. Even ,during that month, they considered their own relatives rushing from

Bombay, Calcutta, Surat to see them as outsiders.[5]

The magnitude of the impact and extreme severity of the cyclone was such that the entire state was paralysed after the cyclone. All channels of communication had failed, even the communication equipment of the state police and collectorates had broken down.

The following blocks and urban areas were affected by the super cyclone.

Table 10.4 : Affected Rural Blocks And Urban Areas

Districts	*Affected Rural Blocks*	*Affected Urban Areas*
Cuttack	Niali, Tangi-Choudwar, Barang Kantapada,Athagarh, Barba, Narsingpur Banki, Damapara, Mahanga, Nischintakoili, Salipur, Cuttack Sadar & Tigiria.	M: Cuttack & Choudwar. N: Banki & Athagarh
Puri	Gop, Kakatpur, Astarang, Nimapara, Pipili, Kanas, Delang, Brahmagiri, Krushnaprashad, Puri Sadar, Satya badi	M: Puri N: Pipili, Nimapara & Konark.
Khurda	Bhubaneshwar, Jatni, Balianta, Balipatna, Khurda, Begunia, Bolgarh, Tangi	M : Bhubaneshwar N : Jatni & Khurda.
Kendrapara	Mahakalpara, Marshaghai, Rajnagar, Rajkanika, Aul & Pattamundai. Garadpur, Derabis, Kendrapara	M : Kendrapara N : Pattamundai
Jagatsinghpur	Ersama, Balikuda, Kujang, Biridi, Nuagaon, Tirtol, Raghunathpur, Jagatsinghpur	N : Jagatsinghpur & Paradip
Jajpur	Binjharpur, Bari, Dasarathpur, Korei, Jajpur, Sukinda, Barchana, Rasulpur, Dharmasala, Dangadi.	M: Jajpur N: Jajpur Road
Bhadrak	Bhadrak,Tihidi, Chand bali, Dhamnagar, Banth, Basudevpur Bhandari	M: Bhadrak

	Pokhari.	
Balasore	Balasore, Remuna, Khaira, Nilagiri, Oupada, Soro, Bahanga, Simulia.	M: Balasore N: Soro, Nilagiri

Note: Bold lettered Blocks and urban areas /Districts are worst affected. M stands for Municipality and N for NAC area.

The knock down effect of the breakdown of lifeline infrastructure has been most severe, completely halting rescue and relief operations(for first few days)in spite of a significant presence of the armed forces. The army and airforce were called on 29th Oct but they were not able to undertake operations till 31st Oct due to bad weather. As the breakdown of power and communication networks had paralysed the state administration, the immediate rescue and relief measures had therefore to be organised from outside the state for many days till the state govt was in a position to take over.

Many state Governments had adopted severely affected districts to carry out relief ,restoration and rehabilitation activities. They had sent financial aid, relief materials and their experts to assist in restoration of essential infrastructure.

Other States of India	Adopted districts of Orissa
Delhi	Puri
Maharastra	Jagatsinghpur, Bhadrak
Karnataka	Kendrapara
AndhraPradesh	Cuttack, Ganjam
MadhyaPradesh	Jajpur

Though this disaster was really the unprecedented event of the century, it was not declared as the national calamity by the central government.[6] The damages of Latuer earthquake, Jabalpur earthquake ,flood in UP, Bihar, Gujrat were declared as national calamities even though the damage had been much less as compared to the

Orissa's super cyclone[7] Every minister and central authorities said that there is "no dearth of funds" for undertaking relief measures. Relief materials were pouring everyday from different parts and different sources of the country and abroad.

The aftermath effects of these disasters should be viewed not only in humanitarian and broad social terms but also in terms of economic terms since it is indeed a formidable obstacle to economic development of the region. One should be concerned with the effects on the population they afflict. We should examine the demographic consequences of such crises in terms, for example, of their effect on morbidity, mortality, fertility, migration as well as their impact on social, economic and political structures.

a. Rural Life during Natural Calamity:

The recent super cyclone, which followed the cyclone occurred in Ganjam district of Orissa just three weeks before, is the greatest horrendous event of the century in the country. It has tormentingly affected three major undivided districts of Orissa: Cuttack,Balasore and Puri. These four districts having long coastal lines are most vulnerable to cyclones and floods. Unfortunately the economic development of Orissa is based on the prosperity of the coastal districts, which are most susceptible to natural calamities. The recent cyclone, which occurred on 29th October, continued for more than 40 hours with speed of 300 km per hour. The sea roared like missiles. Cries of the helpless victims rent the air as the entire coastal belt of Orissa was devastated by the furious wind. Villages have become homeless and towns have become trees less. Nature is crueler than one perceives. The situation has become grimmer as the ninety percent of the cyclone-affected area were marooned under the floodwater. The flash of flood in Baitarani, Salandi, Subernarekha, Budhanalanga, Kusei and Kharasrotta triggered by heavy rainfall have rendered thousands of people in Jajpur, Kendrapara,Bhadrak, Balasore and Jagatsinghpur districts homeless. Hunger among the people has overtaken all emotions. In some villages none is left to shed tears. Entire atmosphere after the cyclone has become cool and calm. Even vultures and crows are absent to fight with the dogs eating the dead bodies. Being rendered homeless by the storm, lakhs of people are on the road. They have taken shelter in the roofless schools, wall less village clubs,open puja pendals or in neighbour's small (2-3 room) bulidings, which are very rare and which have accomodated hundreds of people in the cyclone night with out having any distinction between rich and poor, friend and enemy, male and female and brahmin and harijan. They eat and sleep together. Some cases it is found that people have spent two nights with the most poisonous snakes and furious animals under the same roof. It is also found that houses are washed away by flood where the small innocent orphan baby of two years old has survived innocently siting on the thatched roof eating a ripe palm .In a village of 350 members only one lady is alive who had gone to her father's place.[4]

The scene of devastation and cries of victims is not easily one believable, unless one sees in own eye. No description will be adequate to depict the real story. They hopelessly lie tired, looking to the sky and counting the number of helicopters flying over their village every day. Some Villages have become completely inaccessible. It is even difficult to reach some villages even by bicycle because of flood. People used to move from one house to another with the help of floating buoy of bannana trees. There is no land or space as a result male person used to climb trees to make toilet. There are no radio or television or newspapers. People enjoy the fast moving rumours regarding everything. There is common kitchen cooking one meal a day (Bhat and dalma, or khechri). There is no fuel to cook that bare rice or boil the contaminated water. Even they consider their own relatives rushing from Bombay, Calcutta, Surat to see them as outsiders[5]. Perhaps they have to continue with this situation for some more weeks till they reconstruct their houses and till they overcome the psychological trauma.

b. Urban Life during natural calamity

In the towns electricity, water and telephone services are completely disrupted for more than 10 days. Roads could not be cleared for 5 days in Capital City. People have to trek to different places to fetch drinking water. Town suffered from water logging and contaminated rainwater. Drain water of waist high entered into the first floor of building of Cuttack town. Syntax water tanks were blown off like baloons in Bhubaneswar City. The life of slum people is beyond any description. Dead pigs and bloated cows float in front of the meal they take. They have no choice. They are devoting time to cyclone related activities. They do not repair the repairables in the hope of getting some relief aid from the public authority. They have remained neglected for more than 15 days. As a result they suffer for several weeks with out having a roof. All massive trees are uprooted. The imagination of the town dwellers about the incidence of sunstroke this coming summer make them more panick. Schools and colleges in the town areas have not started functioning even after 20 days of the cyclone. Rural situation is still worse.

c . Relief Operations after the Disasters

Though Orissa has been facing cyclones and floods regularly, unfortunately over the years the building materials, techniques, housing structures in the villages, roads, electricity connections have evolved into such forms, which are completely unsuited to withstand a flood or cyclone. In the recent cyclone people of the affected districts were no way prepared and alert. They are always careless to the warnings because, the predictions of meteorological Department in the past were either wrong or partially true. The devastation both physical and psychological is enormous. Relief poured in promptly from all over the country. The quick provisions of temporary shelter, food for the victims of the motorable villages is by and large a success story. But many inaccessive villages have remained unattended for more than 20 days. Army has now been successful to open roads till Antapur ,Goda and Balitutha and relief materials have reached some of the interior villages. Army has escorted 383 and 300 trucks of relief materials to Jagatsinhpur and Kendrapara districts respectively. It has unloaded 454 trucks of food material from the naval ship at Paradeep port for distribution. Though this disaster is the unprecedented event it is not yet declared as national calamity. The damages of Latuer earthquate, Jabalpur earthquake, flood in UP, Bihar, Gujrat were declared as national calamities even though the damage had been much less as compared to the recent Orissa's super cyclone[6] Every minister and central authorities say that there is "no dearth of funds" for undertaking relief measures. Relief materials are pouring everyday from different parts and different sources of the country and abroad.

Despite loud claims by the state Govt. of establishing road links to all parts of the cyclone ravaged districts and supplying of relief materials to all affected people, relief is yet to reach the majority of the real needy. All that they have received after 20 days of the cyclone a few packets of food. Now the villagers are crawling out of their collapsed houses and begging for a blanket or a piece of polythene. They lay down their children on the roads as a part of their begging tactics. The Govt. is complacent and says, "we have done our best. No body should expect wonders from the Govt. faced with disaster of such a magnitude" The Govt. of Andhra Pradesh become 'the friend in need is friend indeed' with very swift and vigorous action just few hours after the cyclone. Madhya Pradesh Govt has adopted Jajpur District for reconstruction. They intend to take up the reconstruction of schools, hospitals, bridges and culverts on a priority basis. Punjab has adopted Jagatsingpur district for relief and reconstruction works. Arunanchal Pradesh has adopted Mayurbhanj district for rehabilitation. Tamilnadu has adopted Kendrapara district. After the construction of kutcha roads by the Indian army some voluntary agencies and media persons got in touch with the hapless survivors and now have started operating. They are disposing the dead bodies and carcasses. Some have started free kitchens at many places. Even some people have to walk for more than six to seven km and stand in a long queue to get one meal for the whole day. Punjabi langar has made a massive arrangement to feed one lakh starving mouths everyday in Jagatsinghpur district. But question is what will happen once relief operation ceases after few days.

The state administration has unveiled an economic package for cyclone affected people. It includes supply of BPL (below poverty line) rice for five months, 50 percent subsidy on supply of agricultural seeds to the farmers in the affected areas. There are plans to waive loan upto Rs.5000. and provide interest free loans of Rs.25000 to each affected family. There is plan to provide crop insurance to the non-insured farmers. There is plan for housing subsidy and soft loan to be given by HUDCO. There is plan for exempting sales taxes on edible oil, pulses and seeds etc Housing Subsidy: The state Govt. has proposed to cover all affected families in the below poverty line (BPL) categories under housing reconstruction scheme, previously known as Indira Awas Yojana.

d. Law and Order

It is saddening to observe the scene of continuous looting on the highways after the cyclone. They are not the hungry people nor for the later. They are not the real homeless ravaged people. Many of them are local holigans, gundas, dadas trying to exploit the situation to their personal benefit. Now they got the nice opportunity of stylising themselves as the patriotic leaders of the locality. They are the group who sometimes guide and misguide the outside relief teams. All the trees are cut and stolen by the private people. They also cut the unaffected trees and carry the log of woods to their home. Electric polls, wires and telephone lines are stolen away. And the criminal silence of the state administration has generated a feeling of insecurity everywhere. It will result in acute shortage of food items, inducing inflationary pressure. The common man will ultimately suffer from the lawlessness syndrome.

e. Bovine Economy

More than Fifty percent of the livestock population, which was an important source of income in the cyclone-hit districts are dead[8]. The situation that now prevails for animal husbandry is very alarming. Govt. machinery is busy in relief operation but the livestock population is facing starvation following acute shortage of food, fodder and water. The Govt. department has no stock of cattle feed for lakhs of buffalos and other livestocks, which survived the cyclone. They are left at God's mercy. Many of them are suffering from fever and dehydration after consuming the polluted water. It has become another source of worries for the village people.

f. Health Services

Stench emanating from bloated bodies, decomposed beyond recognition and animal carcasses makes the situation worse. Death toll is ever increasing.[9] Inflow of patients in the hospitals are ever increasing. Earthmovers and dumpers are used to remove the dead bodies of man and animal together. Missionaries, NGOs and State administration has prepared for a mass burial in Paradep,Cuttack and Kendrapara towns, five days after the killer cyclone left a devastating trail.There are many cases of death due to cholera and diarrheal disorder. With the slight trepidation of risk, volunteers and personnel of missionary organisation have entered into the villages, as they have not taken any vaccine. Samples are collected by a team of national Institute of Communicable diseases from Ersama, Balikuda, Mahakalpara and Kujanga blocks and examined by ICMR, New Delhi and tested Cholera positive. Health teams from other states like, Andhra, Punjab, Maharastra and Madhya Pradesh are also helping the health administration in different areas. There is no complacency in the rural health services. Lack of desanitisation measures and water purification may cause severe health hazards in the towns. Plight of poor people and patients in the hospital seems to be getting worse by each passing day. Being hopeless some patients are leaving the hospital and going back to their homeless villages by keeping faith on "lord Jaganath".

10.3. ENVIRONMENTAL EFFECTS:

The state of Orissa suffers from environmental imbalance like floods and droughts, because of the expansion of rain shadow zones and denudation of large forest patch. When drought has devastated western Orissa, cyclone and flood have not spared the well off coastal districts of the state. The increasing frequency and intensity of the continual onslaughts have made the environmentalists more concerned. The systematic falling of trees has first sent the warning signals and then wrecked havoc. Dense forest of coastal belt has been plagued by the rain shadow phenomenon. The virgin and rich mangroves forest is being depleted in the coastal belt. There is nothing left to minimise the intensity of the next cyclone or flash flood. The ecological rape in the coastal belt should stop forthwith. During May 1998 thousands of people in eastern Orissa died of heat wave. Experts attributed it to the absence of breeze from the bay of Bengal. Ironically this time coastal people could not face the too much and too strong wind from the Bay. As a retaliation, nature has uprooted the all trees across the cyclone stretch and has exposed the state to another bout of heat wave.[10] Past deed has the seed of destruction. The encroachment into the flood zones of rivers, by the refugees, has been occurring ever since the density of population has been rising inexorably. It is this population pressure related encroachment of the flood zones that is the root cause of ever increasing flood related losses in India. Deforestation aggravates the problem but aforestation can not get rid of it.

It was said that the super cyclone, which occurred in 29th October 1999 in Orissa was the greatest horrendous event of the century in the country. It has tormentingly affected the advance regions of Orissa. But the recent earthquake which occurred on 26th Jan 2001 in Gujrat is most horrible unprecedented event of India's history. The situation has become more grim and grave than any natural calamity of the past. The devastation both physical and psychological is enormous. The shock among the people of Kuch and Ahmedabad has overtaken all emotions. In some houses after the quake none was left to shed tears. Entire atmosphere after the event has become cool and calm. The scene of devastation and cries of victims is not easily one believable, unless one sees in own eye. No description will be adequate to depict the real story.

Death toll continuously increases after the calamity.

Volunteers and rescue operators are disposing the dead bodies and carcasses. Stench emanating from bloated bodies, decomposed beyond recognition and animal carcasses makes the situation worse. Inflow of patients in the hospitals are ever increasing. Earth movers and dumpers are used to remove the dead bodies of man and animal together. Missionaries, NGOs and State administration are making preparation for mass burial. Lack of desanitisation measures and water purification may cause severe health hazards in the towns. Plight of poor people and patients in the hospital seems to be getting worse by each passing day. Being hopeless some patients are leaving the hospital and going back by keeping faith on God. It is very difficult for the people to overcome the psychological trauma.

10.4. ECONOMIC EFFECTS

The earthquake like the super cyclone of Orissa has wreaked a greater havoc on the state economy. Many economic activities where majority of the population ekes out their living have been raped and ruined by this earthquake. It may take more than a decade to achieve the status quo. All most all social overheads and infrastructures are destroyed. Schools, hospitals, dispensaries, colleges, libraries, clubs, go-downs, post offices, banks, cooperatives etc are partially or totally destroyed. All these listing of damages is an indicative of the economic cost (or loss) of recent event. This also depicts the picture of reconstruction works warranted in the region. We need to look afresh. A comprehensive plan for restoration and rebuilding the state's economy needs to be chalked out urgently.

The problem of earthquake, cyclone or flood is multi dimensional in nature, which varies spatially and temporally. These problems constitute a set of structural factors to economic development of the state. Economic effects of any calamity differ among regions. More developed and economically diversified regions can recover more quickly. Their coping capacity is better. The poor regions are most severely affected. The regions more vulnerable to weather and climate are the worst sufferers of flood or cyclone. Economic effects of any natural calamity can be classified as direct and indirect. The direct effects are tangible and monetarily quantified by various agencies. It includes: (a) loss of capital, destruction of houses, roads, bridges, go-downs, factories, irrigation facilities and (b) loss of stocks of consumables, disruption of production activities, reduction of income, loss of jobs, business, livestock, fishing, crop loss etc . Indirect effects include loss of lifetime saving and assets and potential earning, disruption of employment sources, artificial shortages, inflationary situations, spread of antisocial elements, donation to relief fund etc. Black marketeers, hoarders capitalise out of panic situations[11] Balance of payments worsens because of the decline and disruption of exports. Public authorities are confronted with a heavy rise in social expenditures on medicine, relief, subsidies, housing and investment for the purpose of reconstructing the community assets destroyed in the natural disasters

In the **short run** the disaster causes loss of human life, animals and distorts the ecological balances. It injures kills and destroys. It causes emotional stress and trauma. It ransacks home and business, and causes economic hardships and spells financial ruin for many. And the people hit worst are the poor, women and children. The threat of an epidemic looms large as survivors are spending their days in the midst of carcasses, In the **longrun** it leaves an unbearable scar and gives a set back to the natural growth and development process of the region. It further entrenches and exacerbates poverty and unemployment and interrupts and sometimes reverses the economic progress of the backward regions of the state in achieving a self-reliant development. In the face of tardy and sluggish growth of the economy all disasters like flood, earthquake and cyclone or drought distorts the smooth functioning of the economy and puts an extraneous and very weighty impediment on the development process. It nullifies the progress achieved and creates very strong obstacle for planned developmental efforts of the region. Economic theory offers no satisfactory solution to this intractable problem. Economists here offer mere sops in the form of financial compensation to the disaster-hit people. But Govt's project for rehabilitating the victims may head towards spectacular failure if it has no clear-cut vision

10.5 . WOMEN'S VULNERABILITY

There is a general lack of concern and research on sex and gender diff erences in vulnerability to and impact of disasters. The limited information available from small scale studies suggests that there is a pattern of gender differentiation at all levels of the disaster process: exposure to risk, risk perception, preparedness, response, physical impact, psychological impact, recovery and reconstruction. There is some evidence showing that women and men may suffer different negative health consequences following a disaster. It is not clear whether this is because of biological differences between the sexes, because of socially determined differences in women's and men's roles and status or because of an interaction of social and biological factors.

In 1976 an accident in a chemical plant near Seveso, Italy, exposed the local population to dioxin. A twenty-year follow-up study which compared those in exposure zones with a reference population in a surrounding non-contaminated area found that fifteen years after the accident, mortality from rectal cancer and lung cancer increased among men in high-exposure zones. An overall increase in diabetes mortality as compared to those living in the non-contaminated area was reported, notably among women. Studies have also reported adverse reproductive outcomes following disasters, including early pregnancy loss, premature delivery, stillbirths, delivery-related complications and infertility.

- A study from Israel reported an increase in delivery rates during the 48 hours following an earthquake and a signifi cant increase in the premature delivery rate.
- In India, 24% of pregnant women exposed to isocyanide during the 1984 Bhopal explosion had spontaneous abortions, as against 6% in a comparison group. Social taboos around menstruation and norms about appropriate behaviour for women and girls are reported to contribute to health problems in young women in disaster situations.
- During the 1998 floods in Bangladesh, adolescent girls reported perineal rashes and urinary tract infections because they were not able to wash out menstrual rags properly in private, often had no place to hang the rags to dry, or access to clean water. They reported wearing the still damp cloths, as they did not have a place to dry them.

10.6. GENDER IMPLICATIONS

Women's vulnerability to the impact of disasters is also increased by socially determined differences in roles and responsibilities of women and men and inequalities between them in access to resources and decision making power.

- Excess deaths among females following an earthquake in Maharashtra, India were attributed to women being in homes damaged by the earthquake and men being in open areas. Men were sleeping in fi elds during harvest time and were away from the home in preparation for a festival, boys were at school away from the village, and many men were away from aff ected areas as they were employed in other districts or states.

- One study on a 1991 cyclone in Bangladesh noted that many women perished with their children at home as they had to wait for their husbands to return and make an evacuation decision.

When compounded by a calamity, the comparatively lower value ascribed to girls in some societies may take on lethal manifestations. One report from Bangladesh describes a father who, when unable to hold on to both his son and his daughter from being swept away by a tidal surge, helplessly released his daughter, because "... (this) son has to carry on the family line".

Men, on the other hand, may suffer other disadvantages in different situations and for different reasons from women, because of their gender-role socialization. Men's roles as protectors may place a greater responsibility on them for risk taking during and after a disaster, both within their households and as volunteers and rescue workers..

a. Perception of risk and access to relief

Gender differences may exist in the perception of hazard risks. It has been suggested that women perceive disaster events or threats as more serious and risky than men do. Traditional gender roles are also played out in the response phase of disaster situations. Women are responsible for caring for family members, stocking supplies and preparing the household while men were responsible for securing external areas of the house. Following a flood, one researcher observed that while men would build roads and houses the role of putting lives back together was the women's.

Differences are also reported around post-disaster relief. Cultural norms have been found to inhibit women from visibly accessing relief centres, or they cannot leave their homes to go to relief centres due to child care responsibilities. In settings where women are forbidden to interact with male members of the community who are not their kin, they may have difficulties in accessing relief services from male relief workers. Further, where food distribution targets household heads, women may be systematically marginalized, as they would only be registered as household heads if no adult male was present.

b. Impact of natural disasters

The impact of disasters is felt differentially within societies, and those most socially excluded and economically insecure bear a disproportionate burden. The impact of disasters also varies between women and men. Loss of the ability to take care of the family may cause adjustment difficulties for some men, especially those with more traditional gender role norms. Others may view receiving financial aid as a stigma and feel challenged in their role as breadwinner. Women may find themselves burdened with even greater responsibilities than before. Post disaster "flight of men" often occurs, leaving women as sole earners.

At the same time, lower literacy levels and very low levels of ownership of land and other productive assets may leave women on the verge of destitution.

- One study reports instances of women in Bangladesh becoming destitute following a disaster as male relatives confiscated family assets from a woman in the event of her husband's and son's deaths, leaving women and daughters poverty stricken and destitute.

There were no legal provisions to protect women and their families against such problems.

c. Domestic and sexual violence

Although hard evidence on the influence of disasters on domestic and sexual violence is limited, several field reports suggest that the safety of women experiencing violence in the home may be compromised in the aftermath of disaster and they may not have access to disaster relief and recovery resources. These women often live in a world of narrow social networks. Attending to preparedness or evacuation warnings, stabilising their lives in a disaster-stricken neighbourhood, or accessing recovery resources may be impossible tasks. Following a major Australian flood in 1990, one observer noted that women experiencing violence in the home, who were socially isolated, became even more isolated and there was an increase in domestic violence. According to reports from a community intervention centre in the US, women left without housing in a post-disaster situation called the perpetrator of the violence, seeking accommodation. Women and girls are more vulnerable to sexual abuse in disaster situations and may be coerced into sex for basic needs such as food, shelter and security. The sex industry often becomes part of the interaction between the refugee or displaced population and the local community.

d. Psychological impact

Psychological responses to disasters include short term effects such as shock, anxiety, sleep disturbances and guilt. There are differences between women and men and girls and boys in the nature of psychological impact. Several studies have found that a greater proportion of women and girls report suff ering from emotional disorders and distress as compared to men and boys. Female sex, lower social support and being older are associated with higher post-disaster psychological distress after the disasters. A survey of children affected by the 1995 Great Hanshin Awaji earthquake showed that girls were more heavily affected by trauma and that being female was a high risk factor for distress. Women's dramatically expanded care giving roles following a disaster, and putting family needs before their own, may explain overall declines in emotional well being.. Emergency management agencies and others responsible for emergency relief such as law-enforcement agencies and fire personnel have historically been dominated by men. Male-dominated recovery groups which see disasters 'through the eyes of men' may organize relief work in a manner that does not take gender differences and women's specific needs into consideration. For example, sanitary napkins, contraceptives and counselling services for psychological distress and domestic violence are rarely available in emergency situations. There is also a tendency on the part of relief planners to take for granted women's time and labour for work as paid and unpaid care givers in the aftermath of a disaster. Similarly, they may assume men's physical and emotional strength, and therefore overlook their needs.

Therefore there is urgent need for data sets to provide sex-disaggregated data on disaster-related mortality, morbidity and long-term health consequences. At the local level, there needs to be better documentation of:

- whether warning response in disaster relief and vulnerability are influenced by gender-based differences between women and men;
- how gender relations operate in households and communities in a disaster situation and during the relief and recovery phase; and
- how gender roles and gender relations influence coping mechanisms.

10.7. POLITICS OF RELIEF

There is always the pressure on the Centre to declare it a "national calamity of rarest severity", which is the stipulation of 10th Finance Commission.[5] Declaration is essential to get international funding for reconstruction for the ravaged districts. Centre can impress the World Bank for soft loan if devastation is declared as the national calamity. According to the provisions made by Finance Commission the affected state has to submit a memorandum with detail calculations of cost of relief and rehabilitation. This is to be vetted by a committee consisting of the deputy Chairman of the Planning commission and others.

Political rivalry in the state is threatening to muddy the massive effort. Politicians get the scope to garner popularity in the state. The different political parties are accusing each other and politicising the issue of Earthquake. They neglect and remain oblivious of the gender implications of natural calamities. They treat male and female equally during disaster. But biggest natural disaster in living memory of the century too becomes an occasion for the leaders to play miserable politics. Dissident group is critical to show how their present leader is inefficient and not caring enough. Other leaders of other party are busy in gaining cheap popularity and very eager to appear in TV or appear in front page of any newspaper. Due to these pressures the Government tries to depict a conservative estimate of the damages and deaths. The bureaucracy has the inherent tendency to underestimate the loss and tolls. As if the earthquake has been created by the present Govt. Party infighting is an impeding factors in the handling the catastrophe of such gigantic proportion. A responsible Government and a sensible opposition are expected not only to stir themselves beyond politics to cope and manage with this national disaster like this but also are expected to learn big lessons for the future adaptability and preparedness. Every minister and central authorities usually assure that there is "no dearth of funds" for undertaking relief measures. Relief materials pour everyday from different parts and different sources of the country and abroad. People do not repair the repairables in the hope of getting some relief aid from the public authority. Some try to exploit the situation to their personal benefit. Now some get the nice opportunity of stylising themselves as the patriotic leaders of the locality. There are some groups who sometimes guide and misguide the outside relief teams. Govt. should tighten the law and order situation during this abnormal period to ensure security to the survivors and the relief workers.

Announcements of made by state administration are hasty palliatives. Their promises depict confusion between relief and reconstruction. One is urgent, the other required careful thinking. Relief attends to immediate sufferings. It involves quicker rescue and emergency medical aid. Speed is vital as this action saves life and property. But Reconstruction and rehabilitation are concerned with the future quality of the rest of the survivors life and of their children/grand children thereafter. Speed may be useful but it is not the most important goal. What matters more is life long satisfaction, an accurate assessment of and response to the victim's own desires and needs.

10.8. EFFECTIVE DISASTER MANAGEMENT:

Disaster management is very much crucial not only to meet the immediate requirement but also to reduce its long-term adverse implications on the development process. The coping capacity to these calamitous situations in India is very weak. Backward regions are badly equipped to deal with such events. They have a poor and less flexible administrative system, a lower potential to benefit from previous learning and experience and have inadequate technological infrastructure. Relief and reconstruction strategy of the disaster-affected area must focus on:

(i) restoration of physical damages

(ii) promotion of socio economic development and

(iii) prevention and amelioration of future disaster events.

(iv) gender issues in planning and delivery of relief services

But the major shortcoming of these programmes are that they are isolated and most discrete and are not part of any comprehensive integrated development plan. Any plan for integrated development of Disaster prone areas (IDDPA) must be based upon the following key factors:

(a) organisational set up for disaster management

(b) Strong Infrastructural base for IDDPA

(c) Strategy of relief, rehabilitation and reconstruction (SRRR) and

(d) National Policy for IDDPA

Man's response has been focused primarily on relief activity. And Indian meteorological department has only developed a scientific INSAT based cyclone warning system. There is no scientific forecasting about earthquake. As a result the actual and potential consequences of each disaster event are becoming more serious and increasingly global in scale. Disaster management means planned and systematic approach for solving problems in the wake of disasters. An analysis of the present strategy of development of disaster prone areas reveals that it is all based on ad hoc approaches. Even now Indian planners have not recognised disasters as a crucial factor in planning for development. Hence there is the need for the development of these areas on the basis of an integrated approach with a definite regional policy for these areas.

Presently it has extended to mainly to relief operations and reconstruction during the post-calamity period. All Relief operations are only palliatives. It does not solve the perennial problem. But role of the public authority should extend from pre-disaster preparedness to rescue, relief and long term reconstruction and development of the affected area. Important areas of disaster management should be: prevention, preparedness, warning, evaluation, rescue, correct identification, relief operation, rehabilitation, reconstruction, assessment and financial arrangements.

The incidence of all natural calamities varies across gender, regions and time .No standard prescription for redressal of the problem will be appropriate for specific region. The present strategy of development of DPAs reveals that they are all uncoordinated and adhoc addendum. Even now planners in India have not recognised disasters as a crucial factor in planning for the development Hence there is need for a new multi pronged approach to mitigate the severity of post –disaster conditions of the people. The new approach should be an integrated one with definite regional policy for the sustained development of these disaster prone areas(DPAs).The strategy of development of DPAs is not the concern of any single ministry or any Govt. department such as Finance, Revenue Agriculture, irrigation, health, education, rural electrification, animal husbandry, forestry, roads, building, cooperation, and planning. Therefore an integrated development of DPAs has the real danger of floundering on the rock of departmentalism. Hence to overcome these problems it is imperative to devise an organisational and managerial innovations with in a sound functional framework. What we need is a permanent and functional disaster management organisation, not a knee-jerk action Committee with some ministers with dogmatic ideas and some bureaucrats, with their rigid mindset. They must be scientifically equipped to foresee disaster possibilities and move with specially trained rapid action forces (TRAF). Such an agency will be certainly handle the crises better than the present semi-existent agencies/ departments. Intense sufferings today should become the cornerstone for future policy.

10.9. NEED FOR NIDM

In every country there are many research Institutes on disaster management. To cite few examples: Disaster Research Center of Ohio University, Natural Hazard Research, University of Chicago, Natural Hazard Research and Application Information Center of Colorado, World Meteorological organisation, Geneva, UN disaster Relief Office (UNDRO) Geneva, International Disaster Institute, London, Disaster Research Unit, Bradford University, Disaster research Center, University of Delware are doing wonderful research work which significantly contributes to the society. In India the public authority suffer from inadequate and improper understanding about different types of disasters and their consequences and remedies, be it Kalahandi's drought related hunger, Orissa's super cyclone or super flood, Latuer's quake or Bhopals gas tragedy. We have only instant and hasty understanding. We respond very erratically and randomly to the post disaster crisis. Therefore a research team has to be encouraged to disseminate information and generate proper understanding about the problems. There should be one independent National Research Institute of Disaster Management in India which must adopt a gendered approach to disaster mitigation.

10.10. GENDER BUDGETING

The developmental work carried out either by a government or any NGO, hardly ever followed gender budgeting. Since emergency relief and later rehabilitation phase is being carried out on the lines of developmental work, the provision of gender specific budgeting was missing. While one talks of human dignity and humanitarian aid to the affected community, it seems but natural to expect that the needs of the vulnerable groups be met. Gender budgeting is about suitable "policymaking. It aims at developing the coordination of the concepts with policymaking. Policymaking is the work of the government which responds to political decision making.

Gender needs much more conscious effort to be integrated in disaster research, planning and implementation Gender and disaster are generally treated as a post-rehabilitation issue. It is regarded as a complex yet dynamic set of social relations, which needs to be catered to during the response phase soon after a disaster. Gender is seen more akin to women than anything to do with men. The closest it gets is by seeing women as helpless victims, more so because they are poor. Both the government agencies and NGOs are attempting to proactively integrate gender concerns as a factor in response to planning and vulnerability. Similarly, more women need to be necessarily integrated as essential partners during the mitigation and preparedness phases. The world of "developmental work" is slowly and surly shifting its focus to "work during and after disaster". Various governments have now begun to keep a certain budget for emergencies. Earlier it was included only as part of the contingency budgeting. A new paradigm is emerging.

10.11. CONCLUDING OBSERVATION

Under the present policy of globalisation and free market regime, state has a vital role to play. Laws and regulations are to be enacted and enforced to protect the survivors. Market forces can not deliver goods to the people in DPAs. Sustainable livelihood, reconstruction and rehabilitation works and permanent infrastructural overheads can not be provided by the private sector. Worldwide Globalisation movement has little solution to this kind of disaster-related problems. Trickle down theory of the development planning can not be relied upon either. So effective people's participation is warranted in the reconstruction works. The speedy completion of relief phase is crucial to the success of the reconstruction programmes as the community start to take over the responsibility for their own future. An extended relief phase as in Uttarkashi and many other places would severely cripple the ability of the communities to take decisions and resume normal life. They may be caught in a 'dependency syndrome'. In the process of reconstruction the affected people should make their own choices. Benefactors should seize this opportunity to improve their thinking and life style. But there should be community participation. The special needs of the victims should be carefully understood. External solutions should not be considered always superior. Western solutions should not be thrust upon the affected communities. The reconstruction drive should not be designed to force the recipient to switch to the benefactor's value system. Otherwise, the danger is that despite all good intentions, the rehabilitation project will falter not only physically but also leave the people there less confident, frustrated, and unhappier than ever before. These are very crucial factors that the NGOs, donor agencies and state administration should consider. Otherwise it would be a fait accompli.

The gender-specific disaggregated data is needed and research is warranted both at the local and at national and regional levels on structural processes and factors that increase disaster vulnerability in women and men across different social groups. Domestic and sexual violence in the aftermath of a disaster and the special needs of disadvantaged women, and women in violent relationships needs to be studied. Pre-disaster activities such as hazard mapping and vulnerability analysis should integrate gender considerations. Community-based disaster-preparedness projects and disaster training and education programmes should include women and men, and address their respective needs and concerns. Information collected through rapid assessments of health status and health needs in disaster situations should be sex-disaggregated and include a gender analysis. Information is needed on reproductive and mental health needs, in addition to information on communicable diseases and on malnutrition. Basic health services provided as part of emergency relief should likewise cater to women's and men's different needs and be provided in a gender-sensitive manner. Disadvantaged groups such as women and men with disabilities and women in violent relationships should be identified as special-risk populations for disaster relief and recovery services. It may be useful to work with community organizations to identify these groups. The initiative for gender mainstreaming needs to consciously address health issues from a gender perspective. Gender budgeting should be part of the the policy making process but not part of contingency budgeting. A new paradigm should emerge for integrating disaster research, gender dynamics, planning and implementation .

REFERENCES

1. Awasthi A & Ranga Rao SP(1982),*Crisis Administration in India*, Sterling Pub.,Delhi
2. Cuny, F C ,(1983) *Disasters and Development*, Oxford University Press
3. Dhawan, B D(1993),Coping with Flood in Himalayan Rivers, *Economic & Political weekly,*Vol.28(18),May, PP 849-852
4. IFRC(1998) *World Disasters Report*, International Federation of

Red Cross, Oxford Univ press

5. Jain, NK (1982) Disaster preparedness in India, Joint Assistance Centre, New Delhi.
6. Mohanty, Bidyut (1993) Orissa Famine of 1866,: demographic and economic consequences, *Economic and Political Weekly*, Vo.28(1-2) Jan,pp55-66
7. Oliver, J(1981) Disaster management in developing Countries: some contrasts, *Disaster Management*, Vol.1(4),Oct-Dec, PP.155-62
8. Patel, BP(1994) Marthawada Earthquake, *Economic and Political Weekly*, Vol.29(8),Feb,Pp401-405
9. Raghavulu, CV (1982) Disaster Preparedness: a study in Community Perspective, ARTIC, Hyderabad.

11
Violence Against Women

Violence against Women across the globe has remained as grave as ever. It is the key issue in the Indian women's movement. This chapter tries to dispel myths, superstitions and misconceptions about woman and her duties and adopt a rational attitude towards the woman as a human being. Violence against women does not end by merely bestowing of judicial rights or by making women literate.It argues that the social problem can not be solved by legal bell or economic independence. It is not necessarily caused due to poverty or illiteracy prevailing among the households of villages.

Violence against Women across the globe has remained as grave as ever. It reflects the savage mentality of the society. It is the true manifestation of gender subordination and gender inequality. Due to patriarchy in the family system, the family does not give equal importance to all members, as role, power and status are strictly determined by age and gender. Although the family is a source of love, sympathy and support, it is also the source of inequality, exploitation and violence. Gandhiji opines that violence includes exploitation economic, social, and political of individual by individual or of nation-by nation and so on. Domestic violence includes all actions or behaviour of family members which causes either physical injury or emotional trauma or both to a woman.

Violence against women has been and remains a key issue in the Indian women's movement. Throughout the 1980s, Indian society witnessed numerous struggles by women's organizations on issues of dowry deaths, rape, custodial rape, abduction of women, sati (the burning of a widow on the husband's funeral pyre), female infanticide and feticide, sexual harassment of young girls and women in public places (eve teasing), branding of single women as witches, representation of women and their bodies in the media and trafficking in women and prostitution. It is important to note that there has been a legal reform by the government in response to each of these issues of violence against women during the past decade.

11.1. GLOBAL SCENARIO OF SEXUAL VIOLENCE:

In 1995, local child protection service agencies identified **126,000 children** who were victims of either substantiated or indicated sexual abuse. Of these, 75% were girls and nearly 30% of child victims were between the age of 4 and 7. 15% of sexual assault and rape victims are **under age 12. About 7% of girls in grades 5-8** and 12% of girls in grades 9-12 in USA is said they had been sexually abused. Among the girls:

- 29% are age 12-17.
- 44% are under age 18.
- 80% are under age 30.
- 12-34 are the highest risk years.
- Girls ages 16-19 are 4 times more likely than the general population to be victims of rape, attempted rape, or sexual assault.
- About **93% of juvenile** sexual assault victims know

their attacker.

- 34.2% of attackers were family members.
- 58.7% were acquaintances.
- Only 7% of the perpetrators were strangers to the victim.
- In 2004-2005, 64,080 women were raped. According to medical reports, the incidence of pregnancy for one-time unprotected sexual intercourse is 5%. By applying the pregnancy rate to 64,080 women, RAINN estimates that there were **3,204 pregnancies** as a result of rape during that period.

Sexual assault is one of the most underreported crimes, with 60% still being left unreported. Males are the least likely to report a sexual assault, though they make up about 10% of all victims. What happens to Rapists When They are Caught and Prosecuted? About **60% of rapes/ sexual assaults** are not reported to the police. Those rapists, of course, never spend a day in prison according to a statistical average of the past 5 years. Factoring in unreported rapes, only about 6% of rapists ever serve a day in jail.

In 2006, there were **272,350 victims** of rape, attempted rape, or sexual assault in the world. **1 out of every 6 American women** have been the victims of an attempted or completed rape in their lifetime (14.8% completed rape; 2.8% attempted rape). **17.7 million American women** have been victims of attempted or completed rape. And **9 of every 10** rape victims were female in 2003.

- 1 in 6 women and 1 in 33 men will be a victim of sexual assault in their lifetime.
- College age women are 4 times more likely to be sexually assaulted.

Sexual Assault Numbers

- In 2006, there were 272,350 victims of sexual assault.
- Every 2 minutes, someone in the U.S. is sexually assaulted.

About Rapists

The Rapist isn't a Masked Stranger. Almost 2/3 of rapes were committed by someone known to the victim. The rape victimsmostly know their assailants

- 73% of sexual assaults were perpetrated by a non-stranger.
- 38% of rapists are a friend or acquaintance,
- 28% are an intimate.
- 7% are a relative.
- Only 6% of rapists will ever spend a day in jail.
- While about **80% of all victims are white,** minorities are somewhat more likely to be attacked.

Lifetime rate of rape /attempted rape for women by race:

- All women: 17.6%
- White women: 17.7%
- Black women: 18.8%
- Asian Pacific Islander women: 6.8%
- American Indian/Alaskan women: 34.1%
- Mixed race women: 24.4%

Effects of Rape

The Victims of sexual assault are :

3 times more likely to suffer from depression.

6 times more likely to suffer from post-traumatic stress disorder.

13 times more likely to abuse alcohol.

26 times more likely to abuse drugs.

4 times more likely to contemplate suicide.

11.2. INDIAN SCENARIO

India, inspite of its rapid progress in terms of economic growth it has high incidence of poverty in different parts of the country. The increased economic insecurity, unemployment and poverty in families of India result in frustrations, alcoholism, lack of status and sense of belongingness and fulfillment of basic needs of 50% of its population. This affects women directly in the form of increased domestic violence. The pitiable condition of womanhood in India is trapped in the web of socio cultural factors such as superstitious and blind faith perpetuated by male dominance. It is worse in the villages. Her struggle for survival continues from the womb to the grave without respite. The struggle for survival continues throughout the woman's life beginning with the female foetus. Although there is anti-abortion Act, private practitioners continue to conduct abortions with a sex bias. In India , murder against women is now committed with impunity. There is increasing trend of "bride-burning" in the states like Orissa and Bihar . Human Rights organisations and women's bodies are more or less helpless. But gravity of the problem has remained as grave as before. Wrongs against women fail to evoke indignation even among women. They are too tied to wrong traditions and too used to suffering that they accept it as a part of life. The police, the doctor and the teacher all view it as a societal norm. The legal system is also hopeless in the country. There violence against women in India are of following types:

Social violence

Domestic violence

Communal violence

Drug induced violence

Dowry related violence

Mental violence

Let us discuss all these types of violence against women seriatim

a. Social Violence

Violence against women occurs in every society - rich or poor - having different forms of manifestation. One of the crudest forms of violence is the one, which takes place subtly and is sanctioned in the name of culture. Cultural beliefs and practices draw a very negative image of women who are to be suppressed and domesticated, which we all accept unconditionally. Such deliberate subjugation of women is pure violence and negation of human rights. A girl has to fit in the culturally defined role - be at home or outside. Taking a second wife is also possible , though not easily acceptable , in all communities. Though it is not common among the middleclass families, It is acceptable in both poor families and rich families. Violence against women - severe beating, slapping around, being thrown out of the matrimonial home, is also common to all communities, whether society at large acknowledge it or not. It leads to assault, serious injury or burns even death of the victims. It robs the dignity of women not only by indecent behavior but also an esteem form of rape or ravishing her by use of force by outside people. They use indecent, abusive and filthy language against a woman or her near and dear ones. But when any issue is looked at or approached from a religious point of view it gets polluted and vitiated. But the issue must remain gender-based.

b. Communal Violence

There are many cases of state, communal and caste instigated violence . Victims of such violence are mostly women . Caste and communal violence mostly target the women. "Dishonoring" women is the most accepted norm of taking revenge on specified castes, families and communities.

c. Drug Related Violence

An alcoholic beats his wife and children. There are incidences where under the influence of alcohol a father rapes his own daughter. Alcoholism increases violence and consequently family interruption takes place. In most of the cases the victim is branded as a woman of loose morals. In recent years girl children in the age group of 6-12 years have been more victimized. Custodial rape is extremely heinous since the offenders are supposed to be guardians. Witnesses refuse to testify against offenders or men in power, which makes it impossible for the victim to get justice.

d. Violence at Work Place

Informal sector is growing very fast in India. Jobs in the unorganized sectors of India are expanding very fast. These jobs are unregistered, unprotected and exploitative. The work participation rate of female is rising in this sector only. They are ill-paid but don't leave the job due to increasing unemployment. This need for survival drives the woman to a rape situation. Harassment at work place is real and pervasive. The women have no courage to report due to the fear of further harassment, trauma and re-victimization. Earning women do not have the freedom to spend or regulate their lives. They are expected to hand over their salary to their husband or in-laws. The problems of managing both the employment situation and the subordination at home, and the suspicions about the woman's character continue to make matters worse. The male dominance is all-pervading and there are implicit assumptions that the wife should have a lesser designation at the work place and earn a lower salary than her husband. The gender bias at work expects a woman executive to "look like a woman, behave like a lady, think like a man and work like a donkey"

e. Domestic Violence

The most common type of violence against women worldwide is "domestic violence" . It is only now, through the sustained activism by women's organizations that violence against women, including domestic violence, is starting to receive attention internationally. Domestic violence against women is too sensitive a topic to be explored in any survey, and that shame, self-blame or fear of further violence prevent women from discussing their experiences. Domestic violence in the society is a horror they have to cope with in silence. There were even more shocking details. More than 12 per cent of the physically-challenged women have been raped and 15 per cent molested while the count is 25 per cent and 19 per cent respectively for the mentally-challenged women. More horrifyingly, the abusers were often family members or people whom the girls trusted a lot. The woman in India is a slave to the so-called institutionalized cultural shackles. Her mobility is restricted, her self-expression is monitored and her thoughts influenced by others in her milieu. She is the victim of suspicion by her brothers, parents, husband and in- laws. Domestic violence is one of the greatest obstacles to gender equality and right to life and liberty.

f. Dowry Related Violence

Of all the cases of violence against women the problem of dowry in the Indian society stands out in full force as the most brutal and common. It is estimated that a bride is burnt every two days in India. It gives us the unenviable reputation of being the country with an unbeaten record of bride burning. The practice of demanding dowry in states like Orissa has spread so much that death by burning is often the punishment for the innocent young girls who is unable to satisfy the greed of her in-laws. It is true that dowry related violence and killing predominantly affects our community just as triple talaq affects only Muslim women. But what people fail to see is that the status of women across the board is being undermined. Girls are treated as commodity in the marriage market. The expression of such violence can be seen in the form of wife battering, demand for more dowry, divorce, bride burning and regular conflicts in family life. The state of atrocities against women are dealt by Central and State Women's Commission . But ironically, girls relatives or woman's in-laws force her to tell lies eventually at the final stage.

g. Mental And Emotional Violence

Rate of divorce is very less in India . But emotional violence is more serious in India. Mental torture of the wife is a covert phenomenon. It may be even more devastating than physical assaults. Taunting the wife, insulting her in the presence of the children, guests and servants, ignoring her completely and cutting off communication with her are the common manifestations of mental torture. It includes snatching away the assets which a woman possesses or earns. In large parts of India the husband or in laws deprives her the custody of children which leads to emotional rape. They do not allow her to avail the educational opportunities. Denial of her reproductive rights, denial of access to health facilities or opportunities and to use her political rights and denial of rights to take part in family decision making etc are examples of mental torture and vioience. In some families she is deprived of her daily meals and financial means and bare necessities of daily life.

11.2. INDIA'S LEGAL SYSTEM

While words or gestures try to insult a woman's modesty, molestation is an assault that intends to outrage her modesty and rape actualises such intent through sexual intercourse without consent. An act of rape consists in "forcible ravishment of the woman". The hierarchy between these crimes is founded on the concept of feminine modesty, or on the antinomy of virtuous womanhood.The law's reference to modesty has often been interpreted in terms of traditional cultural stigmatization of the victim to make sex crimes vague and justice difficult. This is evident from the characterization of rape as "deathless shame" or an irrevocable, rather than remediable damage. Its supposed irretrievability, coming from its being an actualization of outrage of modesty, downplays the violent aspect of the rape.By categorizing sex crimes as disgrace of "unique" feminine modesty, or women's fall from domestic grace, the law's intervention becomes an act of chivalrous protection of women's natural domestic purity.Defining sex crimes as attacks on chastity shifts the major responsibility of the crime to the victims. The latter often find it difficult to prove such crimes in medical and legal terms, given cultural prejudices harboured by these institutions against women entering public spaces. This is especially the case with the narrow legal definition of rape [Panicker 2002, Venkatesan 2008], which gets obscured through poor infrastructure such as access to medical, penal and legal service. Since 2005 new acts have been introduced to remove the burden of proof from the victim. Though fast-track courts have been set up to deliver speedy justice, they have not worked on a mass scale and have for most part benefited western tourists, only because the tourist industry's profit is at stake. At the other extreme is the National Commission for Women's (NCW) desire to punish rape by death, which is paradoxically grounded in the patriarchal assumption of domestic chastity. Death penalty presumes that loss of chastity is worse than death so that its punishment is equally hard-hitting. The NCW laudably initiated debate to change existing rape laws by calling for a broader definition of rape and lifting the burden of proof from the victim, impacting amendments to rape laws. Yet its endorsement of death penalty overlooks that many women who do register rape cases withdraw due to police deterrence and social stigma. Sex crimes, as well as, the laws against them, assume that the woman's natural place is in the private sphere of the family. The alignment between privacy and modesty has shielded it from the law condoning violence at home [Nussbaum 2002:247-49]. The IPC does not recognize material rape among adults and restricts it to victims who are under 15 years of age. Hence, rape victims are often forcibly married to their offenders [Sen 2004]. Thus domesticity is perceived as both a preventive and remedy to sexual violence. The refusal to recognize marital rape or identify the home as a solution to sexual violence is because rape statutes were written by men to defend male property; since women are construed to be the property of men till contemporary times.

There are pertinent rules and laws Pertaining to the Problem of Violence against women in India. There are many international conventions, the constitution and various other legal provisions provide for certain rights for women. Equality of sexes is enshrined in the Constitution of India as a fundamental right .There are many constitutional provisions to protect the women against violence. There are many Provision under IPC which aims at Protecting the Women . But there are so many factors that prevent women of India to seek justice through legal exercise such as:

(a) Her apprehensions relating to ultimate consequences

(b) Lack of support from her parental family

(c) Unreliable, time consuming and expensive legal system

11.3. CONCLUDING REMARKS

The focus on women as an exploited, victimised and marginalised group is a recent development in India. It has been now recognised that despite all their rights being violated, women have been suffering in silence.. It is time to dispel myths, superstitions and misconceptions about woman and her duties and adopt a rational attitude towards the woman as a human being. Social movement is necessary to break the notion of " virtuous womanhood" and "domesticity of women". Violence against women does not end by merely bestowing of judicial rights or by making women literate. The social problem can not be solved by legal bell or economic independence. It is not necessarily caused due to poverty or illiteracy prevailing among the households of villages. The same problem is also found in highly-educated and rich families living in cities. Being financially independent or belonging to a rich family does not terminate the problem. Feminization of job is only a necessary condition but not sufficient condition for women development. Most urban women are literate today but they are also victims of domestic violence. It is imperative that women themselves must be morally strong and empowered. In order to have the full status of a human being the educational system should make them mentally strong. They should not feel that they are meant for some one or born for some one. They have a social and personal goal and existence in the world. Thus a vigorous multi-pronged and multi-professional effort is needed to establish the woman as a human being in her own right.

REFERENCES

1. Journal of the American Medical Association. *Sexual Abuse of Boys.* 1998.

2. *2002 Recidivism of Prisoners Released in 1994 Study.* 2002.

3. U.S. Department of Justice, Bureau of Justice Statistics. *1998 Alcohol and Crime Study.* 1998.

4. U.S. Department of Justice, Bureau of Justice Statistics. *1997 Sex Offenses and Offenders Study.* 1997.

5. U.S. Department of Justice. *2005 National Crime Victimization Study.* 2005.

6. U.S. Department of Justice. *2003 National Crime Victimization Study.* 2003.

12

Happy Wife But Unhappy Woman

This chapter makes a perspicacious analysis of persisting gender inequality in India . The researchers blinded by populist sympathy for the poor, easily overlook the social and cultural dynamics which endorses the gender relations of inequality. Economic prosperity does not necessarily imply a healthier unisex society. Higher education or reservations of poltical seats or jobs for girls does not ensure gender equality. Higher family cohesiveness or lesser degree of divorce does not imply gender fairness either. Gender hierarchy in India is a paranormal opprobrium where all theoretical ratiocination fails. This chapter argues that it is not possible or necessary to undergo a gender vertigo to arrive at a transformation of the gender relations. It is not necessary to imitate the western route either. A slow dripping of change is very effective in the long run. Incremental change, how so ever slow and piecemeal may be ,can still in the end effect a radical transformation when one takes a longer perspective. Slow and steady process of social transformation can ensure women liberation only through awareness building.

12.1. RELIGIOUS IMPERATIVES

All parables of theocracy and pantheism declare women body to be inherently inferior and fit to be controlled and cared by men. Ancient Greeks believe that man is the measure of perfection while woman is fundamentally imperfect. Aristotle holds that women being natural fool, woman does not deserve to be citizen who could participate in public affairs. They should leave matters to man who could represent her interest better. Hindu scriptural texts and Manu's writings say that women are allotted the habits of lying and bad conduct. 'Man should strenuously exert to guard them'.[1] Christianism maintains that God created man first and women next. Therefore man is exemplary human being and woman is a secondary and dependent being. Islamism believes that man is created to rule over and manage the lives and affairs of woman. Women belongs to the class of religious pariah. Buddhist *Jatak* states that woman are unstable as sand and cruel as snake.

On the other hand all religions make unctuous praises and panegyric worships of women . Hindu praise her as *durga, laxmi, kali, chandi* etc . All Godess are made very powerful and wrathful. Worshiping woman as mother, while devaluing her in every sense, thus became a way of displacing as well as managing fears about female power and sexuality. Thus all religions prescribe , justify and contain the notions of 'ideally masculine' and 'ideally feminine' characters. They do not allow us to question or permute it. They claim that man is the norm, the rule and women is a derivation . Man is the measure of humanity. Man possess the monopoly power to define, interpret, judge and represent the world on his own terms, while woman is to be defined, judged and represented by men.

Even social reformers' view is always conservative and perfunctory. In India they argue that woman need to be educated so that she continue to function as a good mother. Education must help cultivate women's innate modesty and not instill a desire or ambition in them. [2] The ideal woman is one who works tenaciously at home at her profession and find time to keep a good house, attend to her husband and children's need all of which she manages without appearing ruffled ,tired or pallid. She is always expected to be a benevolent altruist with all conciliatory roles.

12.2. GENDER STEREOTYPES

We find many varieties of social stereotypes regarding women in India. Common remarks regarding single mothers are: 'Women are responsible for separation'. They bring separation by 'behaving badly'. They should suffer for their yobbo . 'She has loose character'. 'The termagant and errant wives should suffer their comeuppance' . So on. But after separation they suffer from predation of men. It is fairly a routine hazard of widows/ divorcee ladies. Normally we accept the justification that 'they have money and they earn'. So they suffer from such predations. But there is gender discrimination in this phenomena. The common notion works in the mind of the man that woman should not have left the man despite all adversity. A woman without man to protect her is potentially available for sex and entertainment of other men. She is a 'product' meant for man's consumption and entertainment. She is of the man, for the man and by the man. Children are grown up in female-headed households suffer from social stigmatization.[3] Common reactions towards lone mothers include imposing isolations through speculative gossips or restricted social contacts. The female neighbors used to be very jealous and comment on any type of household purchases :a jewelry or a cloth etc . They keep distance from lone mothers. It is due to : (i) women themselves are worried about women on their own posing a threat to their marriage (ii) own husband may get suspicious about fraternizing with women who theoretically have more freedom. Solo motherhood is the reflector or rear view mirror for the dynamics of power and dependency. It is largely considered as a social perfidy and recalcitrance. The more difficult and stigmatized solo mother hood is in a society, the greater the barriers against opting out of mental torture of a bad marriage.

The immoral and sexual deviances are linked with reactions to economic circumstances of lone mothers. The upward mobility of a lone mother evokes suspicion about immoral earnings also. They lead a life of social sympathy. Male has created a social atmosphere where the females themselves used to pity the lone mothers. So genuine economic prosperity of a lone mother has to be concealed in the society. In order to fend off charges of promiscuity and loose morals many lone mothers tend to lead extremely restricted social lives. Many lone mothers have good net work with the neighbors, but they fear they may lose their sympathy if they were to take up with another man. Both social stigma and economic disadvantages are mutually reinforcing against the single mothers. All these manifestations act as powerful deterrents to women's choosing to be free or thinking to be equal to man.

12.3. CULTURAL ARTEFACTS

Women's role, her fertility and her work in the family and society at large are influenced by economic development of the nation. As economic development proceeds family production for its own use declines. Larger share of goods for family consumption is produced outside the family. This brings changes both in the relation of family members to the out side worlds and in the relation between family members themselves. But in India gender discrimination is culturally stubborn. Women used to remain more burdened with family production. Traditional attitude of the villages, despite paean of modernization, prevails every where today . The need for self protection ,security and lineage has still remained as a strong incentive for having a cohesive family. Therefore educated people today (even many doctors) are found to be father of 5-7 daughters due to their 'son preference'. The highest gender gap is noticed in backward states like Rajstan followed by UP, Bihar, MP and Orissa. [4] Children are socialized to accept their present and future roles without any protests. Boys are encouraged to learn to debate, defy and escape from any responsibility, girls are taught to obey and remain docile.

Economic development is creating a gap in skilling process of man and women and endorsing the revolving doors of occupational segregation. 'High-tech' continuously displaces them to all low-skill and low paid jobs with ergonomics of casualisation and flexibalisation. Role of schools is not only to teach intellectual skills and impart knowledge but also to indoctrinate pupils with dominant cultural values. Cultural education for girls is full of traditional prejudices. The early socialization of girls by parents and teachers contribute to the development of 'superiority feeling' in boys and 'inferiority feeling' in girls. Machismo, being all pervasive in educational, political ,economic and social subsystem, is a real maelstrom for Indian society. The Indian mother transmits the notion of correct 'social behavior' of the family to the girls but the boy need not know the name of his own grand father. The girl grows in a vertical relation of obedience and command. All adolescents girls are taught to be mellifluent and skilled in domestic spheres involving all repetitive and irksome jobs. But the male does the concentrated bust of activity in certain season or weeks of the year and enjoys idleness for long period The male adults stroll up and down to the town, to gossip with friends, to loiter in market places. All these bohemian activities are considered befitting manifestations of the male role. But all duties and tasks of the girls are subsumed in their 'social role'.

The Indian family ,being an undifferentiated unit governed by altruism, is the epitome of gender asymmetries. The right to consume any thing in the house is different for women, regardless of economic status.. Any kind of consumption including food is not simply determined by its availability or adequacy. In India, women fast for the welfare of their husband while men do not reciprocate. If at all male is fasting that is for spiritual purposes but female fasts for the auspiciousness of the household collectively. The behavior of women is certainly and commonly bound up with altruism and prioritizing the needs of others. It is the central element in feminine identities. Men eats before women always. Women's eating before the man or male adult of the family is culturally forbidden . Women and girls learn to refuse to take meat, milk, ghee or any rich dishes. They normally eat the residual quantity of food left by the male members. In formal occasions men and women eat separately. Men eat with the guests .Women eat with the girls and small children. Girls learn and follow the mother to maintain social customs. Women never confess that she is hungry or thirsty. It is considered as a non-women etiquette. Man, while eating, refrains himself from talking and expresses gratification. Male enjoys the 'yum yum' monopoly who seems to live to eat . They eat slowly with restraints urging the other male co-diners to eat more and more(even in poor families) and take digestives after eating. Women while serving the food, carry this modesty to the extremes.[5] Even pregnant and lactating mothers do not get right calorie of food. They suffer from anemia, jaundice and several problems of malnourishment. Women are progressively weakened by successive pregnancies. Women is admired for working late into their pregnancies. They are expected to take rest only for 2 weeks after the child birth, during which they are given splendid nutritional food. After 3 -4 weeks the child is tied to the mother's back. So her food consumption is rigidly determined , so too her work load because it is inseparable from her social role.[6] Not eating (or fasting) and telling lies that she is not hungry is considered a positive moral values for women but it is neutral (or negative) for men. Girls are indispensable for domestic activities in each family. Therefore education is a form of consumption from which girls are conspicuously excluded. But son's education is an investment. Thus birth, growth ,education or achievement of the girls before marriage is by accident.

But Indians are proud to say that there is love, cohesion,culture, less divorce, and familial harmony inside the house. But this 'pseudo harmony' does not imply a healthy society either . In fact it conceals the disharmony and dominance and represents a conflictual cooperation.[7] The effect of masculinity, which is merely an expression of brute male power with yahoo mentality has not reduced unfortunately in the era of globalization knowledge . Male promiscuity today is being excused, legitimized and celebrated . On the contrary beauty, 'chastity and motherhood' are convenient and elaborate fictions which not only convince the women that they are destined to be subordinates to men but also enabled them to gladly accept that relations of inequality. Average Indian educated male(even some female social researchers) may simply dismiss all these narrations and arguments as non-issue and dub it as exaggeration of western feminism.

12. 4. SYSTEM OF MARRIAGE TODAY

Modernization of the society is a semi-myth for Indian

women, because the fate of girls has not improved. The upsurge in consumerism has created the euphoria of advancement for all. In Urban shopping centers , metro women appear to enjoy the freedom of a hedonistic consumer. There has been a movement towards the rejection of traditionally defined gender roles. There is greater acceptance of non familial roles among women particularly younger women with higher levels of education .But the young husbands and the potential ones, how so ever educated may be, tend to suffer from the inertia of the past. [8] They like to marry a potentially employable(not employed) wife who can earn, *if they want at all* but not according to the qualification and ambition of the girls. They allow her to work outside (but nearer to the residence) only under contingencies without affecting the ongoing gender relations. The real desire of the husband is satisfied when he succeeds in putting the wife into the natural jail with 2 or 3 consecutive child births. Many girls, having all chances and potentiality, wait and prefer to remain idle till marriage, which is accepted as a goal. Many working girls quit very good jobs/opportunities and girl scholars fail to complete their doctorate even on the verge of completion .The opportunity cost of all these is very high to the society. [9] The higher education is a problem both for fathers and husbands. One friend casually remarked , "beautiful girls do not go for higher education and beautiful wives do not work outside". There is some truth in this observation too. In fact the conservative patriarchal society does not allow them to study or work in so far as 'beauty of the lady' is the source of entertainment of the maledom. So 'beauty' has become a curse in the backward society. It makes her at best a happy wife but never a happy woman. This does not imply that less beautiful ladies or less educated girls enjoy better position either. Potential husbands have their explicit (some times unrevealed) preference towards acceptance of a more 'familial role' of the wife. [10] The common plea is that 'she should take care of my loving old parents, we have a rich family culture '. It is only a nonchalant criteria of the machismo. Even today 95 % marriages of India are arranged by the parents. It is a great uncanny to the rest of the world. It is a very widely accepted and stable cultural system . But this stability does not imply absence of the social mayhem. All types of ratiocination fails here. Gender specialists get confounded and perplexed. Till today love marriages(even inside same caste) are considered as a social stigma for the family. Even old-love affairs, in order to avoid such stigma, takes the garb of parental negotiations .[11]

The whole host of economic structures and social processes that reinforce patriarchy, commodify girls and promote the horrendous opprobrium of dowry. Arranged marriages is partly due to the social approval of the dowry system. The problem of dowry in large parts of India transcends the rural urban dichotomy Its incidence cuts across all caste and class boundaries .The prevailing patriarchal myths seeks to situate dowry as a girl's share of parental property or as daughter's life insurance policy secured by her parents at the time of her marriage. The structure of acceptance(or indifference) enjoyed by dowry is significant. Most of dowry deaths and tortures are not reported any where , because of the fear of social stigma or lack of knowledge about or fear of complexity of long legal process, unless the level of terror and violence becomes a threat to the life of the victim or in the event of her death. This, coupled with a general neglect of a girl's education/career moulds victims to a stereotyped role associated with reproduction and 'wifely' responsibilities .[12] Many educated married girls commit suicide because the girls-parents, regardless of their socio economic status (due to cultural pressure and due to non refundable dowry involving colossal loan or dissavings) after marriage blame her and force her to return back to the husband who is known to be brutish and sunk in high depravation. Then she suddenly discovers that she has no place of shelter. [13] Pre-marriage 'sweetness' and post-marriage 'bitterness' both are manifestation of masculinity giving her no better than a pet-status. Social stigma-dependency-syndrome, dowry and corruption are the cause and effect of gender inequality.

The boy's father used to say to the daughter's father, "we do not demand any thing, but you have to maintain the social prestige of your son in-law" .Even in so called ideal 'dowriless marriages' it is found that after few years the girl herself is made to demand and collect her share from her parents. Now a days , due to many anti dowry legislations, boy's father used to say we have not demanded any dowry, but the girls' father proudly says I have presented enough and therefore I have sold my land or entered into heavy loan'. The parents commonly select a 'simple homely-girl' for their son, who suddenly (if not before) becomes obedient to agree to their proposal without even seeing the girl. . The 'simple girl' has a cultural connotation. It means a soft, supple, obedient, god-fearing, caring, having good skill and interest for cooking, and having interest towards all types of house hold work.. All these qualities subsumes in one central virtue ie 'submissiveness' which is never explicitly cited as the criteria any where by the male-dominated negotiations. All qualifications and virtues of the girl earned before the marriage merges into nothingness which replaces the explicit criteria of 'homely girl'. Homeliness periphrastically means reticence only.[14] The girls ,particularly in backward states are educationally very successful but socially subdued. This cascading declivity debilitates her social position to a pretty-petty-pet or commodity. This is the unfortunate gift of higher education and modernity for the women.[15] It all reflects the masculinity and gender asymmetries in the society, nothing else.

The higher corruption level and jobbery in Indian society has direct connection with the gender relations too. All corrupt people in the backward societies are male, baring few exceptions. Father may be blamed for few years but the grandson(if not son) is respected as a man of worth and wealth in the society . [16]The gender dominance safely persists in side the outer wall of income hierarchy. But ironically Indian wives used to fervently admire 'my husband is unpeachably honest'. It is strongly correlated with the families/societies having gender asymmetries which thrives on camouflaging of the real image of phoney husbands and concealing the reality of the parvenu . Corruption is the cause and effect of gender inequality. The 'chaste wife' and 'honest husband' both are created and worshiped by the male-dominated society. [17]The family-complexity is a male-made social obtrusive design of roistering where female taciturnity is respected as a great virtue. The modernity has created such a opaqueness where she is unable to see beyond gifts and ceremonies. She remains complacent with the razzle of materialistic success. Paranoid males try hard to pander their wives to parry the risk of losing the stream-of-care . It is a threat-proof system .Uxorious urban husbands proudly says ' I have given you so much of jewelry, house, land, car etc'. He treats her only as the most qualified recipient of gifts . Any women who acquires a minimum financial security or higher education is considered more likely to dare to be a feisty, disobey ,divorce and become a feral cat . In fact anything which reduces women's dependence is seen as a threat, especially within the family. Many male scholars (and even some individual females who have seen success in job market today) shall dismiss all this arguments as pettifogging and pernickety.

12.5. LOOKING FORWARD

Even today man continues to exercises his ever subtler control on the family production and reproduction system. It is gradually institutionalized at several spheres: work, culture, customs, religion and education. Therefore liberation of women will not be easy or complete without the destruction of neo-patriarchy which has four levels of control: production, reproduction, socialization and sexuality. It is not enough if girls succeed in the educational ladder or if women work participation rate increases in the labour market. One has to examine why the chance of daughter's marriage is declining . It is meaningful to l ask why beauty, education and earnings of a unmarried girl is subsumed in one catchall criteria , ie "homeliness"

The social and economic structures today lock production and reproduction together , which perpetrate male dominance and female submission. The liberation of women can only be achieved if all structures in which women are integrated are transformed simultaneously. A modification of any one of them can be offset by a reinforcement of another, so that a mere permutation of the form of inequality is ultimately achieved. Thus a social transformation, which brings real modernity is warranted for India but not this razzamatazz of consumerism.

The state non action should be debated by gender sensitization. Employment facilities and educational level among women should be increased by appropriate policy of the state. Different types of opportunities for women to get gainful work outside home should be broadened by appropriate state policy . It is very crucial variable determining and extending her entitlement . Firstly, her employment enhances the overall command of the household in the family entitlement .Secondly, her relative share responds positively to her out side earnings. Her earnings certainly gives her: a) stronger breakdown position b) clearer perception of her individuality and well being and c) higher perceived contribution to the family economy. The greater economic role for women definitely ensures the momentum towards a unisex social system .It improves the women's status within and out side the family. Even the individual interest of women merges with the notion of family well being, the perception about individual interest becomes more sharpened by greater involvement of women in the outside world. Educational reforms in India should ensure liberation and freedom of thought for all human beings. Both musculine mentality and feminine mentality should change. It should break gradually and slowly the shackles of tradition that binds women and girls in the man-made gaol. It should foster self-esteem among women by means of group and community consciousness.

Economic development is never gender-neutral. So any prescription based only on 'household bargaining' model of the economists will be inaccurate for backward states. Poverty can not serve as the proxy for subordination of women. Therefore anti poverty policies can not be expected to necessarily improve the position of women. Until very high level of income reached, the rise in household income aggravates the gender inequality also. Money is neither necessary nor sufficient for transferring existing asymmetric gender relations. Thus Gender issue should never be approached with poverty reduction policies. Because this approach believes that women are victims of misdevelopment. Rescuing gender from poverty trap means we need poverty-independent gender analyses and policies .The gender issue should be delinked both from economics and politics. There is no substitute for a gender analysis , which transcend class divisions and material definitions of deprivation Therefore 'adding women' is not necessary, but an insight and rethinking development concepts and practices as a whole through a gender lens is necessary. The real improvement in the position of women may indeed involve a shift to humanism and less altruism.

NOTES

(I express my thanks to NACC, Sanghai for sponsoring this research project This paper is an abridged version of the larger study made under the said project involving a wider survey, conducted in MP, UP, AP, Rajstan, Orissa, and Bihar, of India. I also express my gratitude to Professor Takashi Sujeng Ho of Shanghai University for his useful comments on the earlier draft of the paper)

1. Geeta (2002) P.12
2. Agrawal (1997) P.11 and Pearson (1998), p. 21
3. Chant S(1999),P.92
4. The bargaining model of Sen fails to reflect the realities of the rural families because the women has no strength to bargain at all. There is also 'child marriage' practice now in some states . Girls in the villages even today marry before (or just after) puberty . They are always considered as the great burden to the family. Women, both in rural and urban area, suffer from intensive work burden. Maternal mortality rate(MMR) and Infant mortality rate(IMR) are very high. Female morbidity rate and spontaneous abortion rate is also very high. Child always belongs to the father, who is always eager to remarry and experiment if the first wife is barren and finally adopts a male child for family lineage (if not for his old age security).
5. If there is a guest, she often swears that she has eaten already. Or she is on fasting that day. If there is no guest she is taught to lie "I am not hungry at all". An

ideal mother is she , who gives up her share to her children or unexpected guests of the day.

6. Maher (1990) , P.129
7. Agra wal (1997),P.455, and Sen (1990), P.131
8. They enjoy to see beautiful and modern girls around as a girl friend or source of delectation . But while selecting their own life partner they change their attitude. The boys seem to become modern in every sense except allowing their own wife to be modern.
9. The common perturbing rumors like 'society has become very insecure' remarks like 'taxi drivers are very bad, doctors are bad, police is dangerous ' are mostly exaggerated by the 'masculine mentality' to stop/discourage the daughter/wife to have a free thinking. Highly educated husbands in the university safe-campuses and bank colonies are found to lock their wives under alibi that there is possibility of theft. Father says to the daughter 'you are very good, I have faith on you, but the society is very bad, therefore return home before evening '. In side educational institutions (except few universities) girls students and research scholars are locked up in the jail-like hostels at 6 pm, while libraries are kept open for the boys(constituting hardly 10-20 % of the students) in the night . Still then the girls are topping the list of success in every examinations. This indicates their potentiality and loss of wealth for the country due to gender bias. Thus Social backwardness aggravates economic underdevelopment but not vice versa.
10. Given the choice between 'beauty' and 'homeliness', the marriageable boy , in majority of cases, prefers the second one. Beauty of the girl is also ignored very often because it is thought to be associated with arrogance, uppity and other problems.

11. During negotiations, the boy remains either silent about the dowry or goes to the extreme of saying to the fiancée 'those are normal items your father has to give, that is required to uphold our social prestige'.
12. This reduces them to the position of a domestic unpaid maids or at best a mistress, veiling a structure of exploitation associated with household labour. There are many attempts to argue in favour of festivals, like *durga puja, laxmi puja* and *kali puja* etc, where women power is worshiped. Women's sub human status is very often justified by religious fundamentalists by the obsession with rich tradition. People draw upon many customs like 'sabitri amabashya' etc in order to legitimise predatory demands. This coexist with a lumpenised perception which commodifies marriages and converts a sacred act into a materialistic exchange.
13. The marriage is wrongly considered as the cause of her suicide. In fact all daughters endure the feeling of a prisoner or a pet-toy at parent place which culminates in in-laws place. Therefore people are blinded to blame the last man ,for whom the boat is sunk.
14. Therefore it is said that the girls do not find a good match after higher educational attainment. But greater truth is that the 'successful boy' is enjoying the greater opportunity of discarding several proposals in the marriage market. The chance of getting married for the 'educated ' and/or 'beautiful' girls is ever declining .
15. Girls who is praised by the society as a good student, good debator, good nurse, sincere police, air hostess or an athlete is out rightly rejected by the potential husbands. Even today the husbands of nurse and police used to conceal it as far as possible in different

unknown circles, since it is considered a shame for the family(having no control on women).

16. Grand son proudly says " we presented one building and one car to each of my 3 sisters as dowry... and my father was a government servant... we had enough parental property " . All illegal- black money turns into white and legitimate in a span of 2 to 3 decades. This is well known to the male but not to the female. Therefore male has the stronger propensity to transfer the wealth to the son through practicing gender inequality.
17. The female is kept in darkness on several fronts. So she fails to participate in infinite affairs of the family due to lack of pellucid information. She fails to participate in the complicated monetary affairs of the family.
18. View of E V R Periyar, An anti-caste original thinker and famous gender theorist
19. Boserup (1990) P. 20
20. Das Kumar (1999) P.34

REFERENCES

1. Agrawal, Bina(1997) Bargaining and Gender Relations within and beyond the
2. Household, *Feminist Economics* ,Vol.3(1) pp. 454-487
3. Boserup, Ester(1990) "Economic Change and the role of women" in *Persistent Inequalities: Women and World development,* (ed) Eren Tinker, Chapter-2, Oxford University press, New York
4. Blau F D et al (1998) Continuing Progress: trends in Occupational segregation in US over 1970s and 80s, *Feminist Economists* Vol.4(30 PP.29-71
5. Chant, Sylvia (1999) Women-headed households : Global orthodoxies and Grass root realities, in *Women Globalization and Fragmentation in the Developing World* , Haleh Afshar and Stephanie Barrientos, (ed)Macmillan

6. Cohen, Phillip N (2004) The gender Division of Labour: Keeping house and occupational segregation in the united states, *Gender and Society,* April
7. Cotter, D A et al(2001) Women's Work and working women: the demand for female labour, *Gender and Society,*Vol.15(3) PP.429-52
8. Das, Kumar (1997) Asian Profile of Underdevelopment and Poverty, *Asian Profile*, Canada, Feb. Vol. 25(1),1997
9. Geeta V, (2002)God made you different and Nature made us different, *Gender Theorizing Feminism*, Stree Publications, Madras
10. Mackintosh, Maureen (1990) Gender and economics: the sexual division of labour and the subordination of women in *Of marriage and the Market.* Kate Young et al, (ed) Routledge, London
11. Maher, V (1990) Work Consumption and authority with in the Household, in *Of Marriage and the Market* (ed) Kate Young et al, Routledge London
12. Pearson, Ruth(1998) Nimble Fingers Revisited: reflections on Women and Third
13. World Industrialization in the Late 20th Century, in *Feminist Vision of Development*
14. Sullivan, (2004) Changing Gender Practices within the Household: a theoretical perspective, *Gender and Society*, April
15. Sen, A K (1990) Gender and Cooperative conflicts in Persistent Inequalities: Women and World Development (ed) Irene Tinker Oxford University Press, New York.

13
EPILOGUE
Women Empowerment Sine Quo None For Social Transformation

India marched ahead after independence, with central planning for about four decades. The dominant goal and strategy of central planning was to achieve economic development. That development paradigm has not lost its continuity till today, even after new economic reforms of nineties. But with the same obsession for economic development the policy of free marketism has now reduced the dominant role of the state and replaced the strategy of central planning . The pendulum of economic growth in India is swinging from over commitment of public sector to over enthusiasm of the private sector. This model has very substantial core of truth which spreads the message of over optimism of instant change. The post liberalisation period has marked a distinct upturn of the growth trajectory .The urban sector is growing impressively very fast . The growth rate in the industrial sector and service sector has become very impressive but the agricultural sector has lagged behind. **The problem of poverty and**

unemployment among common people poses a real dilemma between the role of the State and role of the market forces. Market forces fail to unleash forces for growth and at the most it tends to generate low-income activities horizontally. It has resulted in the unprecedented growth of the informal activities in the urban sector . This process fits perfectly well with an investment pattern and production structure to subserve a social milieu and life style which has no relevance for the broad mass of the rural people and at the same time impedes the process towards economic self-reliance. It has created one by-pass system of development. The aim is to achieve high economic growth without having any percolation effect. It has created a jobless economy and voiceless society.

The standard prescriptions for growth have not ended poverty or hunger. Poverty reduction is the bench mark against which success of development institution must be measured. Sound economic policy that focuses on broad based employment generating growth is necessary feature of any effective attack on poverty, because real progress occurs when the weak and marginalised become the producers of their own welfare and bounty, not the recipients of charity or the beneficiaries of aid. Aggregate food production continues to increase yet hunger also continues to blight the lives of millions of people. Hunger in western Orissa has featured in the recent volume of Bob Currie, who asserts that hunger and poverty have persisted in KBK districts despite large sums are spent in various Govt programmes. He argues that there is need to give attention to a broader range of public action that may be adopted by citizens to create pressures for better policy administration. Govt can not afford to neglect public need in a liberal electoral democracy. Poverty alleviation programmes do not attack hunger at its roots. Rather they tend to polarise our societies by concentrating income in the hands of few and narrowing the social opportunities for the poor. We must grapple with the monolithic nature of the existing policies and procedures, which serve to shut down the voices of civil society. Food production is endangered because of the damage to the environment. Land degradation, water scarcity and growing vulnerability to stress are real threats to food security. **The danger is that we tend to treat hunger as the result of underdevelopment and poverty as the result of over population.** It is wrong notion. Hungry children become disadvantaged adults. It perpetuates the state of underdevelopment. The chance for a change begins and ends with the people on the ground, because, very simply nothing grows from the top, not trees, not economies and certainly not people. In order to be free from the 'hunger trap' we must have sufficiency of food on a sustainable basis and food security for the common man. There is need for appropriate mix of resources food, water, land, credit, training, market and technology etc in order to create enabling conditions for the poor. With the adoption of new economic reforms for achieving higher economic efficiency India has been experiencing increasing inequality in income distribution. Inequalisation is not desirable by the criteria of social justice. Greater income inequality provokes dissatisfaction and frustration among the poor which may culminate in disruption and civil war ,destroying the social and political basis of economic activities. Large scale indulgence of youth in carnage and violence in the cities is the manifestation of moral amnesia of the youth. These propensities among the youth is rapidly spreading in India. It is all attributable to the trading culture devoid of industrial culture and a peculiar culture dismissive of intellectual rigour, emerging consumerist culture which results in global exposure and excitement but local frustration due to non-fulfillment of numerous dreams . The discontentment and pent of despair is the direct outcome of the economic stagnation arising from the industrial slow down which results in the growth of exploitative informal sector.

13.1. GLOBALIZATION AND WOMAN

An economy which sharply aims at export oriented production and multinational investment is hardly likely to generate jobs for the unskilled and other vulnerable sections of the society. There is inherent gender bias, urban bias and elite-bias in the formulation of macro adjustment policies. It is creating a system which is ultimately as centralised and undemocratic as any that can be imposed by the meddlesome bureaucracy. **The main thrust of globalisation measures is greater commodification of all aspects of everyday life and work. The ongoing development process has inherent tendency to manifest the marginalisation process.** Job market is becoming increasingly characterised by the process of casualisation and informalisation. As a result the economic insecurity manifests in job insecurity, food insecurity, nutritional insecurity and educational insecurity etc . It is not very difficult to observe anti poor bias in the ongoing economic reform process. Common people remain voiceless. While permanent workers of the organised sector are at least offered some benefits in exchange for voluntary retirement, in a shocking display of lack of sensitivity, large number of daily wagers, employed for decades are being sacked as a part of the down sizing drive of the Govt. Agitations are continuing in many states. Court cases have been filed. Family members of the sacked workers are committing suicide in Vidisha, MP.Many educated girls are making suicide. Farmers are making suicide. These are not accidental phenomena to be ignored. These are not by default but by design. The growing casualisation and informalisation of work and lack of secure jobs is in fact becoming the main characteristics of the post reforms economy. There is a soft attitude of the Govt to tax defaulters and strong attitude to farmers. But Govt is strongly emphasising subsidy reduction and disinvestment, rather than improving the governance in order to meet the fiscal deficit. Credit is becoming a major source of mental tension of small farmers. There are many other emerging contradictions. Rich and middle class consumers no doubt have all reasons to celebrate the present pattern of reforms. The availability of imported goods and expansion of choice is indeed a major gain for those who can afford to pay because of their increasing purchasing power. The dot com growth in Indian industries is indeed phenomenal. About 90000 dot com companies are registered in 1998-99 alone and this is expected to grow by 200 per cent this year. NASSCOM survey shows that e-business transaction in India are likely to exceed Rs.300 crores in 2000..But there is no hope any trickle down benefit to rural sector from this growth. Millions of Indian are connected to internet whereas the rural majority could not be connected with fresh drinking water. When India is proud of having 30 % software engineers, India should be sad for having 25 % of the world's malnourished population and highest number of child labour, child selling child begging and semi bonded labour and starvation deaths in the world. Vulnerability to natural disasters is very high . Infant morality, maternal mortality and morbidity rate in the country ,particularly in the backward states like Orissa is very high. Access to basic sanitation and water facilities could not be realized for 60 % of India's population till today. Educational system has become more and more dualistic and discriminatory for the women, Health care system has remained more and more inadequate , urban biased and discriminatory for women and other vulnerable sections.

13.2. RUTHLESS GROWTH AND WOMEN

In response to the issue of poverty and inequity raised above it can be said here that the large scale centralised approach with its heavy emphasis on capital-intensive industrialisation takes most of the investible capital. This approach has never raised the volume employment and has never served the gullible women class, common men or the vulnerable poor. The type of industrialisation that the NEP(new economic reforms) contemplates is going to be of little benefit to the rural majority. **The adjustment with human face is another fanciful rhetoric , cajoling the women and common man at large.** Now the concept of inclusive growth has gained currency in India. In India the 'reserve army' of job seekers is ever increasing. In a labour surplus country it is saddening to note that capital intensity is ever increasing and labour intensity is ever declining. The growth fundamentalists have embraced a perverted set of objectives: higher growth of output, investment, profits etc are the highest values in their commodity-centric world. It amounts to dethroning our society and polity in favour of an economy which disempowers the common masses, a large majority of whom subsist not as parts but on the edges of the market economy. **The present process of economic growth is jobless, ruthless,reckless, rootless, voiceless, has generated a futureless society. There is a growing infatuation with knowledge based new economy. It tends to ignore the real economy pulsating with life and work of millions, which continuously intensifies the exclusion of common man. Market is never friendly to the women, poor people or backward regions.** It creates sharp regional imbalance. Rich states become richer. States like Orissa , having the highest percentage of poverty in the country become more backward. Majority of the rural sector and the unskilled and illiterate section of the urban sector tend to lose their right to livelihood and economic citizenship. With inadequacy of public services carrying unaffordable user charges caused due to inefficient and corrupt bureaucratic mismanagement and inflationary situation the common man is being pushed into vicious circle of vulnerability. Vicious circle of poverty manifests in: malnutrition, ill health,livelihood insecurity, food insecurity, undernourishment, Illiteracy, alcoholism, poor housing, low earning ,lack of productive assets, lack of land -water resources, gender inequality, low creditworthiness, indebtedness, inaccessibility, low productivity, distress sale of land, labour and agricultural produces ,child labour practice and many other inhuman and ruinous practices . **There is also the growth of dangerous tendency of the elite to dismiss the deep concern towards poverty and economic vulnerability as the obsession toward egalitarian romantics.** They strongly believe myopically in the trickle down theory. There is now indifference towards the problem of poverty and inequality in India . Indifference to gender issues or anything is defined as external to one's realities. It is the greatest irony that the society where the problem of gender discrimination, poverty and economic insecurity being the reality of the majority can afford to be indifferent to its endemic malaise.

13.3. CONSUMERISM AND WOMAN

The powerful wave of consumerism in India, coupled with frustration from failures to earn legitimate income has led to corruption in social life. High level of corruption eats away the economic vitality warranted for economic growth, which is the main focus of the new economic reforms. The number of scams during post reforms seems to be larger than the number before reforms. Black money has become the oxygen for corruption. The nexus between the politicians ,bureaucrats and business class has become vicious and interlocked ,where the interest of the common man is blatantly ignored. There are many inherent contradictions, illusions, irrelevance and hypocrisy in the new economic model. It is based on wrong and myopic premises. It does not address the real questions that afflict the India's developing economy with a backward society. **The slogan of women empowerment is becoming increasingly louder with the ongoing process of disempowering people.** The process of commodification and consumerism make the common man voiceless, because he has no capability to participate nor win in the race of efficiency.

13.4. STATE AND WOMEN

One must always remember one simple thing that any model of development which ignores India's rich endowment of human resources and rich natural resources including land and water resources is bound to falter. Any development route which bypasses the people is unlikely to be successful or sustainable. Localism seems to be the correct and steady route but globalism seems to be very exciting but experimental. Genuine peoples participation ,their awareness and empowerment of the people is necessary. Women empowerment is warranted. Health and education sector should be developed in order to achieve meaningful human resource development and involvement of local level institutions should increase in order to have meaningful social mobilisation. Salvation of the developing economy as vast and diverse as India's lies only in the social transformation and revitalization of its rural economy, which requires extensive and positive role of the public sector in building the social overheads which makes the role of the state inescapable. **The trend of withdrawing government from all spheres and promoting inaction of the public authority is dangerous for Indian society**. On the contrary the military and policing activities of the state is becoming more intensified. The government is focusing on peripheral issues of the society. Thus political and bureaucratic reforms is urgently required before economic reforms. Educational reforms is warranted before bureaucratic reforms. Empowerment of people in general has to be achieved.

13.5. MARKET AND WOMEN

All planning and policies are geared to promote economic growth through technological advancement. Technology, market , development are considered gender-neutral. **But technology is divisive and high tech is more divisive. Market is never pro-people ,rather it discriminates against the women**. Women's economic contribution has been invisibilised in the industrial process of economic development. This trend is not linear or unidirectional. Women are also displaced and have lost their share in the industrial workforce due to up gradation of technology, and reduction of labour intensity of production through automation and adoption of high-tech. Technology and labour market imperfections have continuously displaced the female workers from high productive activities to low productive activities. It is tending to accentuate the concentration of women in domestic works and non-market roles and activities. Employers in the process of modernization eschew the responsibility for workers wellbeing in the name of eliminating market distortions . More over in the current globalized economy, women's social subordination coincides with the absence of economic alternatives. Employment of women in industries has been accompanied by deregulation of labour protection .Women fail to defend or promote their interest both as women and as worker. Male-led labour unions either ignore or consider women's demand as divisive and irrelevant to the interest of the 'real working class'.

13.6. POVERTY AND WOMEN

When one aims at true modernization neither the earlier panacea of central planning nor the virtues of ongoing globalization appears to carry much conviction for women section or social development of India. Although gender empowerment has been a buzzword in development circles, the concept has been used in so many different ways that it remains ambiguous. All studies and reports on women status have only remained as a source of data, which rather endorse the passivity of the state. Policy strategy should reject the touristic observations of the metro life , dispel misconceptions and attempt to reveal the real Indian scenario. **Gender subordination in India is not caused by poverty. In India, there is a trade off between women's material well being and their autonomy.** This situation is not faced by the poorer section. This is one way of looking at the limited degree to which poverty and gender development can be approached synergistically with the same policy instruments. If rising household income has a perverse effect on women's well being then poverty reduction policies even if successful, does not increase women's well being. Thus we should have poverty-independent gender analyses and policies in order to rescue gender from poverty trap.

13.7. TECHNOLOGY AND WOMAN

The use of technology in the society is always discriminatory. Man was taught to cultivate with the animal driven equipments or tractor while women continue to toil in the field for the whole day. She prepares the land or harvests the corn with hand tools. Man use pack animals and wagons for transportation while women carry head loads of corn, fuel, fodder , food ,water etc. Women used to do domestic works which is socially under valued .It sharply restricts women's ability to participate in cash earning activities. There is greater rigidity in sexual division of labour in child care, cooking, cleaning, caring for sick and old still dominated by non-wage labour. Sexual division of labour in the home forces her to work for longer hours than men. It results in a lower status for them. **The capitalists extract greater benefits from the existence of sexual division of labor due to cheaper labor cost. Wage is always less than women's marginal productivity**. So there is an exploitation women labour . Capital benefits from using women as a reserve army. They are the most vulnerable parts of the wage labour force and are thus open to high level of exploitation. Any change in the sexual division of labour is perceived as a threat to the established forms of gender identity. **The technology creates digital divide in this decade. It is creating e-illiteracy among women. IT sector divides the society into two parts: hard ware and soft ware. Hardware is hard and soft ware is soft. Hardware is male-dominated but software is not female dominated. The hardware commands money and power and subjugates the software.**

13.8. CAPITALISM AND PATRIARCHY

Capital seizes up the pre existing sexual division of labour to its own advantage. There is difference in pay and compensation for jobs in a situation of unemployment. It reduces the strength of labour-class as a whole. As a result capital enjoys the opportunity to divide and rule. Profit rises at the cost of wage. House hold works done by women is very conducive to capital accumulation. The unpaid labour by women within the house raises the standard of living of the working class above that provided by the wage alone. These services could be otherwise only provided efficiently at high cost to capital by the capitalist or the state. This is insufficient to explain women's subordination. We have to go beyond Marxian analysis to understand gender inequality. **We should understand the sexual division of**

labour as the intersection of two sets of social forces: capitalism and patriarchy. Women's domestic work force is the economic expression of the fundamental inequality of the marriage contracts. Subordination of women, through an unequal division of labor in the wage sphere is ultimately the derivative of subordination within the marriage -based households. The need to support and care for children weakens her bargaining position in the labour market. Men acquire a vested interest in women's free services within the home and in their relatively favorable position in the society, politics and economy. Now in the process of urbanization ,division of labor by gender embodies new but ever-subtler forms of subordination of women. The state, under the hosanna of economic development, also indirectly approves to support such an unequal division of labor by turning a blind eye to women's inferior status both in rural and urban society.

13.9. WOMAN AND CULTURE

Traditional attitude of the villages, despite paean of modernization, prevails every where today . Marriage is compulsory for the girls. Not being married is a social stigma for the entire family. The option of not-marrying is considered worse than her subdued status after marriage. The need for self protection and security has still remained as a strong incentive for having a husband and married life for the girls in the society. There is also 'child marriage' practice now in some states . Girls are still considered as the great burden to the family. The maternal mortality rate(MMR) is very high. The female morbidity rate and spontaneous abortion rate is also very high. Female foeticide is the epitome of gender inequality. The preference for son has remained as strong as before even among the urban class . Urban centers of India flourish with economic activities with large surplus adult men, who leave their wife and children in the villages to take care of their grand parents and property. The propensity to marry among educated urbanite has been falling. So prostitution flourished in the society. But the man blames the women , as prostitution grows in the society. **The male-dominated society makes them either 'good mother' or 'bad prostitutes' in the society**. Both represent cultural prejudices against women. Chaste wife and prostitute mirror each other. The first one connotes life long sexual slavery to one man, while the other sells herself to several men. In either case femininity is condemned to servitude.

Gender relation is most oppressive for the women. Wife (except in the poor households, where there is no margin of choice) also feels ashamed of working for a wage in the presence of a working husband. She feels good if husband is having enough manliness to keep her as a decorative piece at home as baby-producing machine or love-care-giving agent. Individually she has **no compunction**. The social design is powerful enough to control and suppress her 'feeling of deprivation' or to assess her social position as a class. **The cultural imperatives do not allow her to think for the 'women as a class'. Because she is brought up in the culture of altruism.** Therefore it is a great irony and paranormal phenomenon. It is also very difficult to find a single lady remorsing with yell and yelp or audacity to face the challenge of any conjugal estrangement. Under cultural pressure she acts and appears to be jocund. Individual welfare does not necessarily imply social welfare either. It is fallacy of composition. It is just like the problem of child labour or bonded labour or child prostitution who accept the present role as her/his destiny or fait accompli having no alternative. He/ she is happy as a child labour because she lacks understanding about the social malaise. But absence of individual disatisfaction does not imply nonexistence of the problem of social opprobrium.

13.10. VIRTUOUS WOMEN

The notion of "virtuous woman" grafts the notion of modesty on "woman" and domesticity of woman. It connotes domestic loyalty and public shame, adulation and abuse.. The virtuous woman is a myth where the woman embodies a solid shape of sacrifice, a "use-value" for patriarchal economy. The myth of 'pativrata' continues to enduringly govern Indian womanhood , which results in loss of "personhood", Societal control over and regulation of their autonomy renders them powerless. **The Society glorifies** the female with magniloquent words and euphemistic languages. But Social and cultural system has an extreme bete noire towards gender equality and female liberation .All society exhibits a sexual division of labour. It varies from country to country. But it is always undeniably detrimental to the woman status. In order to understand women's socio economic status, we need to understand the sexual division of labor in the houses because gender subordination is embedded in the sexual division of labor. There is no reason why gender should be an important criteria or an important organizing principle of sexual division of labour except child bearing. There are social cultural aspects of women's subordination. Women workers tend to be segregated into certain industrial sector or into certain occupations. Women are typically low paid, defined as less skilled, low in hierarchy of authority and have relatively poor conditions of work. The sexual division of labour is created and recreated as the wage labour market develops. And newer forms of women's subordination perpetuates. Sexual division of labour is not limited to wage works alone. It is pervasive in all non--wage works like self employment, farming, trading or manufacturing or in domestic works. **Women are always made dependent on social relations**. In agricultural sector, development of cash cropping and new farming methods and the shifting of food processing outside the home have in fact brought the changes in the sexual division of labour creating more financially profitable activities for men. It again segregates and pushes women into less productive activities.

13.11. FEMINIZATION OF JOBS

There is pronounced urban bias and rural neglect in the development process. Modernization of the economy or advancement of the society is a semi-myth for Indian women. Feminization of jobs is nothing but feminization of poverty and distress. It reflects only declivity in ergonomics . Employers find the women simple, nimble and supple. They extract more work and pay less. It is highly profitable for them. They take the advantage of labour market imperfections. The razzmatazz of consumerism in the urban centers has created the euphoria of advancement. The current trend of free marketism tends to over emphasize 'economic growth'. With the euphoria of globalization and 'high-tech civilization', the social concerns are virtually dismissed as an obsession of the orthodox class.

13.12. NEO-HOUSEWIFIZATION

Ongoing process of economic development through free market policy is not gender-neutral. It is divisive and discriminatory. It has winners and losers. Therefore this is a game not development. Poverty can not serve as the proxy for subordination of women. Therefore anti poverty policies can not be expected to necessarily improve the position of women. Money is neither necessary nor sufficient for transforming existing asymmetric gender relations. Thus Gender issue should never be approached with poverty reduction policies. Because this approach believes that women are victims of misdevelopment. Even today man continues to exercises his subtler-control on the family production and reproduction system. It is gradually institutionalized at several spheres: work, culture, customs, religion and education. Therefore liberation of women will not be easy or complete without the destruction of neo-patriarchy . Neo patriarchy reinforces the process of neo-housewifization. The social and economic structures that locks production and reproduction together , perpetrate male dominance and female submission. The liberation of women can only be achieved if all structures in which women are integrated are transformed simultaneously. A modification of any one of them can be offset by a reinforcement of another, so that a mere permutation of the form of inequality is ultimately achieved. **Thus a social transformation, which gives us real modernity is warranted. Modernity does not come from technology or economic development or consumerism.** Real modernity implies social prosperity which treats both male female as equal and free human beings.

13.13. THE CONCLUSION

Gender inequality is endemic but not enigmatic. Effective policy design requires an effective understanding of the gender issues within a broad social framework.. Women's income earning activity should not be temporary, exploitative and reversible. Education and technology should ensure liberation and freedom of thought for all human beings. It should break gradually the shackles of tradition that binds women in the man-made gaol. The gender issue should be delinked both from myopic economics and insensitive politics. There is no substitute for a gender analysis , which transcend class divisions and material definitions of deprivation. **Therefore 'adding women' is not necessary, but an insight and rethinking development concepts and practices as a whole through a gender lens is necessary.** The debate on state non action on gender issues should be initiated..

The gender implications are erased from their

analysis. With the immense sophistication in methodology that emphasizes exclusively on quantification, uncomfortable issues such as patriarchy has remained as non issue and invisible. Gender concern and discourses survive with in the development bureaucracies which are themselves dominated by men. **It is easier for them to ring-fence gender issues as a problem of poverty and to argue against 'feminization of poverty' than to admit the realistic view of gender disadvantage which crosses the boundaries of class and ethnicity. We are myopic to treat gender inequality as a result of poverty and illiteracy.** Indian society should not wait till the end of poverty and illiteracy to establish an unisex society. The notion of virtuous woman and domesticity of woman created by the patriarchy has to be demystified. Woman has to be vital but not virtuous. Empowerment of women has to emerge from the society itself through effective health and education The educational reforms can foster people involvement and participation. It breaks the patronage of patriarchal force and exploitation of the capitalistic power. Participative approach can only break patriarchal approach. Empowerment of women shall automatically ensure entitlement and their capabilities. Gender equality is the sine quo none building a healthy and prosperous society. Unisex society can ensure meaningful inclusive growth and true prosperity.

Bibliography

Agarwal, Anil and Narain, Sunita. *Dying Wisdom: The rise fall and potential of India's traditional water harvesting systems.* Delhi: CSE, 1997.

Agarwal, Bina(1997) Bargaining and Gender Relations within and beyond the Household, *Feminist Economics* ,Vol.3(1) pp. 454-487

Agarwal, Bina (1986).'Women, Poverty and Agricultural Growth in India', *The Journal of Peasant Studies,* Vol.13, No.4, July.

Agarwal, Bina (1994). *A Field of One's Own: Gender and Land Right in South Asia,* Cambridge University Press, Cambridge.

Agnes, F (1992) The Anti-Rape Campaign ; The struggle and Set back, in C Datar (ed) Struggle Against Violence, PP. 99-150, Stree Pub, Calcutta.

Agnihotri, A and A Majumdar (1995) Changing Terms of Political Discourse, Womens' Movement in India in 19970s -1990s, Economic and Political weekly, Vol.30(29) July.

Agnihotri, Satish B (2003) Survival of the Girl Child, Economic and Political Weekly, Vol 38(41) Oct.11 Fortin, Nicole M a etal(1998) Rank Regression, Wage Distribution and Gender Gap, Journal of Human Resources, Vol. 33(3) : 610-43

Antonella, Picchio(2003)(ed) Unpaid Work and the Economy, A Gender Analysis of the Standard of Living, Routledge, New York

Balu, Francine(2000) Gender Difference in Pay, Journal of Economic Perspective, Vol.14(4(, pp.75-99

Bardhan, Kalpana (1979). 'Work as a Medium of Earning and Social Differentiation : Rural Women of West Bengal', *ADC-ICRISAT Conference Hyderabad*, India.

Baru, Sanjaya (2002) Strategic Consequences in India's Economic Performance, Economic and Political Weekly, Vol XXXVII(29) June 29

Basu, Kaushik (2001) India and the Global Economy: Rolw of Culture, Norms and Beliefs, Economic and Political Weekly, Vol XXXVI(40) Oct. 6-12

Bhattacharya, BB and S Sakthivel(2004) Regional Growth and Disparity in India: Comparison of Pre and post Reforms Period, Economics and Political Weekly, Vol 29(10) 6 March

BhaumiK SK (2003) Employment in India in the post liberalization Era, Indian Journal of Labour Economics, Vol.46(1):86-97

Biswas, Asit K. *United Nations Water Conference: Summary and Main Documents*. Oxford: Pergamon Press for the United Nations, 1978. Agency: United Nations

Blau ,Francine D (1997) Swimming Upstream: Trends in Gender Wage Diffferential in the 1980s, Journal Labour Economics, Vol.15(1) pp.1-42

Bose, Ashish (2001) Fighting Female Foeticide, Economic and Political Weekly, Vol XXXVI(36) Sept. 8

Boserup, Ester(1990) "Economic Change and the role of women" in *Persistent Inequalities: Women and World development,* (ed) Eren Tinker, Chapter-2, Oxford University press, New York

Black, M. *Thirsty cities: water, sanitation and the urban poor*. London: WaterAid, 1995. Agency: WaterAid

Bhattacharya, S., and Dave, P.N. *Project Nutrition, Health Education and Environmental Sanitation: an impact study*. Delhi: National Council of Educational Research, 1991

Bijlani, H. U. and Rao, P. S. N. *Water supply and sanitation in India* . New Delhi: Oxford& IBH Pub. Co., 1990

Blau F D et al (1998) Continuing Progress: trends in Occupational segregation in US over 1970s and 80s, *Feminist Economists* Vol.4(30 PP.29-71

Bhalla, G et al(2003). Rural Employment and Poverty, *Economic and Political Weekly,* Aug 16th

Bandopadhayay, D (2000) Gender and Governance in India, *Economic Political Weekly*,July 29,

Becker, G (1960) An economic Analysis of Fertility in G Becker (ed) Demographic and economic Change in Developed Countries, Princeton University Press. Princeton.

Bose, Ashish(2006) Falling Fertility and Rising Anaemia, Economic and Political Weekly, Vol XLI(37) Sept.16

Chambers, Robert and Gordon R Conway,.(1992). *Sustainable Rural Livelihoods: Practical Concepts for the 21st Century*. IDS Discussion Paper No.296. Brighton

Chattopadhaya, Molly and David Seddon (2002). Life histories and Long term Change: Rural Households and Gender Relations in a West Bengal village, *Economic and Political Weekly, Vol.* 37(49), Dec 7

Chaudhuri ,P (2008) Sexual harassment at the Work Place, Economic and Political weekly, Vol. XLII(17), April 26

Chakaravarty, S (1998) Mainstreaming Gender in Police: The Maharastra Experience, Development in Practice,

Vol.8(4) pp.430-38

Chant, Sylvia (1999) Women-headed households.: Global orthodoxies and Grass root realities, in *Women Globalization and Fragmentation in the Developing World* , Haleh Afshar and Stephanie Barrientos, (ed)Macmillan

Cohen, Phillip N (2004) The gender Division of Labour: Keeping house and occupational segregation in the united states, *Gender and Society,* April

Cotter, D A et al(2001) Women's Work and working women: the demand for female labour, *Gender and Society*,Vol.15(3) PP.429-52

CSD (2006) Social development Report, Council for Social Development, Oxford University Press, New Delhi

Curie , Bob (2000).*The Politics of Hunger in India, Macmillan India*, Chennai

Chandrasekhar CP and Jayati Ghosh(2006) Employment Conditions: working more for less, Business Line, Nov.28

Das, Kumar (1990) Paradox of poverty and Planning in India, Economic Quarterly, Vol.25(4),Berlin

Das Kumar(2007) Status of Women in Indian Society, Asian Profile, Volume 4(3),pp.234-56

Das, Kumar (1997) Asian Profile of Underdevelopment and Poverty, *Asian Profile*, Canada, Feb. Vol. 25(1),1997

Das, Kumar(1993), *Rural Development in India,* Discovery Pub.House, New Delhi

Das, Abhijit(2001) Protest Against Dominant Soci-Cultural Norms, Economic and Political Weekly, Vol XXXVI(36) Sept.8

Dasgupta (1987) Selective Discrimination Against Female Children in Rural Punjab, Population and development Review, Vol 13, Pp.77-100

Datta Gaurav (199) Has poverty declined since economic reforms, Economics political weekly, Dec.11-17

Datt,Ruddar (2007) Poverty Employment and Growth: pre and post reforms Experience, Indian Economic Journal, Vol. 54(4) Jan-Mar, pp.49-73

Desai, Sonalde. (1994). *Gender Inequalities and Demographic Behavior: India.* New York: The Population Council, Inc.

Deshpande, J V (2006) Towards a Knowledge Based Society., Economic and Political Weekly, Vol XLI(37) Sep. 16

Deere, Carmen and C Doss (2006) eds, Special Issue on Women and Wealth, Feminist Economics, Vol 12(1-2)

Dreze, Jean and Chen Marty (1995), Recent research on widows in India, *Economic and Political Weekly,* Sept.30, PP.2435-50

Dube, Leela and Rajni Palriwala (1990). *Structure and Strategies: Women, Work and Family,* (eds.) Sage Publications, New Delhi.

Dwyer, Daisy and Judith Bruce (1988). *A Home Divided : Women and Income in the Third World,* (eds.) Stanford University Press, Stanford.

Faulkner, Wendy (2000), *The Technology Question In Feminism,* Women's Studies International Forum, University of Edinburgh

Folbre, Nancy, B. Bergmann, B. Agarwal and M. Floro (eds.) (1991). *Women's Work in the World Economy, M*acmillan, London .

Goyal, Anjali(2005) Women's Empowerment through Gender Budgeting- A Review in the Indian Context, Ministry of HRD, Govt of India, New Delhi

Gupta Sanjiv and Michael Ash(2008) Whose Money and Whose Time? Feminist Economics, Vol 14(1), Jan

Geeta V, (2002)God made you different and Nature made us different, *Gender Theorizing Feminism*, Stree Publications, Madras

Harriss-White,Barbara and Ruhi Saith (1999) The gender Sensitivity of Well-being Indicators. *Development and Change*. 30, PP 465-497

Hirway, Indira and Darshini Mahadevia(1999) Gujrat: Human Development Report, Mahatma Gandhi Labour Institute, Ahemedabad

Hukka, J. *Environmental management in India: a baseline study.* Finland, Institute of Water and Environmental Engineering, Tampere, Univ of Technology, 1992

Jain, Devaki and Nirmala Banerjee (eds.) (1985). *Tyranny of the Household*, Vikas Publishing House, Shakti Book Series, Delhi.

Jhaveri , Narendra(2003) India's Growth Chase : High Aspiration Low Inspiration, Economic and Political Weekly, Vol 38(41) Oct.11

Johannesburg Plan of Implementation of the World Summit on Sustainable Development (2002). Available at:*http://www.un.org/esa*

Kabeer,Naila (1999) Resources,Agency, Achievments: Reflections on the Measurement of Women's Empowerment. *Development and Change*. 30, PP 435-464

Kakwani, N . and K. Subbarao (1993*). 'Rural Poverty in India,* 1973-87', in Michael Lipton and Jacques van der Gaag, *Including the Poor,* (eds.*)* The World Bank, Washington DC.

Karlekar ,Malavika (1995), Search for Women Voices, *Economic and Political Weekly,* 29th April

Kedlkar , G (1992) Stopping the Violence Against Women: Fifteen Years of Activism, in M Schuler(ed) Freedom from Violence:, OEF International ,Washington

Krishnaraj, Maithreyi and Karuna Chanana (eds.) (1989). *Gender and the Household Domain,* Sage Publications, New Delhi .

Kumar, V (1997) *Economic Growth and Rural Poverty ,* Concept Pub. House, New Delhi

Kumari, Ranjana (1989). *Women-Headed Households in Rural India,* Radiant Publishers, New Delhi.

Kabeer,Naila (1999) Resources,Agency, Achievments: Reflections on the Measurement of Women's Empowerment. *Development and Change.* 30, PP 435-464

Krishnaraj, M (2001), How Gender Figures in Economic Theorising and Philosophy, *Economic and Political Weekly* ,28 April

Lingam, Lakshmi (1994). 'Women-Headed Households: Coping with Caste, Class and Gender Hierarchies', *Economic and Political Weekly,* Vol. 29, No. 12, pp. 699-704.

Mathur, K (2004) Countering Gender Violence- Initiative towards Collective Action in Rajastan, Sage Pub, New Delhi

Maher, V (1990) Work Consumption and authority with in the Household, in *Of Marriage and the Market* (ed) Kate Young et al, Routledge London

Mishra, Yamini(2001) Unsafe Abortions and Women's Health, Economic and Political Weekly, Vol XXXVI(40) Oct. 6-12

Mitra, Swati. *Communication materials data bank for rural community-based water and sanitation initiatives.* Delhi, Water and Sanitation Group South,Asia, World Bank, 1994. Munasinghe, Mohan. *Water supply and environmental management: developing world applications* . Boulder: Westview Press, 1992

Maharatna, Arup(2002) India;s Family Planning Programme: an unpleasant Essay, Economic and Political Weekly, Vol XXXVIII(10) Mar.9

Narayan, Deepa. *The contribution of people's participation: evidence from 121 rural water supply projects. occasional paperNo.1,Delhi,* World Bank, 1995.

NFHS-II(200) India 1998-99 National Family Health Survey, International Institute for Population Science, Mumbai

Nigam, Ashok and Heyward, Richard. *Improving Cost-Effectiveness of Rural Water Supply and Sanitation Programmes*. New York: UNICEF, 1993.

Parikh, K and C Gupta(2001) How Effective is female Literacy in Reducing Fertility, Economic and Political Weekly, Vol XXXVI(35) Sept.1

Pearson, Ruth(1998) Nimble Fingers Revisited: reflections on Women and Third

World Industrialization in the Late 20th Century, in *Feminist Vision of Development*

Parasar , Archana (1994), *Women and Family Law Reforms in India,* Sage Pub, Delhi

Panda, P(1997) *Female Headship, Poverty and Child Welfare: a study of Rural Orissa*, August, Center for Development studies, Trivandrum ,Working Paper series 280

Postel, Sandra. *The Last Oasis: Facing water scarcity*. London: Earthscan, 1992

Purushothaman, Sangeetha. 1998. *The Empowerment of Women in India: Grassroots Women's Networks and the State*. New Delhi: Sage Publications.

Ray, B (ed) (2005) Women in India: colonial and Post Colonial Periods, Sage Pub. New Delhi

Razavi ,Shahra (1999) Gendered Poverty and Well-being: Introduction. *Development and Change.*30, PP 409-433.

Rao, CHH(2006) Growing Regional Disparity in Development in India, Indian Economic Journal, vOl.54(1) pp.52-61

Rao, CHH (2005) Essays on Development Startegy, Regional Disparity and Center State Financial relations in India, Academic Foundation , New Delhi

Reddy, KS and Kavita S(2006) Unmet National Health Needs, Economic and Political Weekly, Vol XLI(37) Sept.16

Singh, P (2004) An Economic Analysis of Human Development, Sunrise pub, New Delhi

UNDP, (2006)Human Development Report, United Nation's development Programmme, Oxford University Press, Oxford.UNDP(2000) Gender in Develoment Programmes: Learning and Information Pack, Gener Pack, UNDP, New York

Sonpar, S & Ravi Kapur (2001),Non conventional Indicators: Gender disparity under structural Reforms, *Economic and Political Weekly* ,Jan 6

Santhya KG etc (2003) Sexual and Reproductive Health Needs of Married Adolescent Girls, Economic and Political Weekly, Vol 38(41) Oct.11

Serageldin, Ismail. *Toward sustainable management of water resources* . Washington,

D.C.: World Bank, 1995. Agency: World Bank

Schultz, C. and Okun, D. *Surface Water Treatment for Communities in Developing*

Countries . London: Intermediate Technology Publications, 1992. Agency: ITDG

Saskia Everts(1998) Gender and Technology : Empowering Women, Engendering Development, Zed Books.

London

Sen, A K (1990) Gender and Cooperative conflicts in Persistent Inequalities: Women and World Development (ed) Irene Tinker Oxford University Press, New York

Soman, Krishna(2002) Rural Health Care in West Bengal, Economic and Political Weekly, Vol XXXVII(29) ,June 29

Sharma, S D (1999) Democracy and Development inIndia, Lynn Reinner Pub. Colorado

Singh, P and JK Pundit(2002) Women Legislators in UP, Background, Emergence and Role, Economic and Political Weekly, Vol. XXXVII(10) Mar.9

Shidhhanta S et al (2003) Sex Ratios and Prosperity Effect, Economic and Political Weekly, Vol 38(41) Oct.11

Snehi, Yogesh (2003) Female Infanticide and Gender in Punjab, Economic and Political Weekly, Vol 38(41) Oct.11

Sullivan, (2004) Changing Gender Practices within the Household: a theoretical perspective, *Gender and Society*, April

Swaminathan, Padmini and J Jayaranjan(20008), Mainstreaming Gender, Economic and Political weekly, Vol. XLII(17), April 26

Swantz, Marja-Liisa (1995). Embracing Economies of Women: paths to sustainable livelihoods *Development*. (3) , Pp 27-29.

UN Millennium Project, *Investing in Development, A Practical Plan to Achieve the Millennium Development Goals* (New York, 2005).

UN Millennium Declaration, U.N. Doc. A/RES/55/2. Available at: <u>http://www.un.or</u> *g/millennium/*

UNDP, *Beyond Scarcity: Power poverty and the global water*

crisis: UNDP Human Development Report 2006 (New York, 2006). Available at *http://hdr.undp.org/hdr2006/*

UNDP, *Mainstreaming Gender in Water Management. A Practical Journey to Sustainability: A Resource Guide* (UNDP, 2003).

UNICEF, *Towards Better Programming: A Sanitation Handbook* (New York, 1997).

UN-HABITAT, *Meeting Development Goals in Small Urban Centres: Water and Sanitation in the World's Cities 2006* (Nairobi, 2006).

UN-HABITAT, *Water and sanitation in the world's cities, Local action for global goals*

Venkateswaran, Sandhya. (1995). *Environment, Development and the Gender Gap*. New Delhi: Sage Publications.

Visaria, P. and L.Visaria (1985). 'Indian Households with Female Heads: in Devaki Jain and Nirmala Banerjee (eds.) *Tyranny of the Household*, Vikas Publishing House, Delhi.

Viswanatha, K (2001) Whose Body, whose Health, Seminar 505, September

World Bank (1991). *Gender and Poverty in India,* A World Bank Country Study, The World Bank, Washington DC.

WHO and UNICEF, *Meeting the MDG drinking-water and sanitation targets: the urban and rural challenge of the decade* (Geneva, New York: WHO, UNICEF, 2006).

WHO & UNICEF, *The Global Water Supply and Sanitation Assessment* (Geneva, New York; WHO, UNICEF, 2000).

WHO, *Guidelines for Drinking Water Quality*, Third edition (Geneva, WHO, 2004).

WHO, *Guidelines for the safe use of wastewater, excreta and grey water* (WHO, 2006)